AFRICAN CULTURE

AFRICAN CULTURE

THE RHYTHMS OF UNITY

Edited by
MOLEFI KETE ASANTE
and
KARIAMU WELSH ASANTE

 Africa World Press, Inc.

P.O. Box 1892
Trenton, New Jersey 08607

Africa World Press, Inc.
P.O. Box 1892
Trenton, N.J. 08607

First Africa World Press, Inc. edition, 1990

First Published by Greenwood Press, 1985

Library of Congress Catalog Card Number: 89-84609

Cover design by Ife Nii Owoo

ISBN: 0-86543-134-5 Paper

Second Printing, February 1991

To our firstborn son, Daahoud

CONTENTS

PREFACE

Before the appearance of Cheikh Anta Diop's *African Origin of Civilization* (1971), African culture was typically examined by Western-trained scholars from a European perspective. Those scholars, often wrapped in the swaddling clothes of a fully emergent European ideology, were often incapable of understanding the unity of African culture. Diop's masterpiece, *African Origin of Civilization*, and its companion, *Cultural Unity of Black Africa*, turned historiography around and provided the basis for an Afrocentric transformation.

To make clear the perspective of this volume in connection with the African culture, a few comments must be made. It has been common for writers to speak of the diversity of African cultures in ways not used in reference to European or Oriental cultures. In some respects, the literature of culture, in all of its many aspects, has tended to teach that Western, European, Occidental culture and Eastern, Asian, Oriental culture are the two existing phenomena in world history. In their limited knowledge of Africa, Western and Western-trained scholars have often cast a fog over cultural understanding of the African people.

Africa, this volume tells us, is one cultural river with numerous tributaries characterized by their specific responses to history and the environment. In this way we have always seen Europe after the Christian manifestations. England, Norway, Ireland, France, Belgium, Germany, etc., were one culture although at the same time they were different.

Asante, Yoruba, Mandinka are also one, though different in the historical sense. When we speak of unity in Africa, we are speaking of the commonalities among the people. Thus, a Yoruba who is different from an Ibo or Asante still shares more in common culture with them than with Thais or Norwegians. To the degree that the material conditions influence the choices people make, we Africans share similarities in behavior, perceptions, and technologies.

The idea for this book first came during the 1977 Festival of African and Black Arts in Lagos, Nigeria. As African-Americans at the colloquium, we were able to interact with Africans from all over the world. Our similarities and commonalities were obvious once those of use who had been colonized by France, England, Portugal, Spain, and Belgium could get beyond our language differences. What evolved during the discussions was the centrality of origin and struggle in the African world view. Africans from the New World met the continentals and saw themselves. We gathered from Brazil, Venezuela, Colombia, Cuba, and North America and immediately built cultural kinship with Africans from the African continent. There was a cultural authenticity among the 500 representatives to the colloquium from sixty-seven nations.

The chapters in this book were written by some of the most influential scholars in African studies and culture. In organizing this work we have chosen to use four broad divisions: (1) the ethnocultural motif, (2) the artistic tradition, (3) concepts of cultural value, and (4) cultural continua. This scheme is functional for a first comprehensive volume that will undoubtedly be followed by many others dealing with African culture. The present volume results from conversations with our friends and students in Buffalo, Ibadan, and Washington, D.C.; at the State University of New York, the University of Ibadan, and Howard University respectively. We have been influenced by the works and thought of the Diopians, Chancellor Williams, Ivan Van Sertima, Katherine Dunham, and John Jackson.

Molefi Kete Asante
Kariamu Welsh Asante

Part I

THE ETHNOCULTURAL MOTIF

1

AFROCENTRICITY AND CULTURE

MOLEFI KETE ASANTE

It is the express purpose of this volume to allow African scholars and scholars of African descent to speak for themselves on the question of African culture and African world view. In 1959 William Bascom and Melville Herskovits edited a volume published by the University of Chicago Press called *Continuity and Change in African Cultures*. In this volume a group of American scholars examined the diversity of African cultures. The attempt to isolate African cultures, during a time when African leaders such as Kwame Nkrumah in Ghana were emerging, with concepts like African personality has always appeared rather divisive to me. In Senegal, Leopold Senghor, not yet president, had been writing of negritude as the basis of the African's confrontation with European culture.[1] Bascom and Herskovits, widely regarded as progressive anthropologists, were still restrained by their own particular views of African people. For that reason, they could not conceive of African culture as a whole, they saw only the diversity of cultures which existed on the African continent. They were among the Western intellectuals who taught the world that Africa was not united in culture; that Africa south of the Sahara was "Black Africa" and north of the Sahara was the Middle East, that ancient Egypt was not in Africa and that the people of ancient Egypt were not Africans. The limits of their own knowledge were defined by the sociocultural realities of the anthropological profession, one of the most highly Eurocentric disciplines.

The unity of this book is based upon its philosophical foundations, the belief that people of African descent share a common experience, struggle, and origin. The sharing of origin gives color significance but not necessarily dominant significance. As Wole Soyinka says in "The African World in the Ethno-Cultural Debate," the Black Cuban whose complexion may be lighter than the Moroccan's may be a brother less because of color than the common response to the same rhythms, the same rituals, the same African sense.

One argument given by those of the anti-African culture school is that the African culture cannot exist because Africa encompasses too many ethnic groups. Such an argument is not made with regard to European culture or Asian culture. While it is easy to argue that there are numerous cultures within the Arab, European, and Asian cultures, it is an argument with little meaning when one understands that the unity of experiences, struggle, and origin causes each of these major cultures to have an internal unity. So it is with African culture. None of our writers would say that Yoruba is not different from Afro-Brazilian, Ibo, Edo, Ga, or Asante (Ashanti); they recognize those distinctions as they recognize the distinctions between the Welsh, Scots, Bretons, and Anglo-Saxons. Their cultural histories are somewhat different, but they share the same culture. What we might say is that their particular histories are distinct but their general history is the same. When Charles Martel led 300,000 Europeans against the Arabs in the thirteenth century, we had the beginning of a European culture based on a shared destiny founded in appearances, experience, and struggle.

In this book, culture refers to the sum total of African philosophy, behavior, ideas, and artifacts. Although the precise actions and ideas may differ within the acceptable range and still remain squarely in the category of African culture, there are some behaviors among some African ethnic groups which may have the opposite meaning among others. Twinness is commonly considered a positive characteristic in African societies, yet there are some ethnic groups which accept twinness as a negative characteristic. However, in all other elements, the ethnic groups may be related to the others. Behavior and response are predicated upon an ethnic group's particular history. If a group has had experiences on the waterways, then water motifs will be emphasized in the culture of those people. Yet this particularistic emphasis would not make the ethnic group unrelated to others. Patterned behaviors by African ethnic groups are cultural, not rigid or fixed, but related to history and experience. Culture can vary over time, but in the case of the African culture, it will always be articulated in a similar way. Ancient Egypt stands near the head of African culture.[2] Its contributions, and those of Nubia and Ethiopia, the elder sisters, are significant to those who take a holistic view of African culture. Predynastic Egypt, that is, Egypt prior to the union of the Upper lands with the Lower lands by Menes, the king of the Upper lands (southern Egypt), was inhabited by people no different from the present black population of the United States. Thus, the Badarians who lived in Egypt (also called Tamerry and Kemet), prior to Menes were the ancestors of the dynastic Egyptians.[3] These dynastic Egyptians inherited the Badarians' love of ivory necklaces and bracelets, manufacturing of pottery and baskets, and belief in the immortality of the Nile. Furthermore, dynastic Egyptians maintained the belief in the efficacy of amulets made from the remains of the hippopotamus and the jackal. Accepting the principle of life after death, they placed offerings in the graves with the deceased. Beyond these parallels with the social and cultural development of other African peoples were the stunning contributions of the ancient Egyptians in geometry, science, philosophy, architecture, writing, and organized religion.[4] The Nubians brought Egypt the monarchy, a belief in divine kingship, and the worship of Horus and other ancestors, thus greatly enriching the civilization.

Much scholarship has attempted to separate the ancient civilization of East Africa from the rest of the continent, but Cheikh Anta Diop is correct to see that Egypt is to Africa as Greece is to Europe.[5] Furthermore, the ideas of governance, medicine, education in the mysteries, geomancy, and the arts which sprang up in Nubia's belly and migrated to Egypt are now found in all parts of the continent as a result of a series of dispersions spurred by Alexander's invasion in the fourth century B.C. and being completed in the seventh century A.D. during the Arab invasion. Of course, it should be mentioned that Alexander and the Ptolemies of Greece never ruled more than seventy miles from the Delta. The Arabs, with the *jihads*, or holy wars, were thorough in their destruction of much of the ancient culture. Only now are we beginning to read the full account of utter devastation of Egypt's ancient culture by the passionate invaders. The decapitation of the Egyptian priests who practiced the ancient divinations, the subversion and suppression of the ancient Egyptian language, and the constant wars against the blacks who refused to relinquish their ancestral beliefs became unbearable for many Africans who left Egypt as Arab culture and language made its total conquest of the indigenous people.[6] This historic persecution led to the spread of the ancient wisdom of the Egyptian priests to the secret societies of other ethnic groups of Africa.[7] Almost all Africans share cultural similarities with the ancient Egyptians. It is as if small bands keeping just ahead of the Islamic onslaught managed to preserve certain aspects of the traditional culture of Egypt. One finds among the Wolof, Yoruba, and Asante aspects of the ancient Egyptian life. In addition, the Ogiso of Benin have many characteristics purportedly to be derived from Egypt. These are not the only groups that can trace their linguistic or ritual forms back to Egypt; indeed, the continent is replete with evidences of the influence of Egypt in African prehistory.

After the proselytizing Arabs came the European merchants and missionaries. Their attacks on African culture were as brutal as those of the Moslems. Indeed, the Europeans came to Africa after hearing Arab travellers report of the gold and diamonds to be found there. Emerging from the economic and moral devastation caused by the bubonic plague, Europeans were in search of a more secure economic life. They found Africa, and in the fifteenth century the Portuguese commenced to build Elmina, the mine, on the Gold Coast of Africa. They found an Africa in turmoil; numerous splinter kingdoms in migration, without enough population to sustain bureaucracies and at the mercy of larger empires as a result of the Islamic invasions, were plums ready for the plucking. Europe's avaricious merchants took full advantage of the disintegration of these kingdoms and traded in both gold and human beings, initiating the most intense period of human slavery in history.[8]

African culture is therefore determined by a unity of origin as well as a common struggle. All of the African people who participated in the mechanized interaction with Europe, and who colored the character of Europe while being changed themselves, share a commonality. Also present in African culture is a nonmaterial element of resistance to the assault upon traditional values caused by the intrusion of European legal procedures, medicines, political processes, and religion into African culture. Needless to say, resistance has not always meant success in keeping evil at bay. Indeed, while the traditional courts still have the sanction of the people and traditional healers do an increasing amount of business, the pattern seems to be a weakening of traditional values. Part of the problem has been a lack of discussion of the elements that are valuable to African culture despite modernization. Modernization does not mean Westernization. No one society has a monopoly on modernization. African culture takes the view that an Afrocentric modernization process would be based upon the three traditional values: harmony with nature, humaneness, and rhythm.[9]

ETHNO-CULTURAL MOTIF

In a continent of over 1,000 ethnic groups, the question of unity is significant. The scholar cannot deny the ethnocultural debate in the large sense or in detail. Wole Soyinka provides a full discussion of the Arab-Berber, African-Negro, black-indigenous debate in chapter 2. In a powerful argument, he analyzes the question of Arab cultural participation in African international conferences. The specific issue in his chapter is the debate over who should participate in what became the Lagos [Nigeria] Festival of Black and African Culture (FESTAC). Soyinka, a leading dramatist, poet and writer tackles the thorny issue with deftness and insight.

Soyinka maintains that the African world did not come into existence in reaction to or in response to any other "world." He salutes the Africans from Arabic speaking countries for claiming that "they are Africans first and in totality." But having defined the issues of the cultural debate, Soyinka recognizes the hard political facts that often accompany a discussion of culture in Africa.

Perhaps one of the most telling aspects of Soyinka's argument is his discussion of the Soviet Union's use of *progressive*, for example, when referring to blacks in South Africa. The Soviets have dropped the term *black* from their vocabulary and use the more ideological term *progressive*. Soyinka's contention is that there have been no malformations in African history that have led to racist degradation of other people and so Africans should not be imposed upon by someone else's values which have arisen through another history.

Africa does not end where salt water licks the shores of the continent. In Soyinka's view, this "saline consciousness" must not get in the way of a celebration of the achievements of those Africans who live outside the continent. Soyinka's chapter is wide-ranging, engaging numerous issues, elucidating throughout the unity of African culture.

The fact that certain universalities do occur among Africans is highlighted in Aguibou Yansane's masterful chapter. Yansane's major research interest is in West Africa. Raising the perennial question of the relationship between history and culture, he suggests that the universalities are based on the cultural history of the region. Thus, he discusses tradition as a foundation for the present and future. From the perspective of political science, Yansane analyzes the political implications of cultural universals. In Yansane's chapter we begin to see how the history of Africa shaped and was shaped by culture.

THE ARTISTIC AND INTELLECTUAL TRADITION

Africa is rich in every aspect of human art. As the cradle of civilization and the home of many art forms, it has shared its artistic spirit with every continent. The literary tradition, however, is of recent vintage, developing in full bloom only in the twentieth century. But this was a literature based upon thousands of years of a storytelling, praise-singing tradition.

In chapter 4, Kariamu Asante examines the relationship of African aesthetics to life. Using examples from dance, she demonstrates the unity of African aesthetics. Her aim is to distinguish the purview of African dance and to show how the dance techniques of Africa, Haiti, and Afro-America are similar. She lays the groundwork for understanding African aesthetics, showing that art cannot be divorced from life, it is a part of life. Asante's view of dance in the African context is organic and related to every aspect of society. In New World communities such as the United States, separation of dance from traditional African rituals has often occurred. However, as Asante correctly understands, the new forms of the dance that most directly speak to the African essence are those derived from the life of the people. Asante's Mfundalai and Dunham's Haitian are the two most important techniques. Asante's rational account of the position of dance in African culture is remarkable for its thorough treatment of the philosophical grounds of dance. This is the first time that a dance historian has examined the philosophical and cultural bases of the African unity movement.

Samuel Boadu finds that the oral artistry of African culture might be used in the maturation of a new social order already upon us in the major urban areas of the African continent. He is certain that the rubrics of tradition, particularly as they are derived from the cultural material of the societies, are more valuable for the new African social order than the total acceptance of European, Asian or Arab culture. It is explicit in Boadu's chapter that we must move beyond the point of casting out our traditions for the missionaries' new intellectual goods. Simply put, the question is: What is it that they ask of us in return? Boadu takes an assertive stance as he identifies and supports the use of oral artistry in contemporary times.

Maulana Karenga develops in chapter 6 a theme found in the writings of continental Africans such as Amilcar Cabral and Sekou Toure. His work, written from an Afrocentric perspective, throws a critical light on the subject of culture and struggle in the African context. Like Frantz Fanon, Karenga seeks an accountable culture, a cultural positivism, which will help liberate the oppressed. In this respect, his chapter translates the meaning of culture for an African world seeking to assert its total independence from external influences. Karenga recognizes that culture must relate to human struggle, indeed, to direct liberation.

CONCEPTS OF CULTURAL VALUE

Felix Boateng's chapter, which concerns intergenerational communication studies in Africa (still in the developmental stage), focuses on oral literature, proverbs, and secret societies as instruments of educational advancement. Chapter 7 delves into the traditions of the African culture which have seldom if ever been applied in contemporary African education. The source and promotion of traditional education are community-based, originating in the symbolic interchanges in village life. Boateng's work supports the fundamental posture of this volume by underscoring the similarities in traditional education among various African peoples.

In the work of Dorthy Pennington we see what *chronos* means to Africans. She shows how Africans in the Old and New Worlds understand time not as a condition to be conquered, achieved, wasted, spent, or bought, but to be lived. She explores the various dimensions of time in the African mind, resolving the issue for the African culture by laying out the tenets of its operation.

Eghosa Osagie's contribution in chapter 9 is to establish the intellectual roots of European socialism and then to see how that socialism is related to the traditional, indigenous communalism found in most African societies. To do this, he examines the early foundations of European socialism as an intellectual idea, noting that Africans practiced a form of economic communalism many years before the Europeans.

Socialism was endemic to Africa; and when some modern African politicians considered socialism, they saw it in strictly African terms. Thus, Julius Nyerere and Sekou Toure spoke and wrote of African socialism. Osagie proposes to replace the strict notion of socialism or capitalism as conceived in the West by *integratism*, which he believes is more akin to the traditional culture of Africa.

CULTURAL CONTINUA

John Henrik Clarke's study of the role played by Afro-Americans in the reclaiming of African history is highly instructive. He contends that it was the early Afro-American historians who, because of their existential condition, bore the burden of the reclamation of African history. Chapter 10 outlines with great clarity the overwhelming evidence on this subject, raising the major psychological questions confronting Africans on the continent and in the diaspora: Who are we and who are our mothers and fathers, brothers and sisters?

In Abdias do Nascimento's chapter, we have the first major piece on the *quilombismo* movement of Brazil. The Africans in Brazil seem to have maintained their connections to Africa more explicitly than Africans in the United States. The *loas* and *orishas* are still called by their original names in Brazil and Nascimento demonstrates than the revolutionary African movement for liberation in Brazil is the expression of 60 million Black Brazilians' African essence. *Quilombismo* today is a progressive cultural concept based on 500 years of African resistance to oppression. According to Nascimento, there is no need for African self-negation in Brazil; the history is replete with cultural elements of resistance from *capoiera* to *umbanda*. Chapter 11 sets the struggle of Afro-Brazilians in the center of the African diaspora and connects it culturally with the traditional values of the African world.

Mwizenge S. Tembo, relying on the earlier works of Sofola, Quaison-Sackey, Senghor, and the later work of Asante, recaps the African personality argument. Tembo agrees with the previous authors that there is a distinct African personality and moves to establish its character in the modern era. Michael Bradley's *Iceman Inheritance* has recently underscored the geographical argument for cultural differences between Europeans and others. In his essay, Tembo relies on African writers and personal experience, a fundamental empiricism, to make his case.

His chapter is valuable as a continuation of the discussion of African personality.

In a masterful chapter on Africanisms in the Americas, North and South, Dona Richards addresses the specific manifestations of the African culture. She demonstrates the completeness of the cultural relationship between the African continent and the diaspora. It is estimated that over 150 million Africans were forcefully moved from the continent over a 300-year period. It is not difficult to imagine the concentration of African survivals in the New World despite the overwhelming oppression of the African in the Americas. Groups of Africans in Cuba retained religious rites, others in Brazil developed a uniquely Brazilian cuisine, established a religious system, taught music and dance, while Africans in the United States retained and expanded the African sense of language. Richards' essay, therefore, supports the survival theory of culture in historically related people.

Chapter 14 studies how the African sense of language and verbal style rises in the New World on the foundation of African languages. Continuing the unity of culture discussion found in the chapters by Asante, Pennington, and Richards, Molefi Asante explores the development of language forms as related to the syntax of traditional languages. Pidgin and creole, he writes, were an amalgamation of the languages spoken by the African slaves as they came in contact with each other and with Europeans. Thus like music in America, Afro-American language, that is, Ebonics, has a definite African source.

Culture in this book means the accepted behavioral patterns of the African people. This represents the total organization and arrangement of African people's thinking, feeling, and acting. While there may be variations in action as well as in the physical manifestations of African people, the in-group variations are not as great as the group's difference from European or Asian groups. And yet it is clear that most African people live in societies, either on the continent or in the diaspora, in which there have been some extraneous cultural influences of a non-African sort. In the United States, the participation of Africans in the national culture is imperfect and will remain imperfect as long as the African claims Africanity and acts Afrocentrically. The Pilgrim fathers, the Fourth of July, "Yankee Doodle," Tippecanoe, and "My Old Kentucky Home," do not mean to Africans what they mean to white Americans. The social heritage is different. We share Chaka, the Battle of Blood River, the Golden Stool, the pyramids, the Underground Rail-

road, Shango, Nehanda, and Anokye with those conscious scholars and
individuals who understand and appreciate a common origin and struggle.

In presenting this book to the public in the interest of African culture,
we seek to lift the academic and intellectual discussion of Africa to a
higher plane. Understanding other cultures is a skill that we believe
opens the doors to cooperation and communication.

NOTES

1. Leopold Senghor, *Prose and Poetry* (London: Heinemann, 1965), pp.
92–100.
2. Cheikh Anta Diop, *The African Origin of Civilization* (New York: Lawrence Hill, 1971), pp. 21–24. See also Yosef Ben-Jochannon, *African Origins
of the Major Western Religions* (New York: Alkebu-Lan, 1970).
3. Yosef Ben-Jochannon, *Black Man of the Nile* (New York: Alkebu-Lan,
1970), pp. 61–67.
4. Ibid., p. 61.
5. Diop, *The African Origin of Civilization*, pp. 23–29.
6. Chancellor Williams, *The Destruction of Black Civilization* (Chicago:
Third World Press, 1974), pp. 17–40.
7. Ben-Jochannon, *Black Man*, p. 61.
8. William E. B. Du Bois, *The Suppression of the African Slave Trade* (New
York: Schocken Books, 1969).
9. Janheinz Jahn, *Muntu: The New African Culture* (New York: Grove Press,
1961).

2

THE AFRICAN WORLD AND THE ETHNOCULTURAL DEBATE

WOLE SOYINKA

The 1975 Conference of Ministers on African Culture (AFRICULT) which took place in Accra proved for many who attended a most distressing occasion.[1] One found oneself appalled in turn by the high incidence of genuine misunderstanding, frustrated by the infusion of partisan politics, overawed by the intensities of chronic antagonisms (Guinea versus Senegal was the prime example), outraged by the brazen application of double standards, but, above all, numbed by the permanent confusion over the meaning and significance of culture, and the morbid fear experienced by some over the dangers posed to political aims by the simplest truths to those who study culture. The conference was quite generous in permitting observers to speak, and of course this was a privilege which observers tried not to abuse. In any case, the jungle of irrationalities and confusion was nearly impenetrable, and it would take a particularly intrepid observer, especially one lacking the status of a government representative, to attempt the task of hacking through it. One thing became rapidly clear: while all may be cultured, not all are students of culture. This truism can be as confidently stated as, for instance, that all men may be militant but not all are men of arms, or that all men may be politicized but that not all are politicians. The elaboration, it is hoped, will eliminate any suggestion that a special status is being claimed for a concern with culture. If this is admitted, we suggest that it is only reasonable that those who have devoted their intelligence and productive energies almost exclusively to other studies of society, pay a little more attention to the discoveries of those who have made their own culture their concern.

The ideas of sociologists and anthropologists must be contradicted on their own chosen grounds, not by recourse to slogans or wish-fulfilling ideals from outside the disciplined study of culture. If the latter course is chosen—let us say, for instance, that an argument from the language of economics or politics is used to contest a cultural reality—then the argument is thrown wide open, and students of culture have no alternative but to resort to other countering arguments from an even wider range of social mechanics. Unfortunately, each time this response was offered at the AFRICULT Conference, those who had been compelled through the tactics of the politicians or ideologues to utilize—shall we say—direct and contemporary political events in support of their stand, found themselves pronounced politically divisive. In short, the debates at this conference were on such a level of tangential confrontation that, in sheer self-defense, in an attempt to reestablish a sane grasp of those realities that had seemed so commonplace before listening to the debates, I began to formulate an address to the conference based on the various attitudes to the subject of culture and specifically, the Black and African Arts Festival that had generated so much acrimony.

Since I shall touch on actual events in contemporary politics and shall attempt to deal with the reactions of specific governments to questions of culture, I must demand a simple faith in the genuineness of my intentions. I shall not attempt to reconcile contradicting views but express a distinct view which I believe in as passionately as others believe in theirs. But, thanks to the experience of listening to most of the debates at that conference, I believe also that I have a clearer grasp than before of the various geneses of existing points of view, the causes of mutual misapprehension, and fear, both subjective and ideological.

In seeking to avoid the acerbity which marked most of the debates, I also intended not to fall victim to an excessive delicacy which, up until now, has marked the tactics of the defenders of the reality of the African world. In trying to define that world, many intellectuals have been anxious not to give it a reacting character, that is the character of a world which can only be grasped in relation to others. This form of definition is not itself wrong; it is merely fraught with unhappy connotations. The African world did not come into existence in reaction or in response to any other world. But sometimes, when all other arguments and expositions have failed—failed that is, not intrinsically, not from lack of merit, but as a result of what we have described as the illogical imposition of external references—then we must resort to allied methodologies and define the world that is being denied in relation, not merely to the properties of other worlds, but in relation, in complementarity, to the very existence, the assertiveness, even aggressiveness of other worlds. Those whom this method makes unhappy must in fairness recall that it has been forced upon us as a result of numerous conferences and polemical publications—of which AFRICULT, being the representative voice of African governments, has proved the most notable.

I shall begin my argument by the strange method of saluting the Communist party of the Soviet Union which, for laudable ideological reasons, determined to combat racism in all forms by deleting the expression "black" from its political vocabulary of human groups. Thus you will find that in Soviet bulletins, the victims and combatants of apartheid in South Africa are referred to as "progressives," never as black South Africans, or even colored. Similarly, we should salute those Arabs we have listened to here and elsewhere in forums who, contrary to the conception of many that they are culturally separate, have now assured us here that they are Africans first and in totality. They are suggesting for instance that President Siad Barre, chairman of the Organization of African Unity (OAU), who has repeatedly called for cooperation between "us Arabs" and the "Africans," is somehow out of step with current thinking on this theme. Such reflections augur well for the goal of unity for this continent and should strike a responsive echo in the heart of all pan-African idealists. Even for those of us who take the political goal of the unity of this continent for granted, it is reassuring to listen to these declarations of faith, for they contradict nothing that we know of the material nature and potential of the continent and, in that sense, they cannot but become the committed goal of every African. When this idea of African unity is applied culturally, however, we must so phrase our goals that we do not appear to fly in the face of the reality we experience daily. Let us begin with the distractive role of language.

LANGUAGE AND DEFINITIONS

While it is laudable from an "educative" point of view, that is, from the needs of the Soviet revolution to reeducate its constituency in attitudes to race by expunging the obvious from its language of ethnic definitions; the Yoruba peoples, whose culture is not conditioned by any historic phenomena like malformations of the manifest racism of the European world, refer to themselves (and to others with whom they experience an affinity of being, including their descendants wherever they are) as *enia dudu*, the black peoples. Other languages in Africa have similar expressions. For the Ga it is *meedidzii*, for the Hausa, *baiki mutane*. And therefore while the Soviet Union programs this reality of black identity out of existence—as it were—declaring us non-people in an ideological framework with which, ironically, many of us identify as fundamentally universal and applicable in its many important aspects, the fact remains that in usage and consciousness, our societies have recognized this particularist reality of our ethnic consciousness, one that has not, in *our* history, bred racism. Why should we be imposed upon by values and complications which have arisen through the abuse of the language of others by their own history? This abuse need not concern us and cannot demand a reexamination of our linguistic expression. Our language has never been subjected to that particular form of degradation. In brief, instead of wincing every time the French, English, Spanish or Russian refer to our specific racial reality, we need only short-circuit this totally European "culpaphone" by conceiving of ourselves in the untainted equivalents in use in our own societies. Those, in any corner of the continent or elsewhere, who experience a cultural affinity with any groups which have organized themselves as "black peoples," that is, as *enia dudu*, are indeed black peoples and this autonomous sense of being cannot be denied us by others.

Most human activities tend, by their fundamental preoccupations with the ramifications of culture, to arouse or consolidate this sense of self-cognition. To end this self-sensing, three-quarters of human activities, maybe more, would have to be banned. Even deductive processes would have to be suspended and elementary intellectual curiosity decreed criminal. Definitions are a natural end-product of observations and accumulation of knowledge; they cannot be halted halfway once the process has begun, unless the materials that produced such data in the first place are miraculously vaporized or rendered inert. And if the object in question possesses the facility for defining and expressing the definition of itself, of experiencing and recreating that experience, i.e. when it is also the subject, it is not intelligent to expect a cessation of that self-defining activity unless a moratorium is placed on and accepted by all such objects with a self-defining capacity. And by this we do not mean only the conscious and direct, but also the indirect, incidental acts of self-definition, the creation of all objects, even the most trivial artifacts. To cry "divisionism" and "reactionism" at the cognitions that arise from man's continuing cultural discoveries and practices is simply to make so much noise. Cultural truths are not responsible for the class stratifications that make Africa the sociologically obscene environment it is for the masses of our people. We must demand a closer adherence to intellectual objectivity than an emotive recourse to the political aspirations which we all share for the continent.

THE MATERIAL BASES OF CULTURAL INQUIRY

When I indulge in some scientific excavations and discover a potsherd which I identify and label distinctly, either for the sake of fellow researchers or simply from a tidy habit of mind, surely no one will suggest that I have raised divisive barriers between descendants of the civilization to whom that moldy piece of pottery belongs and others whose potsherds must be dug up some hundred miles or so away. Or if, just to complicate matters, I unearth two different kinds of potsherds lying one below the other, touching, and I am unlucky enough to discover, through radiocarbon dating, that both belong to different periods, do I thereby commit an act of disunity to those two pieces of earthenware which were geophysically united? From one potsherd I may read "autochthone," from the other "migrant" or "invader." A pursuit of cultural truths—to which we all pay lipservice—compels me to record my findings faithfully and follow up the ramifications of all evidence. If I organize an academic conference, or a festival of the arts of pottery relating to only one or the other of coincidentally neighboring earthenware, I shall not stand accused of criminal separatism in the habitation of pots. Furthermore, I doubt that anyone can point out to me any law, either in science of archaeology or governing the art of pottery which compels me to tackle investigations of both branches of the history of pottery at the same time.

My research continues. What other things did they do, these potters? Where did they come from? Were they permanent settlers or were they later dispersed? What is the contemporary situation of their descendants, and can their unique contribution to world civilization be in some way manifested even for the simple satisfaction of a scientific curiosity?

These are not thoughts subversive to any feeling of the common humanity of all, nor can actions dedicated to the realization of such ideas be held as directed against outlying groups of humanity, however closely intertwined historically.

But enough of objective considerations. We would be very foolish here to talk about autoculture and limit ourselves strictly to purely bloodless abstractions. Culture is also compellingly subjective.[2] It is also a matter of the psyche, of the viscera. When I declare: The Arab or the Asian is my brother, I do not say it in the same sense or with the same sensibility as when I claim: the Cuban is my brother. Of course, I do not speak of all Cubans. No, I speak of that portion of Cuban humanity whom I met in the shrine of Shango, that familiar deity from the West Coast of Africa. I speak of that descendant who still vaguely remembers the liturgy of the worship of that deity, the rhythm of his drums, the socioethics of his worshippers, the symbolism of the double-headed axe—in short, a community whose life is still so deeply imbued with the African philosophical order from which he was wrenched that the Roman Catholic missionaries to Cuba were compelled to abandon their policy of conversion and adopt instead the principle, "If you can't beat them, join them." These Cubans—or Brazilians, Black Americans—are not conservative, atavistic believers in fallen deities. On the contrary, it was their fidelity to an authentic world order and social justice which made it possible, ultimately, for the revolution of the Cuban people to succeed under the leadership of Fidel Castro. Roman Catholicism in Cuba was allied to the reactionary rule of Batista, and both the exploiters—the bourgeoisie, the landed gentry and the exploited—the landless peasants and impoverished workers, all loyal Roman Catholics, were imprisoned in the superstitions of the Church whose credo endorsed the status quo. But the African religions nerved many Cubans to brave the threat of excommunication and participate in the liberating communion of social upheaval. For the African gods, they knew, were revolutionary deities.

To visit Algeria is to admire its revolutionary history and reality, to recollect and identify with its epic fight against the most brutish, greedy, and tenacious settler forces of the colonial experience. Yet is it being reactionary to confess that this sense of identification is different from the pride, from the sense of belonging which an African feels for the militant black peasants of Caribbean history? It has nothing directly to do with actual skin color, though this of course is related to it. I would be very foolish to say that most Moroccans are not differently tinctured, that their hair and other features are not different from those of most Ghanaians in Cuba. Yet in Cuba there are African descendants with the Moroccans' skin color, hair, and features. I have encountered them dancing ecstatically at the shrine of Ogun, Oxun, Obatala, and I consider them authentic descendants of the people of West Africa. Let us stop the reductionist falsity which attempts to define cultural realities along purely color lines. And therefore, if I find the means, and if I choose to celebrate the achievements, the resilience of these people, the makers of that particular potsherd wherever they are, there is no moral, social, or ideological law which can say "no."

SALINE CONSCIOUSNESS

How can we as intelligent beings submit to the self-imprisonment of a "saline consciousness" which insists that, contrary to all historic evidence, Africa stops wherever salt water licks its shores? Or that, conversely, all that is bound by salt water on the African continent is necessarily African. What other race, and especially on the African continent, has lost 200 million of its people through forcible uprooting? Elementary curiosity justifies that we seek out those who survived of that number and inquire in what forms have they survived? What have they achieved? What have they contributed to their new environments? What lessons, if any, have their specific genius evolved for those who were left behind? The human (and African) habit of celebration, which is an act of recollection, assessment and rededication validates this impulse. It has been proposed that, while representatives of every people on the continent be invited to the general celebration, only that part of Africa which experienced this historic dispersal contribute to the colloquium on the subject of their own culture and civilization. This proposal for FESTAC has however been denounced as retrogressive.

Let me state right away that having participated in numerous conferences on African culture, side by side with Arab and other scholars and researchers, I have no objection whatever to the participation of the entire world plus the moondwellers at such a colloquium. However certain arguments against the narrower alternative have provoked larger issues, questions of principles which are so far-reaching that it would be foolish to let them pass. Indeed, those who have glibly denounced an exclusively black colloquium as reactionary insult the intelligence.

Such an application of a double standard in view of the actualities on this continent cannot be allowed to pass without challenge.

After 3,000 years of pronouncements by others on Black African civilizations, Black Africans propose to meet and to pronounce upon themselves, and the whole world cries "foul play." Do we hear right? The tomes of dubious erudition about Africa which flood the world today were written by outsiders to the African world. At a celebration to which, observe, the whole world has been invited, it is proposed that these pronounced upon now make their own pronouncement, by themselves, that they pronounce also upon the various alien definitions of over three-thousand years standing, yet this proposed minuscule contribution, this colloquium is attacked as something which exists in a vacuum, a retrogressive notion dredged up to haunt an ideological paradise. The intensity of assault on this very simple procedure is what has alerted us to the possibilities, progressively demonstrated and confirmed, of a very real danger posed to the self-cognition of the African world. For it is difficult to understand this attitude of knocking violently on the door when the family wishes to hold a private celebration. It strikes us as an alien affectation. Certainly it is not an African usage, and therefore it is perhaps the best argument yet that there may be certain unique values of the African world which are best examined by the unfettered intelligence and sensibility of African scholars.

It is time to outline the very dangerous limits to which the application of double standards has reached in this matter of self-definitions. And at all possible stages, it should not be considered excessive that I call attention to the fact that I am concerned here with principles, and far less with actual manifestations. The Pan-African Arts Festival in Algiers does not, in my view, contradict or eliminate the validity of the Dakar Festival of the Negro Arts, neither does the reverse process take place nor the pending Festival of Black and African culture in Lagos.[3] Any polarization of these two festival contexts is so contrived that it does not merit recognition. They are complementary. They can both be accused of extravagance, untimeliness, or circus distractions just as both can be lauded for proportion, creative quality, social bonding, and inspirational values. The geographical touchstone is nothing but an arbitrary harassment, a millstone hung around the necks of makers of culture who, it is observed, occasionally step near the sea. Even football, which is not a game indigenous to Africa, played within the context of pan-Africa, continental Africa and/or the black world cannot be held

inimical to African unity. Whoever alleges any such thing must first
prove it in concrete, not speculative, terms. So let us now look at this
entire business of groupings and contextual relations as manifested on
the African continent. Actual political decisions involving fundamental
cultural definitions are at hand to help us; we need not shy away from
them any longer. But let us first proceed by way of illustration.

THE SOMALIAN EXAMPLE

We shall say that within my family I have a brother.[4] This brother
has always assumed that our family identity, his and mine, is totally
defined within the walls of our house or compound. This sense of
definition is so complete that if, as sometimes happens, a distant relation
is unexpectedly unearthed, those walls of our defining house merely
extend to take in that new discovery into a mutual family identity. But
imagine that one day, on discovering one such potential extension, I
exclude him. I say to this brother: "Listen, the peculiar facts which
surround this particular situation are such that a new entity has come
to my knowledge which relates to me but not to you. I have received
a summons to a gathering of a clan to which I appear to belong, and this
invitation most definitely excludes you. I am not deserting this earlier
family compound, I shall still return home for the annual gathering of this
compound, but first I must attend to that very special relationship of other
people and other spaces. And you are not a part of it."

If my brother has not reached the age of maturity, or if certain areas
of—shall we say—our polygamous complexities have been closed to
him, he might resent this separatist act. If, on the contrary, his development has been different, he would be more likely to rejoice in the
fact that, in a sense, he has himself received a bonus from the new
situation, an indirect self-extension. He knows that he now possesses
a friend in an ostensibly alien house. It is not truly alien in fact, but
the very act of my exclusion of him from my new grouping, the act of
his formal and practical estrangement defines the nature of this new
home of mine—in his terms—as alien, just as effectively as my election,
sought or given, my admission into a group definition that excludes
him, redefines my own identity both objectively, and in his own subjective apprehension, as an alienating event. I have effectively estranged
him; I have also intensified the objective's unique apprehension of the
newly adopted clan, its alienation, that is, from all other groupings

known or unknown. This is a very simple matter of fact. To detach
something from a place it has occupied until now is one step of estrangement; to reattach it somehwere else, to a unit previously and
differently defined, is to imbue that detachment with additional finality
and to accentuate a way of perceiving the uniqueness of the acquiring
body. Of course, if the attaching body were content merely to float in
space, this last consideration would obviously not arise. We may also
question the act of detachment in the first place and see even less sense
in its reattachment. Logically, that is a very different matter, and, if
we see it as such and are not lacking in moral courage, we owe it clearly
to the cause of truth to say so.

This last position is one which, in the case of Somalia, I do not feel
qualified to take. I believe that it is not possible for anyone even within
the immediate family of the African continent to pass judgment on an
act of self-definition that must have been carefully thought out, especially by a people who appear to demonstrate a capacity for revolutionary
leadership, thinking, and practice. And there is no reason why I should
be required to go into reasons since, I have no difficulty whatever in
accepting this decision any more than the Somalians have had in re-
defining themselves out of our former community. In short, the problems
which agitated these defecting relations of mine were strictly the problems of Somalia; the problems which agitate me now are the problems
of the rest of that family unit from which they are now dissociated, at
least, on one level. In wishing them fulfillment in their new identity,
it is only rational to insist that, even if I am not wished any luck in my
continuing identity, I am left alone to look out for its continuing health.
At the very least, as a thinking and therefore moderately curious being,
it is not unlikely that I ask myself: What exactly has Somalia identified
itself out of? I could equally seek to understand the exact meaning of
this action as a historical act, as an ontological pronouncement, or would
it be simply as a part of the bloc politics which have come to plague
our existence and confuse otherwise objective issues? Instead, however,
I choose to limit myself to the question: What, in cultural terms, is that
entity out of which Somalia has identified itself? However amorphous,
taken for granted, and intangible it may be, the very simple act of
"detaching from" it gives sudden, even dramatic form to that vagueness
from which detachment takes place. Something did exist, something
from which a part is saying: I am now separated. Even if it simply
says, I am now a part also of something else, that part still redefines
the original totality, itself, and the acquiring unit, for what the part is

saying is that it now has two or three, not one or two identities. And for those who have nothing but their original identity and seek no other, who can say that they must not concretize and formalize their truncated identity? Could it be, by any process of reasoning, those who were the first to chip pieces from it?

I embark on these arguments with the greatest reluctance and only because at various confrontations our self-alienating brothers and their African supporters appear impervious to any other type of discourse. If, and let this be understood very clearly, tomorrow Somalia, and the other parts of Africa which have alienated themselves into the Arab World turn right round and say that they have made a mistake, that they belong absolutely and indivisibly to the African world, I must request equal time for making a similar mistake: That their original recognition is backed by instinct, reason, culture, and history. In any case the initiative for being right or wrong, for simply *acting* in the right or wrong is not preordained for any one section of this continental family alone. When I say that I would like to see that (black) part of Africa from which a certain group have estranged themselves, speak a common language and identify a common essence even within plural cultures, I am acting under the demands of the same historical initiative that has motivated others, and I demand like recognition of the positive nature both of my actions and of their potential contribution to our common existence.

The only remaining difficulty has already cropped up in the last section of the preceding argument. Paradoxically enough, it is an objection most strongly voiced by (black) Africans themselves. "All this talk about an African culture, a black African culture," complained the leader of the Nigerian delegation, "I don't understand it. I mean, is there really such a thing? In Nigeria alone, we have...." And he proceeded to enumerate the several cultural varieties in his country, concluding, "I think it is best to speak of a plurality of cultures. I certainly don't see how we can talk of a black African culture." In this he found ready support from several delegates, including, and I single them out for reasons which will later become obvious, the leader of the Egyptian delegation and the eloquent debater at the head of the Guinean delegation.

SUDANESE REALITY

But first the Sudanese. The mistrust and anguish of the Sudanese delegate over the proposed cultural division of Africa was easily the most deserving of serious attention. Sudan has barely got over its protracted civil war between northern and southern inhabitants, divided along racial lines. It was only natural that anything which threatened to emphasize the cause of that conflict should evoke alarm in the Sudanese, and the rest of us would be foolish to dismiss this unique problem out of hand. But once again, we may ask: Are the discriminatory policies of insensitive leaders ultimately responsible for conflicts of this nature? Both religion and race were factors in the Sudanese conflict, yet the religion alone has produced, proportionately, a far more savage conflict in Lebanon. Sociological inequity is the common factor in both cases, the result of human failing and lack of vision. The new order in Sudan is a rectifying one which is indeed based firmly on the recognition of differences in the Sudanese population.

There would be cause for alarm indeed if we proposed definite and arbitrary cultural demarcations for the continent, in which one nation is entirely planted in one section or the other. While people may not be absolutely politically free, they are absolutely culturally free. The practical applications of this statement are easily demonstrated. There exists as we all know, a Union of Arab Writers. It held its tenth Congress in Algiers in February 1976, attended by delegates from Egypt, Morocco, Libya, Algeria, and other countries on the continent of Africa. The policies at present pursued by Sudan are such that we see no difficulty for a writer of that nation to belong to this union, or to choose not to belong, assuming of course that the Union of Arab Writers admit him into their fold; and here we envisage no difficulties since we on our part would welcome him into our own newly formed Union of Black African Writers if he thus chose. Again, in interpreting Sudanese culture, it is obvious that any scholar worth his salt must distinguish between these two dominant cultures: its melange or synthesis will be manifested in many ways that will be uniquely Sudanese, but its components are only too clearly distinguishable. Sudan is therefore the working proof that the cultural map on this continent need not be the same as the political, and that the false attempt to align them creates the kind of foreboding which we have noted in the intervention of the Sudanese delegate. When we speak of a black African culture, therefore, we refer clearly both to a sum of its various parts, and to its unifying essence. Just as there are minorities in every political state so are there cultural minorities in any convenient cultural division.

But you may further ask, suppose the proposal is taken up for a separate UNESCO Conference on Culture for Black Africa, where should Sudan be? The answer is obvious. Somalia chose to be an Arab nation, so it is obvious where Sudan will go. Sudan has opted for a policy of duality, and Sudan is naturally entitled to be represented in both groups. Since nothing sinister takes place at professional meetings, nothing secretive or conspiratorial, both the Arab cultural group and the African should feel satisfied. It would be up to Sudan to send representatives appropriate to these cultural groupings, or to mix them up as desired. No one at such a conference will, I am certain, dare question the credentials of such participants.

There is one more point worth noting: for nearly thirty years the black population of the Sudan, led by the Anyaya Movement, stated in the language of arms that they were not Arabs. Arabs have, just as cogently, frequently declared their Arabness. We believe that, when a similar statement is made merely in the language of culture, the continent is more than secure. No one quarrels with political leaders when a similar claim is made in the language of economics or politics. Delegates at this conference must be careful to examine all issues within a background consciousness of the totality of African phenomena. The call by OAU leaders for a special conference between the OAU Arab and African heads of state has never yet, to my hearing, been equated with treason; on the contrary, it has been enthusiastically welcomed and a date has been set for it. I presume that Sudan will attend in a dual capacity; certainly I have not yet heard any declaration from the Sudanese government that this encounter poses an insurmountable problem. Must it always be culture whose inescapable realities arouse such terror?

POLICY ILLUSIONS

Let me take this opportunity to register my protest generally against this particular double standard which stems from a rather circumscribed governmental perspective. While governments recognize the existence of certain material realities in the contributory factors to economic systems, resulting in the formation of sometimes overlapping organizations and fiscal institutions such as ECOWAS, the East African Community, the Arab League, African Development Bank, etc., the same policymakers somehow suffer from the delusion that culture, whose material reality is even less prone to dictation, multilateral agreements, manipulations as in currencies of exchange, can be synthesized into one happy broth like instant coffee, simply because there is a noisy, though uniform demand for such an item. A few grains of Kenyan coffee, Arabian mocha, West African beans, and chicory and—*voila*—instant African culture! Culture is simply no such commodity, and it is futile to pretend it is.

AN ETHIOPIAN CHOICE

One more specific example, but this time a purely speculative one: Why should anything prevent Ethiopia from claiming a Semitic culture? There is sufficient evidence to justify such an affiliation of cultural sensibilities, nor can such evidence be wished away by any mandatory concept of a unified African culture. Subject to more qualifications from the more learned, my knowledge of both societies indicates that there is as much evidence from historical, archaeological, and religious art to sustain the claim of Ethiopia for inclusion in the Semitic cultural map as there is for Somalia's adoption of the Arab world. But Ethiopia possesses just as much right to make a definitive choice as all other nations and peoples, and only those inclined toward cultural imperialism will question such a choice. There are black Jewish communities not only in Israel but also in the Arab world; no one has suggested their cultural annexation by the African world.

THE QUESTION OF PLURALITY

I must now recall to your memory a remarkable incident which occurred between the Senegalese and the Egyptian delegates to the 1975 AFRICULT conference, a perfect giveaway moment which did not pass unnoticed by the more observant participants. It was not rigorously pursued, I suspect, because Africans are very conscious of the sensibilities of guests. I refer to the occasion when the Senegalese minister referred, as he habitually did, to the Arabo-Berber and Maghreb cultures of northern Africa. It was a signal for the Egyptian delegate to flare up in irritation: "Why do you continue to refer to the Maghreb, Arabo-Berber cultures? We are Arabs, we consider our culture an Islamic-Arab culture and I don't really see why we should continue to keep harping on these other divisions." He was duly pacified by the Senegalese who, however, pointed out, quite correctly, that they were both basically in agreement. "I apologize if I have offended my colleague from Egypt. Of course he is right, and from now on, since he finds my reference to Maghreb, Arabo-Berber cultures offensive, I am only too happy to call the culture of the whole of North Africa an Arab culture. He has indeed confirmed the very point we are making. There are two distinct cultures in Africa. You say you wish to call yours Arabic, good. But leave us to call ours what we wish. We say ours is the black or African culture. Can anyone really object to that?" And for the first time since this impassioned debate began on the subject, no one did. This was a pity, not merely because those who dissented still registered their dissent at the crucial voting, but because the real lesson of our Egyptian brother's outburst has been lost upon the majority at this conference.

This is the lesson. Throughout this conference, the expression and referentials of specifically one or two or three "unified" cultures were made merely incidental to the forefront. All speakers accepted this, indeed, no one attempted to dispute it, until the wording of a motion by Senegal sought to crystallize the existence of one (black) culture as possessing an identifiable unity in essence. All delegates, including the Senegalese as we noted, adopted the plural perspective; they elaborated upon it, gloried in it, approved policies (including linguistic ones) based upon it and, indeed, enshrined it as the primary reality upon which national policies and attitudes must be based. But, and here is the crux of the matter, the conference was about *African* cultural policies. Suddenly, with the wording of that Senegalese motion came the threat of a shift of focus. The attention of the debaters was diverted, thanks to the outburst of the Egyptian delegate, to the existence of a plurality within the Arab-Islamic culture. What with the previous emphasis on the *plurality* of cultures, and taking into consideration the particular direction in which the debate was now going, it was anybody's guess how soon someone in this chamber would have been moved to observe, and to thereby demolish the remaining arguments against the concept of a unified *black African* culture, that, even in North Africa, Arab culture is also pluralistic. Yet the Arab delegates at this conference, and indeed anywhere at any time consistently identify one *Arab* culture. From that point a cursory look, for the first time, at the reality of the so-called Arab culture on the Arabian peninsula itself would have revealed that it is based on a plurality as diverse, as varied, and as self-evident as that of the so-called black African culture! Yet we have listened to delegates who contemptuously dismiss all propositions for the definition of one black African culture, who piously utter the commendable injunctions that the conference should "concentrate on what unites us rather than on what divides us!" No one at this conference has dared affront courteous usage by remarking on the innate contradiction of these pronouncements. On the one hand, the "plurality" of cultures in the black African world is positive and wholesome, while the unified concept of the same cultures is retrogressive. The Egyptian by contrast protests violently against plural references to the Arab culture. We are *one* culture, he passionately declaims, and this conference endorses his claim. We are also one culture, claim the Senegalese and the Ghanaian, but the Guinean says that this is backward thinking and he is supported by the Arabs and the Nigerians!

What sort of double standard is this? The Arabs are free to formalize, structure, and defend a unified concept of their own culture in spite of self-evident diversities, but a similar right is denied to black Africans. There is hardly any world organization or activity of a cultural nature where we do not encounter institutionalized Arabism. I believe the world of culture is all the richer for it. ALESCO, the Arab League's version of UNESCO, is the readiest and most obvious manifestation of the cultural assertion. The Arab League is itself a multifaceted instrument of the same assertion. We must ask then why it is that we on our part are being declared a nonpeople, for this is the only meaning we can attach to the aggressive negation of all the efforts of black peoples to come to terms with the possible unifying essence of their cultural existence. What is it exactly that is intellectually or politically frightening about the expression of or speculation over this identity? What agitates people's minds against the enrichment from a reciprocal identification that should exist between the people of a self-defined Arabic culture on the one hand, and a contiguous culture—black, Negro-African, African, South-of-the-Saharas, or whatever terminology by which they identify themselves? We may quarrel on the appropriate terminology since the language is not ours, as already remarked. It ought to be sufficient that whenever one or the other of these expressions is used, what registers in my comprehension is the race referred to in Africa as *bakinutane* as *awa enia dudu.* And each expression predates the incursion into the land of *enia dudu* of the progenitors of any (self-defined) European, Caucasian, Aryan, Semite, or Arab. That expression has always encompassed more than the specific users of that language; it has transcended their nation-state boundaries—we only need to pursue the folklore, mythology and contemporary literature of its peoples. It identifies all who, because of a number of factors including—yes—color of skin, were considered coracial with them, and who found no reason to deny it, who did not feel belittled by it nor ideologically retarded on account of its acceptance. It includes those who did not feel that to accept this identification is to accept membership of a racial conspiracy against the rest of the world, to be guilty of a sordid revanchism or of seeking to bisect a continent which, when the earth flew off an overheated sun was mystically endowed with only a choice of two properties: to spawn a single culture or a plurality, where plurality denotes more than two or three! While the owners or other borrowers of the English language may deny me the use of the expression *black* or *African*, I await the day when the same deniers will attempt to expunge the identification *enia dudu* from the vocabulary of my ancestors!

RADICALISM IS SELF-COGNITION: A FALSE POLARIZATION

Sekou Toure, an African militant leader whose radicalism in political affairs cannot be doubted, often gives the impression that it is not possible to believe in a unified black culture and yet to be a progressive. If this were true, let me say this at once, it would be just too bad for progress. Fortunately it is not true, for we know enough about our precolonial social structures to be able to assert confidently that principles of an equitable distribution of resources, of the primary value of labor, of an economy directed toward not accumulated profit but communal prosperity, etc., were not strange to those whose knowledge of the world's inhabitants once encompassed only *enia dudu*. The attitude that seeks to make self-denial a pre-condition of radical political attitudes is simply self-disparaging; it forces upon us an alien definition of a reality, which, I believe, is precisely what the colonizers did to our society for a number of centuries. Just as determinedly, other political thinkers have tried to imply that an attempt to map out Africa culturally in any units other than one or several (more than two or three) is reactionary and disruptive. One answer to that charge has already been given. We want to know why, for instance, these same radicals have failed to censure Somalia for acting in a way which emphasizes the existence of a cultural (and political) duality on the continent, why the

North African countries have not been invited to recognize that their own separatist grouping is also an act of continental subversion. The truth of course is that such accusations are untenable: so why are they made against similar claims to a racial identity?

In the same way as the Arab peoples have defined what they mean by Arab culture, in spite of even its occasionally fratricidal pluralities, have given it such cogency that they can participate in transcontinental events of cultural cooperation such as the German-Arab Cultural Week (1974) and others, so do we who are not Arabs and who inhabit the African continent insist on the right to determine what is "African culture"; to determine who may properly be considered to manifest its essence. Somalia is one of the most seriously socialist countries in Africa today. It commenced its revolutionary program in 1969, and in a few years achieved so much along this ideological goal that it won from President Nyerere of Tanzania this rare praise: "We in Tanzania write books on Socialism, but in Somalia they practice it."

In 1972 Somalia replaced all former official languages—English, Italian and Arabic—with Somali, adopting for its transcription a modified Latin alphabet. This rejection of Arabic and the Arabic script in favor of its own national language is of interest, since Somalia went on in the following year, 1973, to declare itself formally an Arab state by joining the Arab League. So here again we have a very recent example of the variants of culture and cultural strategies. We identify, in these seeming balancing acts of Somalia, a considered aspiration to a separate national identity simultaneously with a craving for membership in a wider cultural community because it cannot be imagined that the formal admission of Somalia into the Arab League marked the beginning of Somalia's efforts to be admitted into the select community.

In a decade which has seen violent militancy from the Scottish and Welsh "nationalists" of Great Britain, the Basques of Spain, the Bretons of France, the Ukrainians and Georgians of the Soviet Union, etc. resulting in several cases not only in acts of terrorism, economic sabotage and even assassinations, we may be excused for finding it strange that a people with—as it seems to us—a greater historic justification for ethnic assertion should be so savagely assaulted on a mere debating floor for seeking to establish a reality which is so demonstrable. The Soviet Union has for instance found it politic to grant to a number of Soviet nationalities the right to use their own languages in their national assemblies and in literature. I find, from this distance, a lofty indifference to the more extreme tribalistic impulses of the European races, and deplore the siege mentality of the French separatist groups or the economic sabotage practiced by the Scottish tribalists against their own ultimate interest in the North Sea Oil explorations. However, I come to the frequent conclusion that it is not my place to pronounce upon these exhibitions, being ignorant of the history of the French or the British people in any profound sense. It is a different matter entirely when I encounter the many variants of the expression *enia dudu*. Instantly, I am filled with a replete sense of community being which transcends the boundaries of my tribe, the geographical nation, or the continental shelf. This sense of community does not contradict an ideological fraternity with all the peoples of the world. Those for whom such a mutual correspondence is impossible, who must choose between one or the other must be, it often seems to me, in some way innately inadequate and unsure; certainly the level of aggressiveness suggests a defense mechanism against inner doubts. If a communist Russia could march side by side with a capitalist America against the rampant fascism of Hitler's Germany, surely it is not beyond the capacity of a self-cognizing African to march beside a self-cognizing Arab against blatant to subtle fascisms on the continent, most especially against apartheid South Africa! Those who doubt this had better go back in history to the struggle of the Congo (now Zaire), examine the present struggle in Angola, then look forward to the fast approaching finale over apartheid South Africa!

RACIAL CREDENTIALS: SUPERIORITY OR ENMITY

I am aware that what needs to be said now is not very palatable, and it is a pity that it must be said. I only demand that it be remembered at all times that the grounds are not of our own choosing. We have never denied other people the right to identify and express their own self-apprehension. It is always others, beginning with the European colonizers who attempted to eradicate our own sense of identity, who have done this. The methods have been different, but the results have been the same. Colonial boundaries, imposition of the superior valuation of other cultures, shame at and denial of one's own culture, aspiration toward and emulation of other cultures as a means to respect and recognition as "human beings," ideological respectability. When we look at the attitude of the deniers toward cultures which they recognize and respect in their pronouncements, we find two very suspect criteria. A clearly defined culture needs to be one of two things: a superior culture or an enemy culture. Thus we find that the same Arab intellectuals who deny the existence of an African culture speak in the same breath—indeed, use as a yardstick of comparison—the European culture. Thus, we hear of Arab contribution to European culture. In a very different vein of course, similar distinct recognition is accorded Jewish (Semite) culture which, every child knows, is twin to Arab culture. These two cultures do not merely represent the much-bandied plurality within the same culture, they are as related as unidentical twins in the family of cultures. Yet the enemy Jewish culture is honored by being conceded its own—admittedly hostile—identity while the friendly culture is not. Is this an unhappy hint about what we have to do before being granted autonomy in our own being? Or would it be merely enough to recall that historically we may also claim similar credentials to recognized enemy cultures, even though we never did counter the *Jihad* with a Crusade? There is, it must be confessed, a highly unsettling quality to the opposition which black intellectuals and artists encounter at these get-togethers, a strategic precision about the method employed to throw the black culturalists in disarray. There is such an intensity of commitment in denying the authentic African peoples the grace and redemption of their own self-apprehension that we can only wildly speculate and, confronted with some obvious answers, join with our more cautious brothers in saying: Now, there has to be some lack of understanding—perhaps to do with a clash of cultures?

A NOTE ON THE NEO-MARXIST LINE

I now diverge from this conference and comment upon a remarkable essay by Amar Sarmi published on this same theme in *El Moudjahid Culturel*. The essay is a reply to Leopold Senghor's address to the precolloquium held at Dakar in November 1974. It is hardly necessary, I trust, to emphasize once again that Senghor's concept of a black African culture as represented in negritude is poles apart from mine. The following is a typical passage, representative of the language of Sarmi and his orientation:

[The] approach which we support, sees the rehabilitation of the values of civilization as implying a common, consistent continent-wide struggle against all forms of imperialist tutelage or domination. Transcending all reference to race, ethnic or anthropological grouping this option puts the discussion back in its true perspective of a struggle against neo-colonialism and imperialism. It thus ties in with the deep seated aspirations of the African peoples for cultural development which is inseparable from social economic progress.

Since culture is not an isolated fact, any analysis which claims to be scientific should necessarily take account of all these facts. For living conditions, socioeconomic relations and peoples' cultural practices, which are the basic foundations of every civilization stem essentially from the relationship governing production, as well as the social relations that exist in any social or economic grouping.

The extent to which a civilization has developed is not measured in terms of density of states of mind, nor of intensity of feeling nor of originality of phantasms it produces or inspires, but by the degree of development observable in the productive forces which actually make it possible for a people to shape their destiny.[5]

Shades of Marx, Trotsky, Cabral... not Fanon, however, for though Fanon was himself quite totally opposed to negritude, his definition of culture, while it tallied with the above rehashing of the Marxian viewpoint, did not totally ignore the imperatives of the racial stamp. Two things are very blithely ignored in the familiar evocation of talismanic phrases such as "socioeconomic relations," "relationship governing production," and "productive forces": (1) certain end results of these productive forces whose aesthetic uniqueness made us reach in the first place for the world "culture"; and (2) the affective outlook of any "socioeconomic" group, its relationship (codified or merely deducible) with its environment, even its material environment, other people, trees, rocks, earth, food, animals, rain, etc., and phenomena, such as nightfall, daybreak, moon, illness, birth, and death, the particularity of which relationship makes us commit the original sin of looking for a defining expression and settling for the various linguistic variants of "culture."

In short, the modern ideologist, embarrassed by group claims of a unique self-regarding in relation to (shall we say) rain, plumbs for its economic primacy, reduces its interaction with society purely to the organization of agricultural and marketing science and around the appearance, regularity, or uncertainty of rainfall. Claims to experiences of, or presumptions or other vectors, of a relationship with this or similar phenomena are placed in diminishing relevance to this simplified rendition of man's productive genius, a position which is comfortable

enough when we are confronted only with the material end-product—
a masquerade headpiece, a silo, an irrigation system, even a funerary
artifact—but becomes distinctly inadequate when we participate in the
processes of their production.

The purely "mystical" foundation of this approach becomes exposed,
however, when culture is also recognized as a continuing, affecting
factor of man's secular consciousness, even of his productive capacity
in society, certainly of his harmonizing capability with the rest of society. At that point it becomes clear that a transposition of "culture"
and "economics" and their allied terms leaves our conceptions of civilization pretty much the same. Thus, since economics is not an isolated
fact, any analysis which claims to be scientific should necessarily take
account of all these facts. For living conditions, sociocultural relations,
and economic practices, which are the foundation of every civilization,
stem essentially from the relationship governing creativity, as well as
the social relations that exist in any social or cultural grouping.

The above statement is no less true than the original, and one begins
to wonder what all the fuss is about; why for instance, it is considered
quite normal to study the economic structure of any given area, but the
identification of a particular cultural area becomes a cause of incantatory
appeals to "modes of production" and "continent-wide struggle against
imperialism." The celebration of a particularly good harvest is sound
productive psychology; but who needs to burst a blood vessel as to
whether the study of creative variants in the "modes of celebration"
belongs more properly to economics and the class struggle than to culture
in the narrow sense? I have observed a mutual interaction of such kindred
and have concluded that it is this interacting process which constitutes
the evolutional characteristics of most societies towards an identifiable
culture in the broadest sense. Amilcar Cabral similarly remarked on the
evolution of a new culture in his own society during the anti-imperialist
struggle, one which for him created a neo-Guinean personality. Can
the continent-wide anti-imperialist struggle be held to operate in the
same culturally "fusing" condition as was inevitable in Guinea, or, for
that matter, Algeria? Unifying, yes, but is unity the equivalent of a
neo-African cultural identity? And does the absence of the latter in any
way hinder the achievement of the former?

To claim ascriptive authority over history as human development is
merely to concede frustration that one has been born a little too late to
prescribe for one's ancestors. Nothing ultimately touches the material

essence of social foundations, least of all the incantations of solecistic formulae. Any suggestion that the definition of the culture is one which "puts the discussion back in its true perspective of a struggle against neo-colonialism and imperialism" is not simply offensive, it is blasphemy! This is a neo-Marxist line that must be modified in Africa or lose its bearings altogether. Needless to say, those for whom African history acquired reality or substance only with the entry of the European imperialist fail to surprise us when they reveal that even their analysis of postimperialist culture is conducted through a recognizable European framework, embracing its worn terminologies. By contrast, we prefer to look into the heart of the perennial phenomenon of our being in all its detail and complexity, without however any romantic illusions, without making exaggerated claims or permitting its evolution into an isolationist credo.

We must constantly bear in mind the fact that virility, i.e. the power to take root even in alien soil, is not a reliable index to the intrinsic value of any culture. The communications media alone would make the acquisition of American culture on such terms a mark of the modern civilized individual. Yet the remorseless inroads of Western culture into the sensibility of the African is one which continues to distress, even revolt a large cross-section of African society. The humanities come into our existence as one tool of counteraction, commencing with definitions and expanding into an infrastructural permeation of society. The demolition squad of the African world, however, insists that this is a retrogressive strategy unless its program conforms to a specific geographical determination.

We must examine this geographical principle, then the actual boundaries proposed. This is not an exacting process, for we find ourselves very quickly in the realm of superstition, mysticism and/or ancestral memory, centainly not in the realm of rationality or logic. The exclusivist case for a culture of "Africanism," for a continental culture, surely rests more on a hidden fear of salt water than on any provable reality of history or projection. Why not an Afro-South Americanism? The material environment—fauna and flora, the preimperialist modes of production on both continents even the recent analysis of the stone sculptures found in South America, the court organization, and nature worship, etc., have led to new theories regarding Pacific crossings in "prehistory." A wish to bound the cultural entity of Africa by the oceans therefore seems more a case for Jung than Marx or Descartes.

The legend of the parting of the Red Sea and its closing over the head of the inhabitants of the northern part of Africa may also partly account for this timidity, for ancestral memory is never completely exorcised, not even by new modes of production mandated by the escape of slave labor. What—moving north-eastwards, assuming we successfully negotiate the Red Sea—would be wrong with a cultural entity which is Afro-Semitic (we already have the Ethiopian link), one which extends as far east as the Bosphorus and perhaps a little beyond? Indeed, if culture and civilization depend so centrally on the interplay of imperialist impingement and modes of productive forces, the cultural map of the world must be a patchwork which may only incidentally and occasionally correlate with national boundaries.

The argument therefore is totally confused in the minds of the decriers of an African-World culture. Africanism, as a concept, is more than laudable, has more than historic and economic aspects for its creative acceptance. So also, however, does the concept of an African world, a black world or a Negro-africanism, one which transcends the oceans whose far-flung members not only took with them the "narrow" culture of their homeland but also the broader, in some cases a world view and a principle of social organization as a vital subculture in their new environment. And no one remotely suggests that the factor of survival makes these cultures intrinsically valuable merely that their continuing existence makes them deserving of study. And if their relationship to the society of their organization is self-evident, it is irrelevant to bring their unique reality into, or exclude it from, a cultural matrix delimited solely by a saline consciousness.

IN CONCLUSION

Let me freely admit that the foregoing has not been entirely free of the emotionalism I have often had cause to remark of in others engaged in this debate. In mitigation it can only be pleaded that we, who organize ourselves as existing in an African cultural world, have for long been content merely to exist and practice our creative trades within its self-evident reality. We continue to oppose the romanticism and social disruption posed by, for instance, negritude. Our opposition to negritude however, is based on self-acceptance, a hard-eyed self-examination, not self-denial. Allied to this has been the same quality of acceptance by us of others in their own declared self-cognitions. The refusal by a minority (the elite ideologues) of other groups to reciprocate, to evince the same humility with which we approach their culture manifestations, their increasingly bold, dictatorial, even contemptuous, dismissal of the most elementary manifestations of our unique self-apprehension, the insistence upon the right to join in pronouncing upon them when we suggest that we would, for once, even as an experiment, pronounce upon it, has the same effect as denying the black world its adulthood, of reducing its inhabitants to second-class world citizens. The knowledge that portions of this black world, through ideological blackmail or leadership antagonisms have been programmed into, or have programmed themselves into, this mood of self-denial is of little consequence, for we believe that the masses of *baiki mutane* are not involved in this argument. They know themselves what they are, and their daily existence is testimony enough to the unique reality of their racial being.

Undoubtedly, even much of the foregoing response to aggressive negations of the African World will be misunderstood, will be oversimplified, and even associated with propositions which I have taken the trouble to reject. So let the final words be a simple reminder that no one in the last ten years has seriously proposed an exclusive black community of being, not even in the United States of America or in South Africa where there would still be found justifications for such tactics in the overall liberation strategy. But an ethnocultural reality, a humane quality which uniquely informs human artifacts, music, poetry, and philosophy, is a crucial factor of human existence which cannot be programmed into externally mandated categories. Those who think it can, must first persuade us, and not in the language of empty rhetoric, why the attempt is necessary. They must explain how the assertion of any one ethnocultural community is negative, but not others, how it may hinder, any more than other types or quantities of community or concerted purpose of total liberation, social reformulation and the organic manifestation of our will to self-direction in all things.

NOTES

1. This was one of several preconferences held to discuss the Festival of Black and African Culture held in Lagos in 1977. The AFRICULT conference occurred in October, 1975, in Accra, Ghana.

2. Molefi Asante, Eileen Newmark, and C. Blake, *Handbook of Intercultural Communication* (Beverly Hills, Calif.: Sage, 1979).

3. The issue had been raised that African-Arabs should not be permitted to attend the third cultural festival in Lagos because they could not decide if they were Africans. The Algiers Conference, the first such conference, was called Pan-African; the second conference, held in Dakar, had "Negro" in the title. Some governments supported the Algiers philosophy and some the Dakar philosophy. The compromise was "Black and African" to allow for Africans living in the Americas.

4. In 1974 President Siad Barre declared Somalia to be an Arab state. This policy contradicted Somalia's claim to be African.

5. Amar Sarmi, "A Reply to President Leopold Senghor," *El Moudjahid Culturel*, March 1975, p. 11.

3

CULTURAL, POLITICAL, AND ECONOMIC UNIVERSALS IN WEST AFRICA

AGUIBOU Y. YANSANE

For 400 years, a body of foreign literature has described Africa as a land without a history to be proud of, without much contribution to universal culture and civilization.[1] Yet Egyptian civilization and its associates, such as the Kushite civilization, which flourished around the Nile Valley, under the Pharaohs, made many contributions to general knowledge in mathematics, mechanics, commerce, law, art, medicine, writing, and religion. After Alexander's conquest of Egypt in 323 B.C., Egypt was ruled by foreign invaders for a thousand years. Pyramids, ruins of temples, and archives are a testimony of Egyptian and associated civilizations existing prior to European and Asian invasions.

For other parts of Africa, it has been proven that organized cultures existed a long time ago, perhaps as long as several hundred thousand years ago. For instance, several modern scientific papers[2] and nonscientific works assert that *Australopithecus*, a fossil man found in East and South Africa in the 1920s was a weapon-user and a meat-eater and, most important, the direct predecessor of modern man. One such nonscientific masterpiece is Robert Ardrey's *African Genesis*.[3] Very important in Ardrey's argument is the point that the weapon was invented by early man before *Homo sapiens* and that it helped to shape the nature of man in his evolution.[4] In essence his theory evolves within a neoclassical framework; so it is still assumed and accepted that original sin biologically determined man's conditions. This is why Ardrey would have us accept his attempt in *African Genesis* of the analogy of the Bible with Cain and Abel. Man goes to war because he likes to kill, so Ardrey says. Nothing in the book indicates Ardrey's understanding of economics, psychology, or history. Finally, he rages constantly against the harm done by the "Romantic fallacy," which he says, is man's mistaken belief in his essential goodness. Although there may be some value in Ardrey's book, it is difficult to sort out the illogical, the prejudicial, and the absurd, from what is useful and essentially correct. Ardrey's conclusion about the nature of man, specifically his concept of the African man as inherently a killer, seems intellectually arrogant, narrow, and the product of preconceived ideas.

Recent archaeological finds and records show that Africa is the birthplace of human civilization. Kush, Axum, Nubia, Ethiopia, and the Zimbabwe stone enclosures demonstrate Africa's contribution to civilization. All over West Africa were born empires and kingdoms whose civilizations at the time were at least the equal of any contemporary institutions outside of Africa. The states of Ghana, Mali, Songhay, Kanen-Bornu, which started as city-states at the advent of Christianity, reached their periods of greatness between the fourth and the sixteenth centuries, and then declined. Along the coastal rain forest areas between the delta of the Senegal River and that of the Niger existed kingdoms, such as the Ashanti Confederation, Dahomey, Ife, Benin. They reached their peak between 1500 and 1885, before European colonialism. This chapter reviews critically some of the literature about the characteristic elements of West Africa's cultural, political, and economic universals. Do these elements set Africa off as distinct from other continents? A succinct review of the institutions of the first West Africa's empires and kingdoms enables us to assess their contributions. In what way have industrial technical characteristics enabled periodization and the ranking of these societies? What evidences illustrate that no single people has a monopoly on genius?

EARLY WEST AFRICAN KINGDOMS AND EMPIRES

The first kingdoms were Ghana (at the early Iron Age in Basil Davidson's periodization), taken over by Mali (intermediate Iron Age), and followed by Songhay (mature Iron Age).[5] These historic civilizations are still described by folk historians, the story tellers, and repositories of tradition. Other sources of knowledge of early African history are derived from archives, books by travellers (Africans, Europeans, and Arabs), and recent archaeological finds. The methodology of African historical reconstruction presents a few shortcomings. The storytellers and folk historians can dramatize their stories, sometimes forgetting important details and at other times adding stories of their own. Archaeology is insufficient to retrace the evolution of complex states which left no material remains; such states can be ignored in historical reconstruction relying solely on archaeology. Furthermore, the use of the spread of technology for periodization is risky because social development cannot always be judged by technology. Books by travellers may be biased. Yet despite these shortcomings, West African kingdoms and empires come to us vividly through the descriptions of Al-Bakri, Ibn Batuta, Leo Africanus,[6] as well as many contemporary historians.[7]

The Ghana Empire

The Soninkes (or Sarakoles) founded the empire of Ghana in the fourth century. It emerged as a famous super-state composed of many ethnic groups, small states, and vassal domains.[8] Ghana's apogee was achieved under Kaya Maghan, one of the most famous rulers of Africa. Since succession was matrilineal, the king, with the advice of the queen mother, chose a successor from his nephews.

Much of our knowledge of Ghana comes from Al-Bakri.[9] He tells us that Ghana emerged about 300 A.D. and lay 1,000 miles northwest of modern Ghana.[10] Its capital was Kumbi-Saleh. This was a large city located about 100 miles northwest of Bamako, capital of modern Mali. By the tenth century the city was divided into two centers united by a long street. Along this street were houses and mansions made of stone and acacia wood as well as modest dwellings made of mud covered with straw or grass roofing. On one side of the city lived the Moslems with their twelve mosques. Each mosque had its *Iman* or chief minister, its *muezzin* or public informant, and its scholars and jurists. On the other side lived the emperor and the people who practiced the traditional religion based on the divinity of the emperor. This religion predated the coming of Islam, which actually did not arrive before the seventh century. The emperor tolerated ministers from all religions. There was a sacred forest located near the emperor's palace. There lived the ministers of the traditional religion who implored the gods and ancestors to come to the rescue of their people, salvage their souls, protect them from calamities, and give them abundant crops. These ministers maintained absolute loyalty to the emperor.

The wealth of early Ghana was based on gold. The provinces of Wangara and Banbouk constituted the main gold-mining areas. Nuggets found at the mines belonged to the emperor and gold dust was left for the people. Much of the gold used in Europe came from Ghana. In return Ghana imported copper, horses, swords and other goods from Mediterranean Europe and Arabia.

Division of Labor

Most people in Ghana made their living from agriculture, particularly peasants. The overwhelming majority of the traditional farmers of Ghana lived in a subsistence economy. They grew their own food, crops, and fiber and bartered with their neighbors. Many villagers and inhabitants of the surrounding areas were not peasants, but lived off the peasantry, by supplying food to cities. In peacetime many people knew nothing but relative prosperity by producing for their own consumption millet, corn, rice, and cotton with simple techniques which neither allowed much surplus nor significant long-distance trade. The producers paid a proportion of their crops to the state as tax, which was not the only revenue of the state.

Some clans specialized in working iron, others in weaving cloth. These products of excellent craftsmanship were exported to other cities of the Sudan and Maghreb. Others raised cattle and sheep. Along the west coast and on the banks of the Senegal and Niger rivers many groups were fishermen. Each ethnic group which dominated a province or a state of the empire had its dignitary lineages of nobles, captives, artisans, and occupational castes.

Slavery existed, but it was not so cruel as in the New World. In some cases slaves were mere prisoners of war, criminals, or debtors. Although stigma was attached to servitude, captivity, and certain categories of criminals, in most cases these slaves and captives became full-fledged members of the extended family; they were integrated into the family by virtue of clan equality. These captives could often move up in the hierarchy of the clan and the kingdom. One emperor of Ghana had been a captive held in servitude in the court of a rival king. This vertical mobility was characteristic of the African form of slavery which was not a servitude for life, nor chattel slavery.

The artisans and their works were visible everywhere.[11] Laundry soap was made with seed oil and ash, and lamps consisted of a bowl of oil with a cotton wick. Much cloth was made locally, but the products were so reputed that many Arabs and Moors came down to Kumbi-Saleh for their supply of fabrics, and to buy leather sandals made by the Soninké artisans. However, it was mainly through gold trade that Ghana made its wealth.

Trade

Kumbi-Saleh, at the crossing of the caravan routes between tropical Africa and North Africa, was an important center of exchange and trade. Gold dust, cloth, sandals, salt, cowries, beads, and copper were exchanged. Gao and Kukia were other centers of intense trading activities.

During the eleventh century for every donkey loaded with salt that entered the empire, a duty of one gold *dinar* was levied on behalf of the emperor; two dinars were levied from everyone who left the country; five *mithquals* were levied on each load of copper and ten *mithquals* on each load of merchandise.[12] These import duties and export taxes were sources of revenues for financing state projects.

Legal Systems

The emperor was the symbol of justice. He dispensed justice in his palace at Kumbi-Saleh. Legends report that Kaya Maghan, one of the most famous emperors of Ghana, used to go for a morning horseback ride through Kumbi-Saleh, listening to the grievances of his subjects. Everybody who complained about an injustice could meet him and report to him. He was a very accessible ruler. He presided over the Court of Appeals of the Empire composed of ten judges or wise men. The wealth and splendor of this court was well known. He is reported as dispensing justice in a domed pavillion surrounded by ten mounted horses in gold embroidered trappings. Dogs with small golden bells on their necks guarded the entrance of the court. In front of the emperor, and facing him, sat the governor of the province of the grievance. The emperor was signaled by the beating of a drum. Lawbreakers were often treated with much generosity, it is reported by oral traditions.

The Defense System of Ghana

Ghana was a vast empire, which required a strong army to defend the territorial integrity of its states, kingdoms, vassal territories, etc. The soldiers were recruited from each kingdom and state of the empire and from each ethnic group. The contingent numbered around 200,000, which included an impressive cavalry and 40,000 bowmen.

Because of its attractive wealth, Ghana often fell prey to northern invaders. In 1076, Ghana, eaten up by vassal's feuds, was conquered by Almoravids from Morocco. Many Ghanaian people were massacred, but the Almoravid rule did not last. In 1087 the Soninkés reconquered Ghana which was now divided into several weak and competing city-states and kingdoms. In 1203, the king of one of these kingdoms, Sumanguru, annexed Ghana to his Sosso territory. In 1240, Sundiata, a Manding conqueror from the kingdom of Kankaba, destroyed what little remained of Ghana, annexed it and founded a bigger and more prosperous empire, the Mali Empire.

The Mali Empire

Mali, which may have existed since the first century, became the strongest and most famous West African empire after the Almoravids conquered Ghana. The history of the Mali Empire is very much the history of the ruler's family, the Keitas. The Keitas had ruled Mali for over thirteen centuries. The empire emerged from obscurity in 1230 when a military leader, a crippled son of Naré Maghan I, ascended to the throne of Kankaba, his father's kingdom.

Sundiata's Mali

The story of Sundiata and his unbelievable deeds are transmitted to us through oral tradition as transcribed by D. T. Niane.[13] Sundiata was the son of Naré Maghan (also known as Maghan Kon Fata) and his second wife, Sogolon. Naré Maghan had three wives simultaneously.

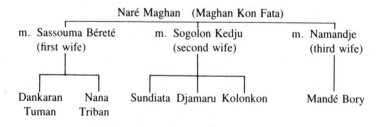

As a crippled son, Sundiata lived a lonely childhood. He was not able to play games with other children of his age. He was often serious and did not smile. His mother, Sogolon Kedju, an Amazon-like woman, had a strong personality; she was disliked by Naré Maghan's first wife, who was headwife. Sogolon was a permanent source of comfort and hope for Sundiata.

Due to the strength of his character and his strong will, he overcame all his physical problems and turned them into assets. Sundiata became an extraordinary man. He conquered the throne of his father which was ruled by his weak and jealous half brother, Dankaran Tuman. At the battle of Kirina, he faced the cruel Sumanguru, one of the most feared kings of the region. At the onset of the battle with Sumanguru, Sundiata was inspired by the praise of his personal griot Balla Fasseké Kuyaté: "You Maghan, you are Mali." With this stimulating praise Sundiata went from one victory to another, and succeeded in enlarging Mali very much beyond the borders of Ghana.

Sundiata enjoyed the respect of the Malian people more because he was close to them than because of the status conferred to him by his power. It was because of his closeness to his people that he was revered as a god. In Western interpretation the beliefs of Sundiata's people could easily be labeled "pagan" or "primitive"; yet the way in which religion permeated the daily occupations of these people, their entire life seems more sincere than just going to church on Sundays.

Sundiata and his people practiced their religious cults in diverse ways. Priests and soothsayers used their knowledge of the supernatural to guide human mortal actions. Sometimes they prayed, other times they made sacrifices. This literary record as seen in the story of Djeli Mamoudou Kouyaté and D. T. Niane shows the transcendental aspect of ritual literature and oral tradition.

In Sundiata's time the African women held positions of regard and respect.[14] This was the case in Ghana and also later in Songhay. Sundiata's mother might not have been liked by Naré Maghan's first wife, but yet her opinions were listened to and fairly considered. Father, priest, judge, ruler—all were the responsibility of a man who was a chief.

Mali's political life is shown in the relationship and maneuvering between different city-states and vassal kingdoms which made up the Empire of Mali. The systems of friendship, association, and alliances were very well defined. Expelled from Kankaba in his early life by his half-brother, Sundiata found refuge in the territory of the Cissé's clan.

This shows that friendly and courteous treatment was often given to political refugees. Enemies were enemies perhaps during a conflict, but after the war, the general outlook of the people of Sundiata's Mali was one of mutual respect and consideration toward other men. Captives were well treated. Slaves and servants had enough to eat, could marry, and some became part of the master's family.

People outside the ethnic group were often looked upon as equals, whether or not they were generally considered to be equal; D. T. Niane's *Sundiata—An Epic of Old Mali* indicates that they passed freely in and out of the society. The centrifugal and centripetal forces which seemed to unite African societies at this time contrast strongly with stereotyped Western images of the black savages of the jungle with no moral values or restraints. The record of events, actions, and words expressed by the people surrounding Sundiata shows a mature and orderly outlook on life and a belief in the freedom of all men. The legends about Sundiata and his people described in Niane's *Sundiata* demonstrate emotions and restraints to stresses, environmental and social, in contrast to the label of inhumanity attributed to Africans. According to the epic, Mali was ruled by very specific laws and codes of conduct. *Griot*'s tales of Sundiata's story reflect a structured yet basically defined sense of justice, equality, generosity, magnanimity, and tolerance.

Sundiata was a military genius. His army was headed by valiant generals who were responsible for several of Mali's conquests. Sundiata's Mali was divided into provinces. Each province was headed by a governor. Sundiata comes across to us through D. T. Niane's *Sundiata* more as a political strategist, a lucid statesman, than a military dictator. Mali grew from the small Manding kingdom of Kankaba to a famous empire stretching over more than 1,000 miles from the Atlantic Ocean on the west to the Great Bend of the Niger on the east, limited at the north by the Sahara desert and at the south by the rain forest areas of Coastal Guinea. Sundiata's story became a source of popular legends, epics, songs and tales. At the closing the griot tells you: "Do not seek to know what is not to be known." Sundiata's Mali was the equal of any contemporary institution in Europe, which was then plunged in feudal wars. At Sundiata's death in 1255, Mali, then the richest and most powerful of the states of western Sudan (or Guinea), experienced many problems and was not able to preserve its territorial integrity.

Mansa Musa's Mali

Sundiata's immediate successors lacked his statesmanship. When the empire started falling apart, one of Sundiata's grand-nephews, Mansa

Musa, who ruled Mali between 1307 and 1332, rebuilt its power and prestige beyond Sundiata's achievements. Mansa Musa (also known as Kankou Musa or Sultan Musa) was crowned in 1307. He extended Mali's rule over a great part of the south of the Sahara desert where he controlled the salt deposits. His pilgrimage to Mecca in 1324 impressed the whole Mediterranean world. His retinue included 500 servants each bearing a 2.5 kg gold bar and 80 carrying packages of gold dust weighing 3 kg each. Long caravans carried foodstuffs and other provisions. The emperor and his retinue were so generous in giving away their possessions that during their stay at Cairo in July 1324 the price of gold suffered a sharp fall.

The emperor, who was called the Golden Emperor, owned much of Mali's gold from Upper Senegal and Upper Niger. He levied taxes from vassal kingdoms and subjects, and also on all of Mali's exports and imports such as salt from Teghazza and copper from Diara. He encouraged exchange programs between North African universities and those he built at Timbuctu, Jenne, Gao, and Kankan. He built mosques and beautiful residences in all of Mali's big cities. He sponsored the services of an Arabic architect named Es-Saheh to design several of Mali's monuments and mosques, particularly after his flamboyant pilgrimage to Mecca.

Mansa Musa's prestige spread beyond the African continent. He was well known in Europe. European world maps of the time showed his picture as the ruler of Mali. Astute statesman that he was, he was very conciliatory toward the gold miners of the Wangara mining group who threatened to stop producing gold if they were forced to become Moslem. Mansa Musa permitted the Wangara people to practice the religious cults of their choice. He had deep respect for the rights of other people.

Malians under Mansa Musa were hard-working people. Many villages had craftsmen, wood carvers, silversmiths, goldsmiths, coppersmiths, weavers, tanners, and dyers. But of great importance was the political organization of an empire which was about the size of Western Europe. Mansa Musa's government was very strong. It was able to keep all the territories of Mali united for as long as he ruled. The empire was divided into provinces headed by *farins* (governors) appointed and dismissed by the emperor. The army, which was strongly hierarchical, counted about 200,000 men, of whom half were mercenaries. The emperor is reported to have had a great sense of justice. In the capital, Niani, a cadi, a great dignitary of the empire, and his council of wise men and elders dispensed justice.

Mali possessed a great wealth in gold, iron, copper, and salt and produced an abundance of subsistence crops. The cities of commerce and trade included Niani, (capital), Ualata, Timbuctu, Gao, Jenne, and Kankan. The social stratification resembled that of early Ghana. Yet the aristocracy, the military commanders, the merchants, and the learned assumed more importance in state activities because of the importance of trade and exchange programs. Arabic was used by scholars and Islam was the official religion practiced by the Mansa (chief). However, the overwhelming majority of the people practiced traditional cults. In the fourteenth century Ibn Batuta, an Arabic scholar of Berber descent who spent a year in Mali's capital described the people in the following terms:

The Malians possessed some admirable qualities. They are seldom unjust, and have a greater abhorrence of injustice than any other people.

The Sultan shows no mercy to anyone who is guilty of the least act of injustice. There is complete security in their country. Neither traveler nor inhabitant in it has to fear robbers or men of violence. They do not confiscate the property of any white man who dies in their country, even if it were of great wealth. On the contrary they give it into the charge of some trustworthy person among the whites, until the rightful heir takes possession of it. They are careful to observe the hours of prayer and assiduous in attending them in congregations and take their children also.[15]

The Songhay Empire

During Mansa Musa's reign, the kingdom of Gao was a vassal state ruled by Dia Assibia who established a dynasty that reigned for sixteen generations. The last descendant, Suni Ali Ber, or Sovereign Ali the Great, came to the Songhay throne in 1464. Suni Ali Ber was a brilliant conqueror who took over Timbuctu and expelled the Tuareg people. He annexed all the kingdoms and city-states which were then vassals of Mali. He made Songhay the largest of the Sudanese empires. Suni Ali Ber maintained a fleet of boats on the Niger to secure peace and promote commerce. Many Arab historians have downplayed his reign because he was not a devout Moslem.

When Suni Ali Ber died in 1492, leaving a highly structured state organization, he was succeeded to the throne by his son, Bakori Da'as. He was soon deposed by Gao's army's general-in-chief, Mamadu Turé, who was crowned emperor of Songhay under the name of Askia Mohamed in 1493 and ruled until 1529. Askia Mohamed was also a valiant conqueror. With the help of a well-trained army of mercenaries, he was successful in most of his military campaigns. He was able to keep nomadic people of the north under control, and he made the caravan roads, which ran across the desert to Morocco and Egypt, safe for traditional (nonmilitary) trade and commerce.

Askia Mohamed decentralized the administrative structures and placed his close advisers as farbas (governors of each province). A strong cabinet of ministers assisted him in this administration which was more efficient than the preceding and contemporary empires and kingdoms. Some of the ministerial departments were agriculture, external affairs, trade and commerce, finance, forests, waters, the navy, the army, and the cavalry. The government appointed chief justices and police, the chief eunuch, (a confidant of the emperor), local tax collectors, price controllers, and magistrates.

Askia Mohamed went to Mecca in 1495, but his pilgrimage was less pompous than that of Mali's Mansa Musa about 200 years earlier. Askia Mohamed revived Islamic learning which had declined under Suni Ali-Ber. Timbuctu, which had been sacked by Ali-Ber, once more became an important center of culture and commerce. The University of Sankoré at Timbuctu excelled in Islamic law, literature, and medicine. Leo Africanus wrote of Timbuctu:

> There are many judges, doctors, and clerics here, all receiving good salaries from the King, Mohamed Askia of the state of Songhay. He pays great respect to men of learning. There is a big demand for books, and more profit is made from the book trade than from any other line of business.[16]

Askia Mohamed, who became blind in 1529, was dethroned by usurping sons who were weak rulers. They engaged in petty rivalries and were never able to unite. The great empire of Songhay declined. In 1590 the Moroccan sultan sent an army of 4,000 mercenaries equipped with cannons and guns reputedly superior to the bows, arrows, spears, and lances of the Songhay armies. The Moroccan mercenaries devastated all the major Songhay cities and crippled the Songhay empire, but this military success did not bring Songhay to its knees. Songhay never accepted Moroccan rule. The gold mines that the Moroccans coveted were never discovered. The Moroccan rulers were never able to unite nor pacify the former provinces of Songhay which organized perpetual guerrilla warfare. By 1618 the Moroccan settlers had eventually been absorbed in the population.

At this time, the Western settlement in the New World needed tremendous manpower. Africa's coast was raided for slaves once slave labor was found to be profitable. The transatlantic slave trade begun by Portugal in 1440 may have robbed Africa of approximately 100 million lives, according to some estimations. This added to the confusion of Songhay's decline. There was a new set of relations between Africa and the Western world.

While Africans and people of African descent can be proud of the West African empires which dominated West Africa and were often talked of, one must not forget that there were other smaller kingdoms which had existed in complete autonomy from these three great empires of Ghana, Mali, and Songhay. The kingdoms of Timbuctu, Kanem-Bornu, and the Hausa states became the major heirs of Songhay dissolution; and the base of power in these states was very reminiscent of those of Mali.[17]

For instance, in the Hausa states, power and authority were in the hands of the *sarki*, who implemented those acts which were acceptable under Islamic law.[18] Despite his great influence, the *sarki* had to answer to his council of twelve men who were very much in control of all the aspects of state activity. This Council of four *rukinis* (or four wise men, including the head of the cavalry, the eunuch *Galadima* or senior civil administrator, the representatives of the governors of provinces) chose the *sarki* in the Hausa states, between 1000 and 1500 A.D., while the *Hakimahs* were in control of territorial organization and local affairs. Beneath this executive branch of the Hausa government there was a whole hierarchy of princes, princesses, wives, officers, chief courtiers, eunuchs, territorial chiefs, and titled clerks, who represented the chain of command and who consequently owed their positions for supporting and implementing the policies and decisions of the *sarki*. At the bottom of the social scale were the *takalawa*, or commoners: the producers, brewers, iron workers, farmers, and peasants. These people paid substantial revenues to the state in terms of grain tithe, corvée labor, booty, fines, legal taxes, customary fees, and miscellaneous taxes on market commodities and foodstuffs. The *cadi* dispensed justice. The military organization was hierarchical.

In the south central portion of the African continent, was the Kongo Kingdom created between 1000 and 1400 A.D., by people who were moving into a plateau region in the southern valley of the Kongo River. The king ruled the kingdom which was divided into several provinces; each province was headed by a governor appointed by the king. The governor was assisted by an electoral council. The king levied taxes to finance the state projects.

Along the coastal rain forest area, between the mouths of the Senegal River and the Niger River, existed small independent kingdoms such as the old Yoruba kingdoms of Ife, Benin, the kingdom of Dahomey, and that of Ashanti. They reached their peak between 1500 and 1885 A.D.

The Ashanti

The Ashanti, before the formation of their federation, between the seventeenth and nineteenth centuries, were ruled by monarchs who had very informal authority over smaller chieftancies.[19] It was probably this lack of formal control that influenced such an astute statesman as Osei Tutu (1695–1731) to form the Ashanti Confederation, symbolized by the Golden Stool. The stool was a means of communication between the king and Onyame, the Ashanti skygod, and thought to contain the Akan soul, *sunsum*. Thus it was obligatory for all kings to show deference to *sunsum* by adding more gold to the stool upon their inauguration. As a symbol of nationhood, the stool was manipulated during the *odwira* or inauguration, so that the king could have everyone present swear his or her allegiance to the state. In this manner, the king assured everyone of the power of the state, of religion, and of himself. Without the assurance of this power, discontent could find its way and disturb the social order.

Oral tradition reports that the mother had informal control over the family, but the father no doubt represented the family and/or clan interests at village meetings. Such authority was based, as in most African politics, on age. Thus, the oldest male represented the family, while within the household, the "queen mother" had informal power over the male, therefore setting the pattern of matrilineal succession.

The Ashanti state confederation was divided into provinces or *omans*, each of which had its own chief, the *omanhene*, and his council of hereditary advisers or elders. But the provinces themselves were divided once again into districts, with their own chiefs. The final division was still the village level. Elders or other notables dominated this political arena. The major offices that existed before the Kwodowan revolution were all subordinate to the king, who appointed them. First, in order to select a king, the real queen mother chose a son among the aspiring king's nephews or his sister's sons. This candidate was accepted or rejected by the Ashanti Great Assembly through a democratic process. Once elected, the king appointed someone as the Master of the Palace, a sort of grounds and security manager. Next, the king appointed a chief informant, the king's most important tie to the people. The informant's job was to report to the king and the people the state of the union, as it were. The hierarchy continued down to the manager of the royal palace and to a military chief (*amafo*), and a manager of the king's finances, and lastly the many chiefs of all the provinces or *omans*.

The Kwodowan Revolution was initiated by Osei Kwado in 1764. This revolution initiated radical changes in policies in the Ashanti state that were fully implemented by his successor. The revolution's main goal was to advance the common people to positions of higher responsibility and pay. To do this, the king had to dismiss and banish some aristocrats, which did not win him any friends, but he placed competent people in positions demanding the same expertise and allegiance to the king. Also a paramilitary body was created at this time which was responsible to the king alone. The *ankobia* had two senior positions which were sometimes given to commoners. This ushered in an era of meritocracy which served several functions. First, it established a core of highly competent, well-trained civil servants. Second, it spread power in the state, thus bringing the benefits and costs of bureaucracy to the commoners. Finally, through *guyasewahene*, the superintendent of finances, literate Moslems were brought in to work for the king. This added Moslems to the ranks of foreigners already working in the state, which included French, English, and Hausa mercenaries.

The Yoruba Kingdoms

The Yoruba founded several city-states between the eleventh and thirteenth centuries, particularly the one under the Oyo king, Oduduwa, who later became a divinity.[20] The Yoruba cult is headed by the *oni* of Ife, who assures the cultural unity of the Yorubas. Oral tradition reports that the holy city of Ife was created in four days and on the fifth, the god of creation rested. This indicated the origin of a four-day calendar in Yoruba lands. Major cities besides Ife included Illorin, Oyo, and

Benin, each headed by a king, who maintained loose relationships with the Sovereign *alafin* of Oyo, whose role was nominal and symbolic. The *alafin* was elected for seven to fourteen years after which he had to retire or be poisoned.

Each of these Yoruba cities managed its business under a king or *bale*, assisted by a grand council, the *ogbani*, elected by elders of the aristocracy (*uzana*), and influential people. The *ogbani* had the real power, electing and deposing the king and occasionally electing itself the high Court of Justice. The *bale* was often elected for two years; he was enthroned on the market place by the *ogbani*; at that time he was given three recommendations: to assist his subjects without exception; to dispense justice equally; and to give special assistance to the ill. The *obas* of Benin were most powerful. They were assisted in their daily use of power by a council of seven members.

The Yoruba religion is a heavily meditative and intuitive cult, built around a hierarchy of gods, linked to one another in the image of the human society. The supreme god is the inaccessible Olorun, the Almighty Sky God. Below Olorun are 600 divinities including the principal gods, Obatala, Shango, Ogun, and Eshu.

The Nok Culture

It is now known that Nok culture preceded both Benin and Yoruba culture and probably contributed to all of the adjacent civilizations. The artifacts of the Nok civilization which influenced the coastal kingdoms were the images of settled people, for only under settled conditions could be developed such works as figurines and large polished metal works cast on walls. There is evidence that this African culture was built during the early Iron Age.[21] By the same token, the people of the Nok civilization succeeded in perfecting their weapons, tools, and means of agricultural cultivation on the basis of their technological advances. The Nok culture (900 B.C. to 200 A.D.) will be regarded as the beginning of West African Iron culture until other discoveries are made.

The Nok culture demonstrates two prevalent ideas. First, it shows that the African has a long and distinctive history in the western part of the continent as well as in the eastern and southern portions of Africa. Second, the fact that the distinctive artistic styles of the Nok people are unique to that region suggests that the artistic traditions were indigenous to the Nok civilization.

CULTURAL ELEMENTS OF WEST AFRICA
IN SYNTHESIS

Social Organization

Kinship relations were the foundation of social organization. The extended family system is based on interdependent functions since few societies provide sufficiently for insurance, sickness, disability, care for the aged, and so on. So the family is a cohesive unit which provides against personal calamities. It is also an insurance against underemployment for its members. In a society where organized care for the aged is nonexistent, children in the extended family take care of their parents, thus children are like an investment for the future. But as income rises, and the need for children to care for the aged declines, the size of the family declines. Both processes can be seen as a maximization of satisfaction (income plus valuation of the extended family costs) discounted over the period of expected life.

The African communalism that is the foundation of modern "African socialism" à la K. Nkrumah, Sékou Touré, J. Nyerere, L. S. Senghor, Cabral, and others, was sometimes based upon chosen policies for safeguarding and sustaining egalitarianism. Sometimes this communalism was thought to have been enlarged by Arabo-Islamic influences (orchestrated with some feudalism) in the cases of Mali, Songhay, Kanem Bornu, and the Hausa states. Sometimes it was influenced by European-Christian principles, as it was in the case of the Kongo's monarchy. In many cases, with the assimilation of certain ethnic groups, the chief of the extended family emerged as a patriarch and a hereditary ruler who enjoyed all the prerogatives of a king. But also, in many cases, each family was represented in the village council through its elder in the traditional subsistence society and economy. With technological development translated into better tools and means of production, the surplus society emerged, carrying more long-distance trade with the outside world. At the same time, a more stratified and structurally hierarchical society appeared whereby much surplus was appropriated by the king or emperor. Succession to the king or emperor was either matrilineal (Ghana and Ashanti) or patrilineal (Mali, Songhay, Kanem-Bornu, Hausa states, Yoruba kingdoms). The societies included the aristocracy, the princes, the courtiers of the king, his council of government, the officers of the army, the bureaucratic civil servants,

Village
Council → powerful → Kings
Chiefs

the merchants, and the predominantly productive class made up of the commoners, the artisans, workers of iron, leather, wood, and cloth, and the slaves in dialectic relationship with the political and economic base of power.

Political Organization

First, at the village level the power base was represented by a village council in which every extended family was represented. This system was very democratic and power was well distributed. Then through the gradual evolution from a subsistence society to a surplus society, powerful chiefs of extended families appropriated more surplus and became kings, thereby establishing monarchic centralized states and governments which maintained peace and order.

Mali presented jointly decentralized and centralized structures side by side. The governors of provinces (the farins) were appointed and dismissed by the emperor. But the empire included many vassal states which showed only loose allegiance to the emperor.

Songhay, which was a theocratic state, run according to the Koran, was extremely centralized. The emperor appointed all the governors of province (the farbas), the commanders of the army, the officers, the higher staff of the civil service, the judges or cadis. All these civil servants were responsible to him; he could dismiss them at will, although he was to be restricted by the Koranic principles. The Hausa states reflected this extreme centralization and differentiation, by investing a supreme authority in the apparatus of the state. In this way, such acts as land appropriation or involuntary servitude were not only justified, but also institutionalized. Through the corvée, the *sarki* or king of Hausa states was able to appropriate the labor of the *takalawas* (or commoners) for personal purposes and to ensure proper payment of taxes.

The coastal kingdoms of Ashanti, Ife, and Benin were very decentralized. In the Ashanti king's very formal authority over smaller chieftancies, the role of the kinship system was one that was directly in conflict with the Kwadowan Revolution's meritocratic system. The conflict beteween the kinship system and the bureaucracy was due to the recent emphasis on merit. The king seemed to have remained fairly well removed from this conflict even though his own rule might have been questioned at some point. One reason was that the Ashanti king was also a functional part of the religious system; thus his rule was justified by an entity higher than the principle of meritocracy. The same decentralized structures existed in Yoruba cities, which had become the centers of civilization and the centers of oligarchic republics with some religious cults, but which insured basically the freedom of individuals and the flourishing of African art.

In the Dyula (Mandinka merchant) Revolution of Samori, during the late nineteenth century, the Mandinka empire was divided into 162 cantons, each of which consisted of twenty or more villages. The cantons were grouped to form ten large provinces. The provinces of the empire were governed by three parallel lines of authority, first the traditional political, second the military, and third the religious—all leading up to the *almami*, or the emperor, and his state council composed of the provincial heads of the three lines of authority. For example, village heads were chosen by traditional methods; canton chiefs were also chosen by traditional methods, but held purely honorary positions. Real authority lay with the *sofa* (professional military officer), the administrator and the *cadi*. The *almami* was the supreme political, judicial and religious head of the empire as well as its military commander.

Samori's Mandinka empire was endowed with an extensive bureaucracy to insure the proper dispersal of power through representative democracy; it was one of the most effectively governed of the largest West African empires of the nineteenth century. This state was unique in its guarantee to religious syncretism. Although Mandinka unity was based on law, taxation, a traditional way of life, and the thinking of Islam, the particular influence of indigenous religions was seen as a beneficial influence in both political and cultural affairs, unlike most Islamic states founded after the jihad. Also, the particular influence of Islam on the indigenous government was reflected in the distribution of power from the top which was dispersed throughout the community by way of local spokesmen. Finally, the state was deeply involved in repulsing foreign invasions, militarily and diplomatically, to gain more power for the Mandinka coastal trade, unlike many other Islamic states which were concerned with accommodating demanding European colonists.

In sum, four types of government were prevalent in West Africa; the village council; the somewhat centralized monarchy of Ghana, Mali, Samori's Mandinka empire; the strongly centralized structure of Songhay, Kanem-Bornu; the seemingly decentralized monarchies of the coastal Guinea in which the King's power was limited by the customs, the constitution, and by religion. No one of these political systems excluded the other.

The governmental institutions can be characterized by a greater or lesser degree of centralization within the king's sphere of influence, but outside the capital, the tendency was toward decentralization. Thus one could expect decisions at the village level to be made at the village level. Only royal decrees would affect all parts of the states. In general, the nineteenth century saw no drastic changes in the body politic with the advent of the *jihads*, but the growing influence of Islam meant the incorporation of more Moslems and a more widespread use of Arabic within the Sudanese states (Dan Fodio, Umar, and Samori empires) as well as in most of the coastal kingdoms. Islam played a characteristic role in the state's organizations by determining the level of bureaucracy established. Islam created a bond of unity in the new states by providing a training ground for political officers since education, discipline, and national, not tribal, loyalty were stressed in the army. The army was organized to defend the right of the state's religious organization and to protect any economic interests immediately threatened by other states. Despite the strongly social influence of Islam, the old traditional African background remained central to much thinking.

Mythical, Cultural, and Religious Organization

The traditional cults dominated the religious life of the overwhelming majority of the people in the empires and kingdoms described, as was illustrated by Sundiata's time. For instance, the myth of Mandé creation, is an illustration about a ceremony taking place every seven years in Kankaba to celebrate the rebuilding of the *kamablio*, a sanctuary built by Mansa Sama, a descendant of Sundiata.[22] This myth, still recited every seven years by the Kouyaté or Diabaté people, describes how the forty-four or forty-eight people originated in Mandé, and were separated into five mythical generations, justifying the social division of labor, the stratification into castes and classes.[23] The Mandé myth explains many unknowns in the society and the world in general through Mandé logic. The Mandé myth of creation also explains how God (Mangala) first created the *balaza* (acacia albida) seed, which was abandoned, because it was a failure, to create twin varieties of elusive seed which made up the egg of the world. God then created six additional seeds, making a total of eight. These seeds were paired into four groups, associating them with the four cardinal points of the earth. In the egg of the world or the placenta, there were four paired petals (one male and one female). One male, Pemba, dominated the creation. Pemba stole one piece of placenta and put it on his own placenta. This piece of placenta which became the earth, was impure. The other male twin, Faro, assumed the form of twin in heaven. Faro was sacrificed to make up for Pemba's sin and his body was cut into sixty pieces scattered throughout the space, in form of trees, and vegetation. Faro was brought back on earth by God, on an ark made of his celestial placenta, which ark came to rest on a mountain, Kouroula. The first human being such as Faro had a common vital force (myama) and complementary spiritual forces (ni and dya), each of which had both a male and a female form. Faro himself on earth and in water, was to be the intermediary between himself and mankind. His fish became basic taboo of a great number of people. Faro is reported to have taken a journey, and sanctuaries are built all along his journey along the Niger so he could continue to make revelations to date.

The Mandé myth of creation shows that nearly every level of the natural order is involved with sacred things. There is a certain amount of importance placed upon the morality of acts and the acceptability of certain acts, thus outlining social laws. The actions of Pemba parallel the Christian myth of the original sin of Adam and Eve and the consequent acts to stabilize the social order and make up for guilt. Pemba's sin of incest which caused the earth to become impure sanctioned the taboo of incest and the imposition of social restrictions. The belief in Faro's presence everywhere is spiritually fulfulling and uplifting and makes mortals respect the social order and the environment, making sense of their environment through so many spiritual connections which are ever present in Mandinka's cosmology. The myth explains some earthly methods of reproduction through the description of seeds and placenta. Mangala's susceptibility to make mistakes showed him fallible and earthly and is not to be seen as a permanent Lord Savior. In sum, oral tradition in Mandé reports that the universe stemmed originally from a vibrating movement which generated spirit and twenty two fundamental elements forming the tangible world of things and spirits. During that creation, Faro organized sky and water. He is still ruling the world according to an oscillatory movement regulating from a helicoid spiral curve ascending and descending every 400 years.

The Hausa myth of creation is centered around Bayajida (Abu Yesid), a man from Baghdad said to have been angered at the loss of his followers, so he embarked upon a journey.[24] Bayajida arrived at a village deprived of water by a great snake known as *sarki* (the chief). In an act of selfless bravery, Bayajida slew the snake with his sword and in doing so restored tranquility to the village. In reward, the queen of the village, Daura, married him and also gave him a concubine. By Daura, Bayajida had a son called Bawo and another called Karbogari (town seizer) by the concubine. Bawo had six sons, three sets of twins who became the rulers of Kano, Rano, Katsina, Zazzau (Zaria), Gobir, and Daura. These six cities formed the foundations of the Hausa *bakwai* (pure states). Karbogari established seven states, Kebbir, Zamfara, Gwari, Jukun, Yoruba, Nupe, and Yauni forming the Hausa *banza bakwai* (impure states).

This myth attempts to overcome the social hierarchical differentiation by showing that all the segments of the society had a common ancestor. Bayajida was a benevolent and cheerful but brave and strong leader who made all the Hausas proud of him.

Between the Middle Ages and the era of the nineteenth century jihads, Islam had made a lot of converts among the population of western Sudan. It would be extremely difficult to argue demonstrably, in light of available documentation, that the Islamic expansion was the result of the power of the gun, although it may be said that both Islam and Christianity were alien religions which succeeded in adjusting to African traditional cults.[25] Besides the Almoravid invasion of Ghana in 1076 and that of Songhay in 1591, the Sudanese rulers tended, because of the egalitarian tendency of most African societies, to be attracted to Islam: it was a potentially revolutionary force, and there was a relatively easy syncretism of Islam with the traditional religious cults.[26] Yet the reality is that through Islam, the rulers such as Mansa Musa and Askia the Great, were able to assert their right to rule through a divine principle and not by force or violence. Since the religious dogmas of Islam tended to be so forceful, the rulers were hopeful that the people would accept Islam in order to perpetuate their own rule. Moslems did not allow their members to question the existence or truth of the religion without being stereotyped *cafirs* or infidels. Moreover, Islam presented two important opportunities for the aristocracy. First was the opportunity to use Arabic as a language of religion and learning. Second the Arabic language was used by many traders (the Wangara) and was eventually considered to be the language through which much commerce and trade transactions were carried. Although a few people took advantage of Arabic as a written and spoken language, the overwhelming majority of the people used local languages. Traditional education drew its model from tales, proverbs, legends, epics, and ritualistic ceremonies such as the Mandé creation myth. Traditional education was initiatory in such ceremonies celebrating the origin of creation and the glory of subsistence work.[27]

Economic Organization

Most people in West Africa made their living from fishing and subsistence agriculture using simple means of cultivation, crop rotation, irrigation, and burning of forests. They cultivated cereals such as millet, and vegetables such as rice, sugar cane, melons, onions, yams, palm oil, and kola. Nomadic people raised cattle, sheep, and goats. Later with the European contact during the fifteenth century, maize, beans, bananas, and coconut were introduced.

Land was subject to family collective ownership. In centralized states such as Songhay, the emperor had all the lands which he held in trust for people's use. Usually the family controlled those resources most vital to its livelihood, minor agricultural products and some animal resources procured from hunting. Luxury commodities were beyond the reach of most families because the existence of surplus commodities within the household production unit to trade against the former was practically nil. The survival and efficiency of the family was based on the contributions of each member.

The economic base of the empires and kingdoms was the taxation and the collection of tribute from vassal states. The tax-based states developed large and complex bureaucratic bodies out of necessity to control the flow of both monies and information. Cloth cotton, manufactures, sandals, tanned hides, ivory, gold, gum, kola nuts, and slaves were exported through traditional trade routes to North Africa. Clothing, carpets, silk, spices, perfumes, cowries, books, including the Koran, and horses were imported. Thus the diffusion of power through the creation of a separate body of finance, was a feature of the growing state. Yet, the growing pressures of trade with the Portuguese, Danes, English, French in gold, ivory, and kola nut, also brought additional needs that the states found themselves ill-prepared to handle without a bureaucratic organization. Goods imported from Europe included cloth, cotton prints, silk, linen, writing paper, beads, swords, blades, looking glasses, needles, files, chisels, razors, scissors, etc. The cooperative pressures of domestic taxation and external trade facilitated the growth of regulatory bodies for the benefit of the state.

The emperors of Songhay and Kanem-Bornu did contribute to the protection of the long-distance trade and were the main organizers of the merchants. These indefatigable merchants (the Wangara) collected the produce from the southern coastal regions to sell them in the region peripheral to the Sahara, around the Niger Bend (Timbuctu, Gao). Transportation was done by the caravan routes and on the Niger.[28]

In economic terms, the Mandinka-Dyula, the Ashanti, and others had been well ahead of their times, representing most explicitly the dialectical growth of a state society whose economic base was not exploitation of labor. They realized that the necessity of efficiency should not only exist within the family, but also should permeate the organization and operation of the state. In this way the values of the common people were reconciled with the needs of the state to the benefit of both.

The decline of this traditional trade was due to several factors, among them the changing political conditions in the Sahara and western Sudan, the disorganization and instability in the states as a prelude to imperial expansion whereby the production systems became controlled and attached to the fulfillment of the supply and demand needs of Europe, and colonial rule which established total control over the societies.[29] Several forces have contributed to the disorganization of African traditional societies: autocratic colonial administration, missionaries, a new economy and a new educational system. But through colonization (and slavery), the African has sharpened his own awareness because the new conditions have caused him to desire dignity, pride, and identity. This implies that the ferments of change may be contained in colonialism itself. For example, despite the extent of this disorganization or the superimposition of mercantile systems on precolonial production systems, the indigenous African societies still kept a residual culture which resisted colonialism, struggled against it, before starting to prevail after about seventy years of official colonial rule (from the Berlin Conference of 1885 to the Ghanaian independence in 1957). The era of independence and neocolonialism has been marked by the recovery of African sovereignty and the commitment to cultural revival. Basil Davidson's *Lost Cities of Africa* makes several significant contributions to African scholarship.[30] First, it shows in a dramatic way that Africa had a blooming civilization that was little known by Europeans, but that was, by European standards, advanced and civilized. Second, it shows that from Africa would have emerged much earlier greater nations had not foreign interventions occurred to slow the pace of development.

Although Davidson's reconstruction of African history is sound, his theory making technology responsible for progress is questionable and debatable. His technological interpretation of progress does not take into account the possibility of inventions for functional purposes. He views invention as advancement. This leads him to categorize African societies into "higher" and "lower" societies, depending on their resemblance to the observer's society. Thus, even Basil Davidson is guilty of a sophisticated Eurocentric viewpoint which does not allow him to view Africa objectively. His bias for technical aspects of production is not an isolated case. In Jacques Maquet's *Civilizations of Black Africa* one finds a similar disposition.[31] Here the technical aspect of production is demonstrated by the use of technical concepts to categorize a civilization such as the civilization of the bow, the granary, the spear, the use of industry.

On the other side are some pioneering historians and anthropologists, including Thomas Hodgkin, Ivan Van Sertima, George Balandier, Jean Suret-Canale, Robert Cornevin, Bernard Fagg, Melville Herskovits, to mention just a few. Africa's historical and cultural redeemers, such as E. W. Blyden, John Henrik Clarke, Cheikh Anta Diop, St. Clair Drake, Chancellor Williams, and Joseph Ki-Zerbo, have excellent arguments against the idea that precolonial African structural organizations were chaotic and stagnant. Drawing from early African-Arab and European writers, as well as from modern historical and archeological sources, and from oral tradition, these scholars show that Africa has had civilizations in the past as great as those of Iron Age or medieval Europe, that African religious beliefs in one superior being preceded the Euro-Judeo-Christian monotheist faith, and that the imprint and influence of African religious cults on modern Christianity and Islam are evident.

These historians dismiss the myth that West Africa's most famous past and lost institutions and monuments were designed by Semites, Hamites, and white conquerors. They treat soundly the disastrous consequences of the transatlantic slave trade on Africa (loss of manpower, economic exploitation, stagnation, assumed inferiority of Africans and people of African descent, racism in its most vicious form between the fifteenth century and the nineteenth century). They all concur that these past African civilizations possessed a distinctly African character and a certain unity in diversity which was probably the result of an interplay and exchange of ideas between countries which now appear so completely severed from each other as never to have known any kind of common history. They argue that African consciousness and cosmology have shaped these societies in the most humanely universal way by communal living characterized by a high spirit of cooperativeness and sacrifice.

These people's synthetic creativeness expressed by the monuments of Ghana, Mali, and Songhay, the Nok culture, the bronze art of Ife and Benin, the techniques of wood carving and the iron processing techniques drawn perhaps to West Africa from Meroe, capital of Kush state, show how solid were the integrating links from one region to another.

It is possible that these cultures might have been stimulated by other foreign influences; but if so, the genius of the people lay in their capacity to absorb into their own culture what they needed and wanted, making their societies distinctly their own. These societies were therefore successful in answering the physical and emotional needs of life in their environment.

Even by the late nineteenth century when the slave trade had degraded much of African society and had twisted European opinion of all Africans, many regions of the interior, relatively "untouched" by the brutal effects of "the peculiar institution," were still able to efficiently maintain their region in peace and security. When European colonialism was at its height, many of these societies had already lost their strength; they declined or disappeared. The Europeans used these chaotic conditions to rationalize not only their conquest and occupation but also racism—the result of the biological and genetic myths created to rationalize the inhumanities and atrocities practiced by Europeans for economic gain, as it is today practiced in South Africa.

African people are described as following their own road in the past. The works of Cheikh Anta Diop and Chancellor Williams have gone a long way toward reconstructing African history. What they have written has often been debated but that is certainly characteristic of ideas which challenge accepted interpretations. These historians and their works justify the values of Africans. They provide good background information from which to examine problems facing the people of African descent.

CONCLUSION

The empires of Ghana, Mali, Songhay, Kanem-Bornu, the Hausa states, the coastal kingdoms, and the Nok culture show that the African way of life has a very long, famous, and distinctive history and culture, but is still similar to other world people's experiences. These civilizations may have been exceptional diamonds; but yet they were and are diamonds, which illuminate the unfortunate epithet "dark" applied by Stanley to the African continent.

After the industrial revolution, the economic success of Western countries was dominated by the access to cheap raw materials. The "Dark Continent" which until then was being depopulated by the "peculiar institution" of the transatlantic slave trade became an object of penetration, conquest, occupation, and colonization. A few countries such as Dahomey, which operated under a planned economy, were able to make a smooth transition without upheaval from a slave economy to a colonial economy.[32] Others were underdeveloped in the process of "legitimate trade" and colonialism.[33]

From the fifteenth century to the middle of the twentieth, which one can easily call "Africa's Dark Ages," there was much African resistance to conquest. In the nineteenth century, Uthman Dan Fodio, Samori Ture, Hadj Umar Tall, and Behanzin and their followers in West Africa struggled against the consequences of conquest, but their efforts of resistance could not prevent the destruction of many of Africa's highly organized systems.

And the Europeans used the old formula *dividere et regnat* (divide to rule) to turn Africans against Africans, laws against laws. This led to Africa's loss of independence, loss of sovereignty, economic stagnation of the continent through colonialism, international humiliation, and the assumption of the inferiority of Africans and people of African descent. The many disastrous effects on the psyche of the modern African and people of African descent are evident. But the historic past of Ghana, Mali, and Songhay should provide inspiration to Africans and people of African descent to overcome the handicap imposed upon them by the colonial legacy (neocolonialism). They could not revive all the aspects of traditional life which existed in Ghana, Mali, Songhay, Kanem-Bornu, the Hausa states, or the forest kingdoms before European colonization. But they can synthesize the best of both worlds, the positive traditional values and those values representative of the twentieth century. They could also show an appreciation for subsistence work. Africans through traditional means as a core model could develop a new power and prestige that should make Africans and people of African descent proud of this heritage. They should develop a new sense of working together, show a desire for progress, and make democracy a participatory concept for all.

It is still possible for the small, weak, and competing new nations of Africa to merge cooperatively, or to be integrated into groups which are economically, politically, and technically viable, just as it was possible for ancient Ghana, Mali, and Songhay to exist and to be regarded by the world with great respect.

NOTES

1. Sir Philip Mitchell, *Africa Afterthoughts* (London: Hutchinson, 1954), pp. 10-32. See also Arnold Toynbee, *A Study of History* (London: Oxford University Press, 1962), pp. 11-82; and Joseph Arthur Comte de Gobineau, *The Great Races* (Berkeley, Calif.: Muscatine and Griffith, 1966), pp. 467–75.

2. Cheikh Anta Diop, *Antériorité des civilisations nègres: Mythe ou vérité historique?* (Paris: Présence Africaine, 1955). Also L.S.B. Leakey, "The Evolution of Man in the African Continent," *Tarikh*, vol 1, no. 3 (1966), pp. 1–11. See also J. Desmond Clark, "The Prehistoric Origin of African Culture," *Journal of African Culture*, vol. 2 (1964), pp. 161–83.

3. Robert Ardrey, *African Genesis: A Personal Inquiry into the Animal Origins and Nature of Man* (New York: Dell, 1961), pp. 2–29.

4. For example, speech is a cultural attribute. The fact that man uses weapons to kill animals for food is not to say as Ardrey does, that man is inherently a killer.

5. Basil Davidson, *The Lost Cities of Africa* (Toronto: Little, Brown and Company, 1959). See also Basil Davidson, *A History of West Africa to the Nineteenth Century* (Garden City, N.Y.; Doubleday, 1966).

6. See Abu Ubayd 'Abd Allah ibn 'Abd Al-Aziz Al-Bakri, *Descriptions de l'Afrique septentionale*, trans. Mac Guckin de Slane (Algiers: A. Jourdan, 1913), p. 80; Ibn Batuta, *Travels in Asia and Africa*, trans. H.A.R. Gibb (London: G. Routledge, 1929); and Leo Africanus, *Description de l'Afrique*, trans. A. Epaulard (Boston: Little, Brown & Co., 1959).

7. Davidson, *The Lost Cities of Africa*, pp. 12–72; Robert July, *A History of the African People* (New York: Charles Scribner's Sons, 1970); Roland Oliver and J.D. Fage, *A Short History of West Africa* (Baltimore: Penguin Books, 1962); J. F. Ade Ajay and Michael Crowder, eds., *History of West Africa* (New York: Columbia University Press, 1972); Jan Vansina, *Kingdoms of the Savanna* (Madison: University of Wisconsin Press, 1966); John G. Jackson, *Introduction to African Civilizations* (Secaucus, N.J.: Citadel Press, 1974); Chancellor Williams, *The Destruction of Black Civilization: Great Issues of a Race from 4500*

B.C. *to 2000* A.D. (Chicago: Third World Press, 1974); D.T. Niane and J. Suret-Canale, *Histoire de l'Afrique occidentale* (Paris: Présence Africaine, 1965); S.M. Sissoko, *Histoire de l'Afrique occidentale* (Paris: Présence Africaine, 1966); Philip D. Curtin, *Economic Change in Precolonial Africa: Senegambia in the Era of the Slave Trade* (Madison: University of Wisconsin Press, 1975).

8. The Soninké are reported to have found Ghana, not Hamites or Semites, according to oral tradition. See Oliver and Fage, *A Short History*, pp. 17–64.

9. Al-Bakri, *Description de l'Afrique septentionale*, p. 19.

10. In 1957 when the former British colony of Gold Coast became independent, it chose the name Ghana in memory of the ancient kingdom.

11. Archaeologists have found the ruins of Kumbi-Saleh. See Raymond Mauny, "The Question of Ghana," *Africa*, vol. 34 (1954), pp. 11–20.

12. A *dinar* is the equivalent of an eighth of an ounce of gold. A *mithqual* is the equivalent of a fourth of an ounce of gold.

13. D.T. Niane, *Sundiata: An Epic of Old Mali*, trans. G.D. Pickett (London: Longman, 1965). Oral tradition is the testimony of the past through legends, epics, tales, and proverbs. The *griots*, or "living encyclopedias" combining the functions of the praise-singer, the minstrel, the gleeman, the cantor, and the poet, are the most articulate popularizers of past history in traditional Africa. Oral tradition is one way to reconstruct African history since written documents are usually lacking and many documents found in European archives appear distorted. However, caution is advised since the *griot's* story needs to be authenticated; the genius of the *griots* can turn many facts into amusing legends. This is why the life reconstruction of Sundiata is still full of mysteries. Yet Niane's *Sundiata, An Epic of Old Mali* remains a very positive contribution to oral tradition as a means to reconstruct West Africa's history. Another article on oral tradition that one may consult is Jan Vansina, "The Use of Oral Tradition in African Culture History," in *Reconstructing African Culture History*, ed. Creighton Gabel and Norman R. Bennett (Boston: Boston University Press, 1967). See also J. Vansina, R. Manny, and L.V. Thomas, eds., *The Historian in Tropical Africa* (London: Oxford University Press, 1964).

14. This respectful treatment of African women needs to be contrasted here with that given in Yambo Ouologuem *Le Devoir de violence* (Paris: Editions du Seuil, 1968). See also Aguibou Yansané, "Books Noted," *Black World*, October 1973.

15. Ibn Batuta, *Travels in Asia and Africa*, pp. 82–97.

16. Leo Africanus, *Description de l'Afrique*, pp. 7–32.

17. The Kanem-Bornu, situated at the northeast of Lake Chad, had one of the most feared armies in Africa. Their kings are reported to have imported Turkish military instructors to train the soldiers.

18. See Michael Smith, "The Beginnings of Hausa Society," in *The Historian in Tropical Africa*, ed. J. Vansina, R. Mauny, and L.V. Thomas.

19. R.S. Rattray, ed., *Ashanti* (Oxford: The Clarendon Press, 1923); Kwame Arhin, *The Financing of Ashanti Expansion, 1700–1820* (Oxford: The Clarendon Press, 1965); Kwame Arhin, *The Structures of Greater Ashanti 1700–1824* (Oxford: The Clarendon Press, 1965).

20. Davidson, *A History of West Africa to the Nineteenth Century* pp. 96–104, 146–47, 219–23.

21. Bernard Fagg, "Nigeria," in *Encyclopedia of World Art*, vol. 1 (New York: McGraw-Hill, 1963), pp. 650–51; Britannica Press, *Encyclopedia Britannica*, vol. 1 (New York: Britannica Press, 1965), p. 285; Georges Balandier, *Ambiguous Africa* (New York: Pantheon Books, 1966), p. 56; Davidson, *A History of West Africa*, pp. 16–17; Davidson, *The African Past* (New York: Grosset and Dunlap, 1917), p. 40; Davidson, *Lost Cities of Africa*, pp. 58–59; Melville Herskovits, *The Human Factor in Changing Africa* (New York: Village Books, 1962), pp. 4, 433–34.

22. Germaine Dieterlin, "The Mande Creation Myth," *Africa*, vol. 17, no. 2 (April 1957), pp. 124–38.

23. These five mythical generations included five Masaré (true Keita) lineages, five learned Moslem lineages (Berété, Turé, Haydara, Fofana, Sanogo), four lineages of occupational castes (Namakhala), sixteen other families of noble captives (Traore, Kono, Kamara, Kuruma, Mogasuba, Dansuba, Dagnogo, Kulubali, Dyara, Dante, Dangonno, Sogoro, Diallo, Diakité, Sangaré).

24. Michael Smith, "The Beginnings of Hausa Society."

25. J.O. Hunwick, "Religion and State in the Songhay Empire 1464–1591," in *Islam in Tropical Africa*, ed. I.M. Lewis (London: International African Institute and Oxford University Press, 1966), pp. 296-317; Ivor Wilks, "The Position of Muslims in Metropolitan Ashanti in the Early Nineteenth Century," in *Islam in Tropical Africa*, ed. I.M. Lewis, pp. 318–41.

26. Edward Wilmot Blyden, "Mohamedanism and the Negro Race," "Mohamedanism is Western Africa"; "Islam in the Western Sudan," in *Black Spokesman: Selected Published Writings of Edwrd Wilmot Blyden*, ed. Hollis R. Lynch (London: Frank Cass, 1971), pp. 273–306.

27. A.Y. Yansané, "The Impact of Colonialism: Education in West Africa," *First World: An International Journal of Black Thought*, vol. 1, no. 3 (May-June 1977).

28. Joseph Ki-Zerbo, "Le Monde noir," in *Collection d'histoire, Le Monde contemporain* (Paris: Hatier, 1962), p. 654–55.

29. A.Y. Yansané, "Introduction: Decolonization, Dependency and Development, the Theory Revisited," in *Decolonization and Dependency: Problems of Development of African Societies*, ed. A.Y. Yansané (Westport, CT: Greenwood Press, 1980); Claude Meillassoux, "Introduction," in *The Development of Indigenous Trade and Markets in West Africa*, ed. Claude Meillassoux (London: Oxford University Press, 1971), pp. 49–86.

30. Basil Davidson, *The Lost Cities of Africa*.

31. Jacques Maquet, *Afrique: Les Civilisations noires* (Paris: Horizons de France, 1962). In addition, see the excellent discussion of progress by Dona Richards, "European Mythology: The Ideology of Progress," in *Contemporary Black Thought: Alternative Analyses in the Social and Behavioral Sciences*, ed. Molefi Asante and A. Sarr Vandi (Beverly Hills, Calif.: Sage Publications, 1980).

32. Dahomey, now Benin, once operated under a planned economy based on slave trade and it was capable of making a transition to a cash crop economy based on palm oil production. See Rosemary Arnold, "A Port of Trade: Wydah on the Guinea Coast," in *Trade and Market in the Early Empires: Economy in History and Theory*, ed. Conrad Arensberg and Harry Pearson (New York: Free Press, 1957), pp. 154–57; and Catherine Coquery-Vidrovitch, "De la traité des esclaves à l'exploitation de l'huile de palme et des palmistes du Dahomey: XIXe siecle," in *The Development of Indigenous Trade*, ed. Meillassoux, pp. 107-122.

33. Samir Amin, *Neocolonialism in West Africa* (New York: Monthly Review Press, 1973); Walter Rodney, *A History of the Upper Guinea Coast: 1545 to 1800* (Oxford: Clarendon Press, 1970).

Part II

THE ARTISTIC AND INTELLECTUAL TRADITION

4

COMMONALITIES IN AFRICAN DANCE: AN AESTHETIC FOUNDATION

KARIAMU WELSH ASANTE

African dance is a complex art in an advanced form. Its development encompasses many forms, including ballet, jazz, and modern dance. Its influence is visible in the highly stylized dances of the Americas such as the samba, rumba, and *capoiera*. The polyrhythmic, polycentric character of African dance is immediately recognizable and distinctive. From the foot-stomping dance of the Muchongoyo of eastern Zimbawe to the stilt-walking Makishi of Zambia to the masked dance of the Gelede in Nigeria, to the Royal Adowa and Kete of Ghana, to the knee-sitting dance of the Lesotho women, to the 6/8 rhythms of the samba from Brazil, to the High Life of West Africa, to the rumba of Cuba, to the Ring Shout dance of the Carolinas, to the Snake dance of Angola, to the jazz dance of Black America, to the Ngoma dance of Kenya, to the Katherine Dunham technique, to the dust-flying dances of the Zulu— and still there are more;—in all of these dances a commonality can be established. Intrinsic in this commonality is the ancestral connection to Africa through epic, memory, and oral tradition, even though these dances represent different languages, people, geographies, and cultures.

What this commonality exposes as we examine each dance is a foundation for many African dance techniques. African dance is polyrhythmic, polycentric, and holistic with regard to motion rather than being postural or position-oriented as an essential requisite. Position and posture are integral, but it is the movement that is challenging scholars and choreographers of African dance to define, structure, and codify it. The genre of African dance has always had technique, indeed, it has enough substance for a hundred techniques. Techniques and qualities from the African dance have been drawn upon by dancers, teachers, and choreographers from all over the world. It is crucial that artists now are organizing, identifying, and codifying some of the techniques that have developed. For example, Dunham and Primus techniques are two of the known techniques. A third technique, following in the tradition of Primus and Dunham, is Mfundalai technique.

African dance is visually stimulating and exciting and capable of arousing emotive responses as well as visual ones. Cultural anthropologists and ethnomusicologists have to date offered insights and research in the field, but lack the expertise and perspective of a trained dancer, choreographer, or dance historian to properly analyze the movements and steps found in the dance.

There are certain foundations which make up the African dance aesthetic which I call senses. They give the African dance its touch, feel, voice, motion. Two of the techniques that I have mentioned: the Katherine Dunham technique, based on Haitian folklore and about forty years old, and Mfundalai, the African dance technique that I began to develop ten years ago based on universal African movement, are both African techniques. They both exhibit the seven senses of the African dance aesthetic and substantiate the evidence for future techniques.

The foundations of an aesthetic can be found in the culture of a society. The value system and religious ethos normally provide and stimulate the creative setting for "stylized art," that is, art which is no longer directly associated with religion or ritual. The particular qualities of an ethnic group provide the ingredients which distinguish the aesthetic and enable individual expression as well as manifest collective expression. All African cultures express themselves through the universals of dance, music, visual arts, and graphic arts. Differences are as varied as the ethnic groups, and it is not the particular artistic qualities of individual African ethnic groups that will be analyzed in this chapter, but the aesthetic commonalities of dance in ethnic groups with origins in Africa.

African dance in general has been difficult to categorize because there are thousands of ethnic groups representing 150 million people of African descent in the diaspora (North and South America and the Pacific) and 400 million on the African continent itself. By establishing a definable codification, further scholarship and analysis can be encouraged and techniques and choreography can be improved. By definition, for purposes of clarity, Africans are all people of African descent.[1] An historical, mythological, and religious world view must be undertaken to understand the African aesthetic. Any discussion of African dance must appreciate the role of dance within the African society. Rural dance is traditional dance and traditional dance is rural dance. Traditional dance in urban areas is more stylized, removed from ritual, and influenced by other nationalities. The commonalities discussed here will also cover the creations of contemporary choreography which exhibit the African aesthetic.

The beauty of African aesthetics is in its enormous complexity. Absence of documentation and notation has unfortunately forced students and scholars to rely on performances, oral reports, and scholarship by interested but uninformed persons as the only body of research material. Part of the responsibility for the lack of written documentation and notation is the dominance of the oral tradition, which is an art in and of itself and a form of documentation. An oral tradition, literally a word of mouth phenomenon that preserves history and entertains in African culture, actually appears in all disciplines of the arts as a subtle undercurrent. The "oral narrative" is in effect the story, dance, art, and the speaker becomes the *griot*, dancer, choreographer, or sculptor. And the "oral" becomes the property of the speaker to reshape or to retell within a shape. The boundaries are there in plot, structure, outline, and form, but it is the dancer who breathes new life into the dance and it becomes hers/his for the moment. There are no permanent stamps of the creators, only the changing designs, rhythms, movements that change with the performers. What the work represents is guarded and revered, but not the identity of the creator herself/himself after the creation has been completed even though the profession is respected and acknowledged. The mark of the artist is in her/his creativity, not in time, nor in her/his person. The element of permanence or signature usually deals with the work itself and the culture it represents, not the person of the creator. The oral tradition then is the organic, creative process, evident in all African artists. It is the reason, ironically, that so many impressive works of art are not signed. The signature of the African artist is inherent in the creation and the spiritual or divine creator deserves and is given the credit. It is understood that the artist is a conduit and therefore not responsible for the greatness of the work. This does not mean that the artist is irresponsible, in fact, the responsibility is awesome. Acceptance of the responsibility as a conduit is where the appreciation is acknowledged and the completion of the task is when the applause is given. The artist is considered "chosen" and the rejection of this role is often considered sacrilegious. This is not to be confused with the economics of being an artist when one has to make decisions based on survival, but on the philosophical and spiritual aspect of being an artist.

The oral principle constitutes a fundamental principle in African aesthetics manifesting itself in African dance. It concerns the process of creativity itself and in that respect is a fundamental sense of the African aesthetic. The derivatives of this traditional oral response to the African ethos are seven aesthetic senses: polyrhythm, polycentrism, curvilinear, dimensional, epic memory, repetition, holism.

The first sense, polyrhythm, is the motion sense. Movement and rhythm in the African dance cannot be separated. The rhythmic quality of the aesthetic is the most distinguishable of its qualities. It is the world within another world, the deeper you travel, the more you feel, hear; it is multidimensional. The multiple contractions of dance and polymeter of music best manifest the movement and rhythmic quality. "In a context of multiple rhythmics, people distinguish themselves from each other while they remain dynamically related." This sense of movement, like the other senses I will discuss, refers to qualities which make up the integral composition of the dance and are inherent in all of the dances of Africa, regardless of theme, ethnic group or geography.

African dance requires a musical sophistication in order to adequately participate within the rhythmic framework of a particular movement. Requirement for participation in such a context is the ability to stand back from the rhythms of the scene and find an additional rhythm which complements and mediates those other rhythms.

The rhythmic sense is evident in all disciplines; particularly in the marriage of music and dance where the sacred circle joins the two. The sense of motion initiates rhythms and then polyrhythms. In fact, the rhythm of one beat after another cannot compete with the complexity of several beats within one note or several contractions in one beat on a dancer or the entire body moving with the head and hands doing vibratory movements while the pelvis double contracts and the feet mark time.[2] The performance of this element is crucial if one is to understand polyrhythms as a sense.

The second sense is polycentrism. Movement as defined here is motion spending time, the occupant of a time frame and not the moving from point A to point B.

Robert Thompson cites Richard Alan Waterman in the following statement:

An African learns to be conscious mentally of every instrument employed in an African orchestra and this has a tremendous influence on his dance. All the various muscles of the body act differently to the rhythms of the instruments. One of the terms in the Twi language when speaking musically is to "dance multi-metrically."[3]

Thompson continues to speak about the polycentric sense when he says that "people in Africa further suggest that dance is defined as a special intricacy, built of superimposed motions."[4] Once again, the "extra" or "super" realm is realized and must be taken into account in studying most forms of African dance.[5] It is this multiple existence of polysenses that is the African's signature in dance. The representation of the cosmos in the body is a goal. The myriad possibilities in the universe also exist in the body for the African dancer. The artist has his particular say with the polysense. Multiplication of sound, movement, color, texture, is for us the task which parallels the movement of nature. In the African aesthetic, the polycentric sense allows for both slow and fast (all within the same time frame), with the movements coming from several directions. A readily used principle in African aesthetics is the holism which will be discussed later.

The third sense is the curvilinear as seen in form, shape, and structure. This sense applies to and appears in most African dance. It appears as the antithesis of Western dance, which has a heavy reliance on symmetrical, proportional, and profile-oriented form.[6] Form and shape vary in the arts of Africa with a similarity that occurs frequently enough to make a generalization about the curvilinear quality. The circular quality of the African artists' world is ever apparent. "Let the circle be unbroken" is a creed in the African world. There is "power" in the circle, the curve, the round, supernatural power if you will.[7] The beautiful symmetry of the *chi-wara* heightened by its curvilinear essence contrasts and yet compliments the Shona serpentine sculpture where the smooth, round figures curve lines create circles within circles. Curvilinear qualities of dance, art, and music round, curve, and carve out images that are similar and resemble aspects of African society and mythology, if only in essence. The Watusi in their long sculptured movements carve out half-moons in space and toss their elegant heads, making small circles in the sky. For the dancer, it may be mostly hand movement as in the *Adowa*, or it may be the *Gum-Boot* dance of the Zulu in which the foot stomping focuses the eyes on the energies and messages being sent through the ground and up again as the contact sends sound and dust back to the dancer. The structure is always related to experience, message, theme, and feeling. Structure for structure's sake has been a recent occurrence, and generally it is the result of formal education, outside influences, and urbanization. African dance forms and structures are traditionally, inherently entwined in the work and develop as the idea emerges. There is calculation and methodology as well as precision, but neither masters the artist; rather, they serve the artist and the work of art in expediting the idea.

Some Western writers have misunderstood the essential elements and contributions of the African dance. Lincoln Kirstein has written about African dance:

From the point of view of actual technique, primitive dancers have not a great deal to offer either in methodology or structure for our theatre. The ends for which they dance are entirely different from ours. Nevertheless, physiologically, as ritual, health, they are fascinating. It is obvious how highly developed the pelvic, visceral and gluteal regions of primitive people are. The movement of the belly is a great aid toward digestion. Exercises of the female pelvis eases birth.[8]

Kirstein's ethnocentrism is understandable. Evaluation by European standards only make Kirstein's statements inaccurate albeit sympathetic. The foundations for African dance techniques have always been present. While the basis for codified and organized techniques have long existed, the need for them and indeed the society that would support that concept does not exist in traditional Africa. In Western society, dance functions as entertainment and has evolved separately from religious life, but it remains harmonious and functional to Western society where church and state are separate and linear organization is the foundation for most institutions. The function of entertaining becomes paramount in formulating the creation. It is dysfunctional and sometimes contradictory with regard to religious and social goals of the same society, but the coexistence of church and state allows and permits these contradictions.

The pelvic development that Kirstein speaks of is correct when he refers to it as a vital instrument in African dance and aesthetics and as physiologically important. What has to be emphasized is that aesthetically there are differences in cultures, but a culture is not void of a technique because it speaks a different language.

The simplicity of form may be regarded as primitive or the busyness of a dance might be interpreted as inspirational but nonstructured. Form produces imagery, and it is the structure and shape that helps to provide the dynamics for the viewers. The images are mirror-like reflections of history, mythology, and literature. Only through memory is the viewer allowed to be an intimate part of the art. The form is paramount in helping the artistic experience along, spurring on the imagination of the participants, viewers, or listeners. The audience engages in a remembrance with the dancer not merely in the mechanical act of seeing and applauding, but through an intimacy that has not escaped documentation.

Alvin Ailey in his magnum opus "Revelations" used contemporary dance language and "epic memory." The presence of the multiple contractions and hip swaying movements were foundations of the dance and the reason for its indelible stamp onto the minds of the dance audience.

The fourth sense is dimensionality. One aspect of depth in the African dance is texture. Music is textured; the dance is textured; the art is textured. The dimensional sense accounts for the fuzziness or graininess that one sees, hears, or feels. Something extra is occurring or existing like that extra contraction or extra beat and three-dimensional essence. Its additional value is entwined and embedded so that its existence becomes inherent. There is a plateau feeling, an area perceived as depth that arises out of African dances. The dimensional aspiration speaks to the supernatural in space, the presence beyond the visual presence. The dimensional aspect is characteristic of all the senses in that it is by definition extrasensory, involving the oral tradition. The texture sense is reverberation. It is interconnected with the first sense. The texture sense is the extrashape and vibration that occurs during a dance. For example, in the movement of the waist and hips of the *Jerusarema* dance of Zimbabwe there are surrounding sounds and motions which are indivisible from the central movement.

In the dimensional sense, there is a human quality, something extra that is present in harmony with the music, dance, or sculpture. It speaks in a physical, three-dimensional sense in Western terminology, but it is not measured dimension, but rather a perceived dimension. These extra senses, in addition to the universal aesthetics of all cultures, provide the African aesthetic with its complexity and the reasons for its nondocumentability in strictly Western terms. There is great difficulty in documenting an art on the extrasensory dimensions of an art form which is creative by definition, consequently, a changing art form. The nonmeasured, but ultraperceivable senses are difficult to define by virtue of their frequency, complexity and place in society.

The time and the oral sense contribute to an organic, nonfuturistic perspective that creates and lets be. Preservation and documentation concerns are important to twentieth-century scholars, and the relationship is directly correlated with advances in industry and technology.

Criteria established for the purposes of measuring the value and significance of works of art as they relate to aesthetics must take into account the personal reflection of an entire nation. The historical and social mirror cannot be overlooked. In fact, the particular reflection of the ethnic groups, as well as the collective reflection of the nation, must be considered when considering African aesthetics. There is no universal aesthetic without a personal reflection. In the African aesthetic imitation is based on sensation, not materialism. The literal or realistic is not prevalent in African aesthetics. For example, the dance of the *chi-wara*, the African half-man, half-antelope, is, in fact, not a realistic representation but a symbol of the feeling of fertility, the relationship of man to the earth, and the harmony that must exist between man and nature for any conception to happen. It is a representation of the mythology behind the reason for ''being'' for the Bambara people. This is very abstract and yet as a commentary of the Bambara people, it is an accurate idea of how they perceive fertility, but not the actual story of the planting of seeds. The desire to create and be productive in the arts is therefore the artists' personal reflection and a rational contribution to the arts.

Tap dance is an African-American art form born of experience. The polyrhythms of a time step of the Cincinnati as danced by Honi Coles are in fact the feet playing multiple rhythms to the inner rhythms of an urban setting, registered in concrete performed in shoes and props. The relationships are crucial as they provide the sounding board that generates the harmony and ''challenge.''

Imitation and harmony as reflected and echoed in nature are symptomatic of the ''oral'' sense, not a materialistic imitation but a sensual one. The imitation of the rhythm of the waves, the sound of the tree growing, the colors in the sky, the whisper and thunder of an elephant's walk, the shape of the river, the movement of a spider, the quiver of breath, the cringing of concrete, the choreography of the expressway become sources of inspiration. The imitation of life is in fact surrealistic, as the Europeans would call it, and as the Africans have interpreted it. Harmony is achieved in the artist so as not to disturb, destroy, disrupt the order of the cosmos, except by permission. The Akan drummer asks the tree before he cuts it to make a drum. Bill "Bojangles" Robinson beseeches his feet, "Feet don't fail me now." "May I?", an African-American children's game could well be the collective request of the African people. Harmony does not hurt the earth, land, provider, nor does it retard inspiration and creativity for the artist. This is no longer expressed ritualistically as in the past, but subconsciously in African artists today, particularly in the Americas, there is the "May I?" beneath the skin, above the soul, and in their hearts before they attempt art that achieves harmony. Camara Laye, in the *Radiance of the King*, says it is not merely the skill that makes the drummer, but the history, the memory.[9]

The ontological aspect of African aesthetics is memory. The blues, the presence of memory recreated in the southern United States environment of Africans, and the samba, a 6/8 rhythm in dance, is continued and expanded from memory. The permanence of an art work or creativity is in its harmony with nature, the people, and their god.

In the African sense, the work itself must have life and be worthy of the praises and approbations of an audience. The African aesthetic in the oral element provokes collectiveness in terms of spirit and individuality in terms of artistry. Pride and self satisfaction come from the harmony achieved with the ancestors, nature, family and village.

The click sound has its counterpart in dance and is another demonstration of the polyrhythmic African sound. In the Xhosa language, the rhythm of the click sound is not unique, it is in the tradition of African culture and consequently African aesthetics. It is not just the pathos (memory) of the Xhosa people singing, but the click itself that renders multiple sounds in one syllable that must be understood. The Khoi Khoi people of Botswana go even further with their language sounding of clicks only. Another example is the Mfundalai poetry verse in seven lines of 5,7,5,7,5,7,5 syllables each. This pattern recreates one of the rhythms found among African people.

The epic memory which is the fifth sense contributes to the ideal in the African artistic expression. Perfection cannot be achieved unless the experience or memory sense is drawn upon. It is the "body" of the work itself. In Dianne McIntyre's choreography, the suite "Up North" uses modern dance technique, but it is her epic memory sense that gives "Up North" its complexion and substance. It is not an historical reenactment of blacks coming to the U.S. North from the South, but a memory retrieved that delivers to the viewer the pathos, feeling, and experience without telling the literal story. McIntyre digs for the memory that will jar and reach the audience that she is serving and "universally" compute to any human that is watching. The experience sense is broad, it unearths the emotional feeling realm without limiting the artists or the audience. It is nonspecific, pertaining only to the illusion of experience and not the actuality of it. The experience realm in the arts is the reconciliation of the metaphysical with the physical and plastic.[10] This sense is not, however, the idea or the thought which can merely be an intellectual or mathematical exercise. Rather, it is the image within the structure of the thought that provides for the ethos. There is a spiritual dimension to this concept of experience.

This spirituality is another manifestation of the epic memory. It flows into and overlaps with experience, preceding, feeding, and imprinting the African aesthetic qualities. It is not religious by definition, but can involve ritual; it is the conscious and subconscious calling upon the ancestors, gods, mind, to permit the flow of energy so that the artist can create. It is more than submission to authority, present or ancestral; it is an innate recognition that the creative force is indeed a force and not the person performing the act of creation. The artist can reject it, kill it, or accept it, but the creative energies come from within in response to a spiritual initiator. The spiritual element is embodied in the epic memory sense. The African artist recognizes the "blessings" of the gods for his intentions. Spiritually, the artists' resources are limitless and he draws from the material world and the metaphysical. The spiritual element does not imply that the composition or work of the artist is related to anything metaphysical, extraterrestrial, or supernatural. The process of the creation of the work, not only the manifested work of art, draws upon a spirituality and epic memory that becomes embedded in the work.

The sixth sense I call holistic. In this sense, the parts of a creation are not emphasized or accentuated beyond the whole; neither is the individual. Silence or stillness is as much a part of the music or dance as sound or movement. For example, the ululations performed by the Shona upon greeting each other incorporate silence as part of the rhythm. If you break the silence, you break the rhythm and destroy the good will of the greeting. Attention must be directed at the silence and the stillness if one is to appreciate the full complexity and beauty of the polymultiple experience.

Repetition, the seventh, is a very important sense of the aesthetic in African dance. It is not the refrain or chorus of a movement, but it is the intensifying of one movement, one sequence, or the entire dance. Intensification is not static, it goes by repetition from one level to another until ecstasy, euphoria, possession, saturation, and satisfaction have been reached. Time is a factor, but enough time rather than a set amount of time. A dance that is performed only once is cold, impotent, unable to elicit praise or criticism because of the incompleteness of the dance. Repetition is a constant in African dance. As the artistic director of the National Dance Company of Zimbabwe, I had to prepare traditional dances for the stage, and the first consideration was time. What to do about all these sixty-minute dances? How to condense the dance into seven- and ten-minute versions without losing the intensity? The answer: Warm-up before performance time, so that performers would literally, in the African sense, go on stage dancing.

The oral principle and the seven senses combine to comprise an African aesthetic. The concept is theoretical and does not ignore the myriad attributes and qualities that thousands of ethnic groups and nationalities possess. I speak of African as one speaks of Western, European, Eastern. It is categorical and historical in certain similarities only. The need to understand the various cultures has been largely taken up by historians and anthropologists, but the aesthetics and artistic perspective have been missing and are necessary to properly understand the dance of Africa. The classic, neoclassic, traditional, modern, post-modern forms exist within the confines of the African's own aesthetic and sensibilities. There are schools and differences among the groups within the African culture, but there is a common ground that history, race, and politics contribute to in order to make for collective expression.

The foundation for an African aesthetic has been laid by scholars such as Gayle and DuBois.[11] African dance offers significant insight into the African culture. This dynamic and organic art form must be analyzed, researched, documented, and preserved so that any contemporary expression in African dance will not be at the expense of traditional dance. African dance encompasses the traditional and contemporary expressions. The thoroughness with which we document and study the traditional dance will directly stimulate and encourage contemporary expressions and techniques.

NOTES

1. Tsegaye Gabre-Medhin, "World Dimensions of the Community of Black People," *Proceedings of the First Precolloquium of the Third FESTAC* (Dakar, Senegal: University of Dakar, 1980), p. 3.

2. Kariamu Welsh, *Mfundalai: A Dance Technique* (Buffalo, N.Y.: School of Movement, 1980).

3. Robert F. Thompson, *African Art in Motion* (Los Angeles: University of California Press, 1974), p. 16.

4. Ibid.

5. Ibid.

6. Susanne Langer, *Feeling and Form* (New York: Scribner's 1953), pp. 64-98.

7. See chapter 13 of this volume.

8. Lincoln Kirstein, *Dance: A Short History* (New York: Dance Horizons, 1969).

9. Camara Laye, *Radiance of the King* (London: Collins, 1956), pp. 65-87.

10. Maxine Sheets, *The Phenomenology of Dance* (Madison: University of Wisconsin Press, 1967).

11. Molefi Kete Asante, *Afrocentricity: The Theory of Social Change* (Buffalo, N.Y.: Amulefi Publishing Company, 1980), pp. 1-70.

5

AFRICAN ORAL ARTISTRY AND THE NEW SOCIAL ORDER

SAMUEL OSEI BOADU

The emergence of a new social order has been the major preoccupation of contemporary social scientists. Sociological and anthropological analysis in particular have provided insights into the conditions and mechanisms of continuity, disruption and change in an old social order. All the analyses in one way or the other make the point that the presence of new technological methods and machines in the developing nations of Africa creates the atmosphere within which traditional institutions are forced to undergo change. This gradual and continual erosion of the characteristics of traditional institutions arising from rapid technical change taking place in society can clearly be observed in Africa. For example, traditional characteristics of the family, government, and education are observed to give way to orientations consistent with new technological orientations. One traditional African institution that has fallen victim to modern technological developments is oral art. This chapter assesses the extent to which the new social order has affected traditional oral art, as well as the effect of such changes on the consciousness of the oral artist. This study is appropriately part of the cultural revolution which is attempting to ensure some measure of continuity in African culture.

Oral art embraces all the activities that depend on the spoken word for transmitting important messages to a collectivity and, more importantly, for maintaining societal continuity from one generation to another. Oral literature (folklore), the priestly functions, Okyeame in the Ashanti court, the town crier, all are activities and roles that are affected through oral art. Since oral art has an imaginative quality and relies on a play of the mind and spontaneity of composition, the performer of the art can appropriately be called an oral artist.

The oral artist depends primarily on the spoken word to activate all the other senses which complement each other to ensure meaning in messages.[1] Toward this end, the language of the oral artist must be solidly grounded in significant symbols so as to elicit expected audience response. Since the oral artist and the audience are participants in the same symbolic system, there is a high likelihood of isomorphism between the internal responses (meanings) to a given set of symbols on the part of both sender and receiver. Overall, the oral artist is to a large extent the prime organizer of the cultural universe of the society in which he functions.

The test of a true oral artist is the ability to use and change words according to the dictates of situations and circumstances. Appropriately, therefore, it could be said that oral art is totally dominated by the oral moment—the moment of performance. The oral artist relies on the spontaneity of rendition unlike the literary artist who writes a text, choosing his words, and balances his phrases. The difference is between the fluidity of the oral art as opposed to the rigidity of form which is characteristic of literary art. In Africa the oral artist tends to be subjected to a more critical presence of the audience than the literary artist. The literary artist has more time to ponder, polish lines, balance syntax, and coordinate plot. Even when the literary artist is subjected to the criticism of an audience, this occurs after the work of art has gone through some form of editing by others to ensure perfection. The crux of the argument is that in terms of on-the-spot performance, the oral artist undergoes more mental taxation in the production of material than the literary artist. The common ground shared by the oral artist and the literary artist is the belief in language as both a critical element in the formation of thought and a medium for expressing thought.

The oral artist in the traditional African society performs basically for the benefit of society. In the communalistic society where people are tied by tradition to set patterns of activities and where the people lead a deeply integrated life, there exists a strong social solidarity. Each member is expected to contribute to the strengthening of the social bond by giving his utmost in services to the society. One result of the existence of strong social solidarity is the demand it imposes on the oral artist for complete devotion to his art; the end product of the effort is geared toward the aesthetic consciousness of the society rather than toward considerations of personal gain.

Oral artistry serves three broad purposes: ritual, entertainment, and education. The priest's work is purely ritualistic—performing the naming ceremony of a newborn baby into the community, pouring libation (call of the ancestors), and serving as the link between people and the gods. Traditional singers at festivals and important social meetings perform to entertain. The pedagogic role of the artist in the traditional African society is illustrated by the art of storytelling. An elderly person tells stories to the young ones around the courtyard in the moonlight. The storyteller performs not for any financial gain but for other reasons—artistic commitment, for teaching the children the moral values of their society, and for exposing them to the sociocultural background of their society. Art to such a narrator is not a means of sustaining life but of complementing it. He performs an obligatory social duty from which he derives joy.

Even in the instances when performances seem geared toward some personal gains, the art remains uncontaminated because the primary obligation of the artist is the provision of service to the society rather than personal gain. The performances of the dirge singers at funerals and the Ijala (Yoruba) chanters are primarily intended to meet some ritualistic need of their society, but they also perform elsewhere for monetary gain. The Bambara farmers of the Upper Volta consider their oral performance as both ritualistic and as a means of livelihood. During the dry season, these farmers leave the fields to subsidize their livelihood from performances and at the end of the dry season they go back to their normal activities—farming and ritualistic obligations to the society. This pattern is also followed by the traditional Ajagbo dancers of Ikare. Like the Bambara farmers, they do not rely wholly on the success of their performances which come up once a year (during the sugar cane harvesting period) as their only means of livelihood. But despite the element of double allegiance—when the artist is devoted to his art as well as to other occupational endeavors for sustenance—the artist is nonetheless conscious of his social responsibility first before any consideration of personal gain. The visible trend in the African societies is that whenever the artist is performing basically for ritual purposes he is first and foremost devoted to his art although possible monetary gains may result from incidences of appreciation from the highly impressed and artistically inclined. Traditionally, oral performances were sheer art, and individuals were engaged in them out of artistic commitment.

There are observable changes in oral artistry today, and these changes are all traceable to the pervasiveness of technology. To meet the challenge brought about by the new world revolution, scholars must look beyond the immediate situation for new ideas in order to survive in the world.

African societies today show an increasing trend toward the creation and use of a variety of new expressions in attempts to modernize various types of activities. The Ewi chanters on the NTV, Ibadan or Radio O-Y-O, Ibadan (Nigeria) have modified the practice of the art to fit into the sociocultural background of the new emerging audience. For example, for the musical accompaniments during performance, electronic guitars are used in addition to the flute and drum. The inclusion of music in a performance is not new to the African scene. Indeed, music is an integral part of African life.[2] In the traditional societies, music has always been the dynamic and driving force that animates the life of the community. This aspect of music as an integral part of African culture is capitalized upon by the modern artist but with some modifications to suit today's audience.

The prominence of new artistic forms can also be witnessed in the changes that have been taking place in the costumes for performances. Modern styles take precedence over the purely functional clothes used for performances in traditional societies. For instance, the *griot* of Mali today has a taste and sophistication in the choice of dress completely unknown in traditional society. The new social order is clearly having some effect on the consciousness of the *griot* artist.

Along with technological influences are economic changes, and the combined effect of the two is the ever-widening gap between traditional oral art and the modern version. It is a popular assumption that if notions of traditional institutions persist, then there will also be present the fundamental and undiluted form of oral art and the possibility of finding devoted artists. But the hope of survival of oral art along with devoted artists cannot be entertained forever; on closer inspection, it is quite evident that the pure form of oral artistry is fast slipping away in the face of persistent economic and technological influences.

The economic impact on oral artistry has been strong. Unlike the old artists, the new oral artists have been made conscious of the possibilities offered by a new wage economy. The change from the traditional to the modern economic structure and the effect of the new wage economy is still being analyzed. In the traditional economy without money, the principal occupation was farming, mostly subsistence. Today however, farming as an occupation has suffered a serious setback. The new wage economy has led to a mass exodus (mostly of youth) from the farms into the urban centers, and this shift in emphasis from farming to jobs in the wage economy has some serious implications for the state of oral artistry today.

Oral transmission as a mode of preserving culture has survived through the ages by young men learning the intricacies of the tradition under the guidance of older (veteran) artists. The apprentices obtained their training (after the day's work on the farm) through narratives, songs, and dances. Though the various activities were on the surface purely for entertainment, at a more serious level they built the strong mental discipline that would produce the oral materials of the next generation, an understanding and appreciation of the historical basis of the culture and the ability to use language for desired effects. But today the young men have dispersed to the urban centers with the golden dream of exploiting the new wage economy. To them oral artistry has become a thing of the village.

Farming, the occupation of the traditional people, was particularly suited to the practice of oral artistry. For ages, farming was regarded as the basis of collectivism in the traditional community. Such strong group spirit provided the atmosphere within which the composition, transmission, collective rendition, and appreciation of oral art were most conducive. The introduction of the wage economy marked the beginning of the weakening of the psychological bonds that united the members of the farming community and the weakening of the strong community spirit and sowed the seed of heterogeneity among members of the society in their personal psychic organization. In a nutshell, the wage economy has not only disrupted the natural and traditional mode of transmission of the art from one generation to another, but it has also encouraged the artist to redefine the reasons for performance to include financial reward.

The oral artist's interest in economic gain has been particularly sharpened since the awakening of Africa into political consciousness in the 1950s. Specifically, the 1950s witnessed the sudden emergence of cultural awareness all over Africa. Along with economic developments went the promotion of social developments, particularly the idealization of the cultural past and rustic innocence that were believed to have been trampled upon by the colonialists. The cultural revolution assumed much significance because it was conceived as the only means of reversing the hegemony of an alien culture over the African culture. Today the media seek the artists for cultural programmes and governments call on the artists to perform on such occasions as visits of foreign dignitaries into the country and state functions. The constant demand for oral art has automatically meant increased financial benefits to oral artists.

Clearly the commercial orientation of oral artistry in modern times has made technological encroachments an unavoidable consequence. Recording studios have capitalized on certain aspects of oral artistry. The "Oriki" used by the Yorubas of Nigeria to glorify individuals—the society's way of acknowledging and encouraging exceptional accomplishments—has become today a gimmick used by some Yoruba singers for monetary gains. Those whose praises are sung are expected to show appreciation for recognition by giving gifts commensurate with their supposed affluence. Sunny Ade's album "Ogun Onire" and some recordings by Ebenezer Obey are clear examples of modern recording artists' interest in certain aspects of oral artistry.

Apart from the recording industry, the broadcast media use oral materials on radio and television. Oral materials set to text are read over O-Y-O Ibadan, Nigeria, by Ewi chanters. It is difficult to say whether or not the Ewiists are true oral artists since they fail to meet an important criterion: the exhibition of true aesthetic value in oral artistry by a complete reliance on memory and an exhibition of tonal variation suited to the mood of the audience, qualities found in traditional Ewi performers.

The current recruitment exercises and short-term training programs for oral artists have had a strong influence on the steady decline of pure oral artistry. Most African states feel a sudden urgency to exhibit the artistic and cultural values of the independent nation to the outside world. As part of the preparation for national exhibitions, the planners of the cultural activities recruit artists from the rural sectors. The recruits then go through a period of training to familiarize them with stage movements and performance before television cameras. Performing on the modern stage and the consequent restriction on freedom of movement pose a serious problem for the spontaneous expression that oral artistry demands. The traditional Congo epic singer demonstrates perfectly the need for a wide area for performance. He has to mime and gesticulate and sometimes to mix with the audience to drive a point home. If put on stage in a modern theatre or stadium, it will be hard, if not impossible, for the fullest abilities of the artist to be demonstrated.

In summary, technological and economic changes could be said to have affected oral artistry in two main areas. In the first place, written texts and recorded oral materials often represent only a feeble grasp of traditional oral artistry. One distinguishing characteristic of the traditional oral artist was the possession of a linguistic depth that is possible only in an individual with years of training and practice in the language and culture of a social system. The lack of linguistic depth of the modern oral artist is inadequately compensated for by superficial technological adornments. In the second place, unlike the traditional artist, the new oral artist suffers from a serious set-back: he is removed from his sociocultural milieu and must perform before a "foreign audience" who may not understand the ritualistic or social significance of his art. The performance itself may be entertaining, but this is comparatively unimportant—the essence is the ritual aspect. The indigenous audience is a participating one; through ovations and interactions with the artist, it acknowledges both superficial performance and ritualistic essence of the performance. A considerable part of any artist's strength is derived from his perception of the audience's informed appreciation.

CONCLUSION

The influence of science, technology, and the new economic order have touched on all spheres of African life leading to the creation of a new social order. One of the cultural institutions affected by the new social order is oral artistry. New oral forms will undoubtedly be created to accompany the new realities. For oral artistry to revive today and prosper tomorrow the art and the consciousness of the artists must accomodate some of the demands imposed by scientific and technological realities.

But accomodating changes is not easy because it is often difficult for people to accept the fact that technological influence has actually touched certain social institutions. It is easier to accept changes through theorizing or historical study or a combination of both, but the complete acceptance of changes in these institutions is difficult because of a psychological lag. The African's true humanness is still rooted in an emotional nature, and, while the mind may make the necessary leap and accept a change, emotion still lags behind. The idealization of chieftaincy within an executive presidential political system in Nigeria is a case in point.

The main problem with the psychological lag is that it blocks us from accepting the true state of affairs at specific points in the society's evolution. It blinds us to the fact that change is constantly taking place. Thus the greatest danger inherent in the psychological lag is its success in deceptively leading us to believe that there is neither past nor present. As Edward Hall points out, not only is there a past and a present, but also men living in these two periods possess distinct sensory experiences so that an event that takes place in one period is not easily transposed to any other period.[3] The lesson to be learned is that oral artistry of the past needs to be considered in the light of some set of circumstances and conditions at that point in time. What is needed now is a more thorough search for new directions in oral artistry consistent with the set of circumstances and conditions of a technological age.

NOTES

1. Molefi Asante and Jerry Frye, *Contemporary Public Communication*: Applications (New York: Harper and Row, 1976), pp. 3–7.

2. Alan Merriam, "African Music," in *African Cultures*, ed. William Bascom and Melville Herskovits (Chicago: University of Chicago Press, 1958), pp. 49–59.

3. Edward Hall, *The Silent Language* (New York: Doubleday, 1959), pp. 22–78.

6

THE AFRICAN INTELLECTUAL AND THE PROBLEM OF CLASS SUICIDE: IDEOLOGICAL AND POLITICAL DIMENSIONS

MAULANA KARENGA

There is general agreement among both continental and diasporan African social theorists—whether revolutionaries such as Amilcar Cabral, W.E.B. Du Bois, and Frantz Fanon, or reformists like Harold Cruse or E. Franklin Frazier—on the indispensible role of petty-bourgeois intellectuals in broad and profound social change.[1] In spite of the criticism of their class and its tendency to hedge, betray, compromise, and play broker between the masses and the ruling class in any given situation, there is the continuing concession that this class is most conscious of the possibilities of change and that a segment of this class must accept the historical responsibility of imbuing the masses with a new active self-consciousness which will culminate in self-liberation. Whether they are called the petty bourgeoisie, the Talented Tenth, or the revolutionary petty bourgeoisie, it is these intellectuals who are charged with the decisive role in the theoretical and practical project of liberation, grasping the fundamental dimensions of the situation and developing strategies and structures to change it.

Even Marxists such as Lenin and Gramsci assign a fundamental role to members of this class in bringing about serious social change. Lenin argued that left to itself, the working class would only develop a trade-union consciousness and thus there was an urgent need for political intervention from the party in the fundamental roles of education and organization.[2] Antonio Gramsci contended that without a revolutionary

intelligentsia to challenge the cultural hegemony as well as political
domination of the ruling class, complete liberation was impossible.[3]
Hence, Marxism also concedes the fundamental function of intellectuals
in the political preparation of the masses for self-liberation.

The problematic, however, is that assigned historical vocation and
assumption of social responsibility often diverge. African and other
social theorists have recognized this problem and suggested some necessary solutions to it. Perhaps the most direct and definitive confrontation with this problem was effected by Cabral, whose contribution is
unique and valuable on several levels. First, Cabral does not repeat cant
about the unqualified majesty and might of the working class. He recognizes their limitations and need for allies and leadership. Second, he
does not rant and rave about the irredeemability of the petty bourgeoisie.
In fact, he argues that the level of consciousness of the working class
and the objective and subjective position of the petty bourgeoisie offer
them "the historical opportunity of leading the struggle against foreign
domination."[4]

Third, he defines the dilemma of the petty bourgeoisie as one of
allying with the oppressor or the people, retaining power through al-
liance with and service to the oppressor, or identifying with the interests
and aspirations of the masses and seizing revolutionary power. Fourth,
Cabral does not think the whole petty-bourgeois class is prone to or
capable of revolutionary action. He thus distinguishes between the revolutionary sector of the petty bourgeoisie and the other sectors who
"retain the doubts characteristic of these classes or ally themselves to
colonialism so as to defend, albeit illusory, their social situation."[5]

Finally, Cabral argues that making the choice of not betraying but
leading the revolution and the masses requires that the revolutionary
petty bourgeoisie commit class suicide. This positive solution in favor
of the revolution and masses, Cabral states, is essentially a question of
social commitment and "shows . . . that if national liberation is essentially a political problem, the conditions for its development give it
certain characteristics which belong to the sphere of morals."[6] For
Cabral, then, class suicide by the petty bourgeoisie is a process of
transformed thought and transforming practice. It involves at a minimum
the thrust to: (1) "strengthen its revolutionary consciousness"; (2) "reject the temptation of becoming more bourgeois and the natural concerns
of its class mentality"; (3) "identify with the working classes"; and

(4) "be reborn as revolutionary workers, completely identified with the deepest aspiration of the people to which they belong."[7]

In this position, Cabral refines the crudity of the purely economic determinist position on class, as he did when he argued against the Marxist contention that history begins with class struggle, a position which obviously eliminates from history peoples and societies who had no classes.[8] Marx had dismissed the petty bourgeoisie as reactionary and entirely self-serving based on the assumed position and calling of their class.[9] On the other hand, continuing his demystification of class, Cabral seeks to establish a theoretical equilibrium between economic position and political possibilities. He recognizes and respects the possibilities of human intervention in all social processes and seeks to identify the areas in which intervention is most probable and effective. This is a major contribution to socialist theory and elevates human initiative above the specious objectivistic notion of immutable laws.

THE PETTY BOURGEOISIE: PROBLEMATIC AND POSSIBILITIES

The problematic and possibilities of petty-bourgeois participation in liberation and social transformation has been treated by various social theorists, African and otherwise. As mentioned above, Marx recognized the problematic and dismissed the possibilities. Cabral and other African theorists recognize both the problematic and possibilities. There is obviously an ambivalence about the petty bourgeoisie, based on its dual history. Samuel Huntington, equating the middle class with the petty bourgeoisie, notes the fact that "the image of the middle class as a revolutionary element clashes, of course, with the stereotype of the middle class as the keystone of stability in a modern polity."[10] He argues that "the relation of the middle class to stability, however, is not unlike that of affluence to stability." On one hand, "a large middle class, like widespread affluence, is a moderating force in politics. The creation of a middle class, like economic growth, however, is often a highly destabilizing event." Huntington concludes that intellectuals are both the first sector of the petty bourgeoisie to appear on the scene and at the same time the "most active oppositional group within" that class.[11]

Both Afro-American and continental African theorists demonstrate ambivalence toward petty-bourgeois intellectuals. E. Franklin Frazier criticized the Afro-American intellectuals for integration mania, intellectual sterility, and ideological submissiveness. He states that:

They have failed to study the problems of [Afro-American] life in America in a manner which would place the fate of [Afro-Americans] in the broad framework of man's experience in this world. They have engaged in petty defenses of the [Afro-American's] social failures. But more often they have been so imbued with the prospect of integration and eventual assimilation that they have thought that they could prove themselves true Americans by not studying [Afro-Americans].[12]

Their task, he feels, is to free themselves from the desire to conform, to overcome their inferiority complex, to stop wishing for racial disappearance, and to begin to leave a social legacy worthy of any people.[13]

Harold Cruse is even more critical of the Afro-American intellectual. He asserts that:

Even at this advanced stage in [black] history, the [black] intellectual is a retarded child whose thinking processes are still geared to piddling intellectual civil right-ism and racial integrationism. This is all he knows. In the meantime, he plays second and third fiddle to white intellectuals in all the establishments— Left, Center, and Right. The white intellectuals in these establishments do not recognize the [black] intellectual as a man who can speak both for himself and for the best interests of the nation, but only as someone who must be spoken for and on behalf of.[14]

He too feels that the black intellectual is trapped in the integrationist syndrome much to his/her own disadvantage and that of his/her people. Pursuing the illusion, he/she is forced to pretend its reality just to save face and tenuous space:

The tentative acceptance the [black] intellectual finds in the predominantly white intellectual world, allows him the illusion that integration is real—a functional reality for himself, and a possibility for all [blacks]. Even if a [black] intellectual does not wholly believe this, he must give lip service to the aims of racial integration, if only to rationalize his own status in society.[15]

However, recognizing that it is difficult to get around the need for them, Harold Cruse assigns them functions. "The special function of the Afro-American intellectual," he argues, is a critical one.... He should explain the economic and institutional causes of this American cultural depravity. He should tell Black Americans how and why [Afro-Americans] are trapped in this cultural degeneracy, and how it has dehumanized their essential identity, squeezed the lifeblood of their inherited cultural ingredients out of them, and then relegated them to cultural slums.[16]

Moreover, he continues, "The [black] intellectual must deal intimately with the white power structure and cultural apparatus, and the inner realities of the black world at one and the same time." More important is the need for the black intellectual to organize and lead a cultural revolution to break the monopoly the oppressor has on black minds and create a new system of thought and values. As Cruse concludes: "For the [black] creative intellectual, the watchword is this: There can be no real black revolution in the United States without cultural revolution as a corollary to the scheme of 'agencies for social change.' "[17]

    W.E.B. Du Bois begins by praising black intellectuals, the Talented Tenth, not by lambasting them. He contends that:

The [black] race, like all races, is going to be saved by its exceptional men. The problem of education, then, among [blacks] must first of all deal with the Talented Tenth; it is the problem of developing the Best of this race that they may guide the Mass away from the contamination and death of the Worst, in their own and other races.[18]

The special function of the Talented Tenth is to be "leaders of thought and missionaries of culture among their people."[19] Du Bois goes on to say:

The Talented Tenth rises and pulls all that are worth the saving up to their vantage ground. This is the history of human progress; and the two historic mistakes which have hindered that progress were the thinking first that no more could ever rise save the few already risen; or second, that it would better the unrisen to pull the risen down.[20]

However, later Du Bois conceded that in advocating this concept of the Talented Tenth, he neglected to deal with the problem of "leadership and authority within the group which by implication left controls to wealth" and which automatically tends to put class interests before mass interests.[21]

    Frantz Fanon contended that the true historical vocation of the Continental national bourgeoisie is to repudiate its own nature insofar as it is bourgeois and makes itself "the willing slave of the revolutionary capital which is the people."[22] In other words, he concluded they should "put at the people's disposal the intellectual and technical capital that it has snatched" from the dominant society. However, he recognizes the problematic of the situation. He recognizes that conditions create consciousness and that, given the oppressive situation, the class is an obscene caricature of Europe, marked by "intellectual laziness . . . spiritual penury and . . . the profound cosmopolitan mold that its mind is set in."[23] Thus, even though he calls for self-repudiation by the class, he is pessimistic and suggests finding an alternative in a multiclass revolutionary elite.

Julius Nyerere recognizes also the special contribution of the African intellectual. He accepts the fact "that intellectuals have a special contribution to make to the development of our nation, and to Africa. And I am asking that their knowledge, and the greater understanding that they should possess, should be used for the benefit of the society of which we are all members."[24] Moreover, he believes that intellectuals "in the developed societies do not have such opportunities as we have in Africa, and such social satisfactions as we can have." For ". . . here in Africa, we can, by the use of our skills, help people to transform their lives from abject poverty—that is, from fear of hunger and always endless drudgery—to decency and simple comfort."[25] The problem, he feels, is to prevent African intellectuals from class isolation and alienation from the masses, for it could only damage them and the people they should serve. Speaking to the intellectuals, he observed:

We can try to cut ourselves from our fellows on the basis of the education we have had; we can try to carve out for ourselves an unfair share of the wealth of the society. But the cost to us, as well as to our fellow citizens, will be very high. It will be high not only in terms of satisfactions forgone, but also in terms of our own security and well-being.[26]

Thus, the need is to merge and serve, not isolate and alienate through thought and action in contradiction to the social service to which one is committed.

Sekou Toure states that the African intellectual must be a conscious, capable, and committed representative of his/her people. For Toure, "the political leader is, by virtue of his communion of idea and action with his people, the representative of his people, the representative of a culture." Moreover, the African intellectual must aid in the decolonization and rehabilitation of Africa and the African personality: "It is in terms of that decolonization that the African intellectual will bring to Africa an effective and valuable aid."[27] He continues, "Moreover, he will realize the necessity of liberating himself intellectually from the colonial complex; furthermore he will rediscover our original virtues and he will serve the African cause." This requires the class suicide and dedication of "true political leaders of Africa, whose thought and attitude lean toward national liberation of their peoples," who are, in fact, "dedicated men, fundamentally engaged against all the forms of dehumanization of African culture. They represent, by the anticolonialist nature and the national tenor of their struggle, the cultural values of their society mobilized against colonialism."[28]

Kwame Nkrumah, like Cabral, recognized that the petty-bourgeois intelligentsia is not necessarily a homogeneous or static social grouping.[29] He contends that there are basically three sections of this intelligentsia. According to Nkrumah, the first sections "are those who support the new privileged indigenous class—the bureaucratic, political and business bourgeoisie who are the open allies of imperialism and neocolonialism." The second section is composed of "those who advocate a 'non-capitalist road' of economic development, a 'mixed economy,' for the less industrialized areas of the world, as a phase in the progess towards socialism." Finally, Nkrumah describes the third section as the revolutionary intellectuals "who provide the impetus and leadership of the worker-peasant struggle for all-out socialism. It is from among this section that the genuine intellectuals of the African Revolution are to be found." He asserts that "very often they are minority products of colonial educational establishments who reacted strongly against its brainwashing processes and who became genuine socialist and African nationalist revolutionaries." It is this third section whose task it is "to enunciate and promulgate African revolutionary socialist objectives, and to expose and refute the deluge of capitalist propaganda and bogus concepts and theories poured out by imperialist, neocolonialist, and indigenous, reactionary mass communications media."

Still, however, Nkrumah is ambivalent, for although "the intelligentsia always leads the nationalist movement in its early stages, it aspires to replace the colonial power, but not to bring about a radical transformation of society. The object is to control the 'system' rather than to change it.'' The reason for this is that "the intelligentsia tends as a whole to be bourgeois-minded and against revolutionary socialist transformation.'' However, the problem of the African intelligentsia is further complicated by the fact that even intellectuals "from working-class families aspire to middle-class status, shrinking from manual work and becoming completely alienated from their class and social origins.''[30]

Thus, the dilemma Cabral posed is a reality; it is problematic for other African theorists also. This problematic choice of betrayal or revolution which confronts the continental and diasporan Africans confronts African peoples also. For if they choose wrongly, the struggle for liberation and a higher level of human life suffers. However, if they accept their historical obligation and join the struggle, the revolution benefits and goes forward faster. The question thus is how this problematic class can be won over and made a social force for revolution and liberation rather than reaction and oppression.

CLASS SUICIDE: TOWARD TRANSFORMATION

Class suicide is obviously easier to propose than to effect. If a class is conscious of its interests and has the capacity to defend them, it tends to do so even at the expense of other classes. In fact, its definition of itself as a class places it in opposition to and makes it distinct from other classes. The petty bourgeoisie, which understands its interests better than the working class and has more economic, social and political status and power than the working class, tends to defend and maintain its position. Hence, we have to question why and how this position can be transformed. Simply stated, three factors conducive to transformation can be defined and developed: (1) objective social conditions of marginality; (2) the revolutionary party; and (3) the increased political maturity of the masses.

Social Marginality

The first factor conducive to class transformation is the objective social conditions of the petty bourgeoisie which, in fact, deny or diminish the reality of their class position, and thus change the objective content of their class consciousness. A problem vulgar Marxists have in recognizing the political potential for class suicide of the petty bourgeoisie revolves around the reductive translation of class as an exclusively economic category and the mechanical attachment of characteristics which may or may not exist, depending on various factors. Class as a social category has at a minimum three dimensions to it: economic status (or capacity or position relation to the means of production), social status, and political power. In a racist context, the economic status and possibilities are often conditioned by the social status and political position imposed in racial terms. As Milton Gordon notes: "Since an individual or group may rank high on one variable—say, economic power—and low on another—for instance social status—certain strains and pressures toward marginality may come into being." Given this dynamic interrelationship of variables, a calcified position on one's class position and consciousness becomes problematic and unproductive. "Thus, the study of *stratification inconsistency* as a dynamic variable constitutes an important area of social class analysis."[31]

Explicit in Cabral's positing of the possibility and desirability of class suicide among the petty bourgeoisie, as well as in the work of other African theorists who suggest a similar fate and future for the revolutionary intellectual, is the assumption that the stratification, inconsistency, and subsequent marginality which the revolutionary intellectuals experience will be a motivating force in their alienation from the existing oppressive order. In fact, Cabral argues this, contending that the historical opportunity for the petty bourgeoisie to lead the revolution is determined not only by the masses' objective need for leadership, but also by the nature of the petty bourgeoisie's' objective and subjective position which includes most definitively "more frequent contacts with the agents of colonialism and hence more chances of being humiliated."[32] Moreover, as Huntington notes, it is not a question of the established order being deserted by the intellectuals, but of "their emergence as a distinct group"—in fact, an alienated group. Thus, "in most cases the intellectuals cannot desert the existing order because they've never been a part of it."[33]

The Revolutionary Party

The second factor conducive and mandatory to the class suicide and transformation of petty-bourgeois intellectuals is their organization and molding within the context of a revolutionary party. The party organization is effective human intervention in the social process. Lenin, who argued that the proletariat could not achieve class consciousness by itself, and that real class consciousness had to be brought about by socialist intellectuals, pointed to a solution to the crisis and conversion of the intellectual.[34] To paraphrase Marx, if the educator is to correctly educate, he/she must also be educated.[35] And it is within a party structure that intellectuals can be absorbed and transformed.

Huntington is correct when he argues: "Lenin's constant emphasis on the achievement of a true revolutionary political consciousness as distinct from a limited immediate 'trade union' or economic consciousness was a practical recognition of the broader scope and needs of politics and of the transcendence of political goals over economic ones."[36] In stressing the preeminence of the party and party goals, values, and politics over vague trade union-oriented goals of the unconscious working class, Lenin introduced a substitute for old class consciousness. In fact, he

substituted a consciously created, structured, and organized political institution for an amorphous social class. By stressing the primacy of politics and the party as a political institution, by emphasizing the need to build a "strong political organization" based on a "broad revolutionary coalition," Lenin laid down the prerequisites for political order.[37]

Party membership is based on party loyalty and achievement, not class background, and thus members from any class, especially the petty bourgeoisie, can be and are absorbed and transformed. The problematic, then, would be to make sure the party clearly represents the masses, for it is its vision and values that the petty-bourgeois intellectual will absorb and put into practice. Gramsci, likewise arguing for a party to organize and direct the masses, lays the theoretical basis for a structure which organizes and trains the organizers and directors. He calls for the creation of a body of intellectuals. He contends:

Critical self-consciousness means, historically and politically, the creation of an *elite* of intellectuals. A human mass does not 'distinguish' itself, does not become independent in its own right without, in the widest sense, organising itself; and there is no organisation without intellectuals, that is without organisers and leaders, in other words, without the theoretical aspect of the theory-practice nexus being distinguished concretely by the existence of a group of people 'specialised' in conceptual and philosophical elaboration of ideas.[38]

Toure also argues for a mass party which represents the popular will of the people and denies any one class or section from a class, the right to oppose that will. Therefore, he reshapes the intellectuals and redefines the nature of the revolution as one not of class but of the masses. "The Guinean revolution," he states, "is not a class struggle, nor one of social strata. It is a global revolution, inspired, realized and directed by the people, whose means of expression and action is the Democratic Party of Guinea. Upon the base of a determined doctrine and orientation, the phases of the revolution are defined at the grass-roots level of the people and the avantgarde role played, to the hilt, by the Party."[39]

As Irving Markovitz points out, Cabral also struggled to create not only a political organization to win power, "but also the type of social organization that would enable guerrillas to become responsible officials."[40] Cabral thus built the revolution as he fought, training the trainers in the values and vision which could be put into social practice on a grand scale "immediately following liberation."[41] Cabral informs us that "the armed struggle for liberation, launched in response to the colonialist oppressor, turns out to be a painful but *efficient instrument for developing the cultural level of both the leadership strata in the liberation movement and the various social groups who participate in the struggle*" (italics mine).[42] Thus, the petty-bourgeois intellectuals and clerks who live with the peasants, "come to know the people better, discover at the grassroots the richness of their cultural values," economic realities, problems and suffering and thus are transformed. In a word, they "develop personally their capacity to serve the movement in the service of the people."[43]

Political Maturity of the Masses

Finally, it must be admitted that regardless of the original commitments of leaders—revolutionary, reformist, or reactionary—they are not bound to keep them if the masses themselves have neither the consciousness nor capacity to hold them responsible for their action. This is why Cabral stresses the dual educational process—one not only for the cadres, but also for the masses. Through the party's political education, the masses "lose the complexes which constrained them in their relations" with each other and the party. Moreover, "they realize their crucial role in the struggle [and] break the bonds of the village universe to integrate progressively into the country and the world."

Finally, Cabral observes, "they acquire an infinite amount of new knowledge useful for their immediate and future activity within the framework of the struggle and they strengthen their political awareness by assimilating principles of national and social revolution postulated by the struggle."[44] This enables them not only to play a decisive role during the struggle, but also after the struggle when the question of social commitment is ultimately answered or betrayed.

Fanon also stresses political preparation and education of the masses so that they themselves can define, defend and develop their own interests and hold the intellectual responsible. To him

political education means opening their minds, awakening them, and allowing the birth of their intelligence; as Cesaire said, it is 'to invent souls.' To educate the masses politically does not mean, cannot mean, making a political speech. What it means is that everything depends on them; that if we stagnate it is their responsibility, and that if we go forward it is due to them too, that there is no such thing as demiurge, that there is no famous man who will take the responsibility for everything, but that the demiurge is the people themselves and the magic hands are finally only the hands of the people.[45]

Speaking of the struggle in Algeria, Fanon notes the bringing into being of "a new, positive, efficient personality, whose richness is provided less by the trial of strength that he engages in than by his certainty that he embodies a decisive moment of the national consciousness." Furthermore, he states, "the liberation of the individual does not follow national liberation. An authentic national liberation exists only to the precise degree to which the individual has irreversibly begun his own liberation." That is why "the Algerian combatant is not only up in arms against the torturing parachutists. Most of the time he has to face problems of building, or organizing, of inventing the new society that must come into being."[46]

Nyerere also realizes the need for dual education and transformation. He contends that political or technical education cannot be imposed.

If real development is to take place, the people have to be involved. Educated people can give a lead—and should do so. They can show what can be done, and how. But they can only succeed in effecting changes in the society if they work from a position within the society. Educated people, in other words, can only be effective when they are full members of the society they are trying to change, involved in its good and bad fortune, and committed to it whatever happens.

In order to do this the educated people of Africa have to identify themselves with the uneducated, and do so without reservation.[47]

Thus he instructs the intellectual:

We have to be part of the society which we are changing; we have to work from within it, and not try to descend like ancient gods, do something, and disappear again. A country, or a village, or a community, cannot *be* developed; it can only develop itself. For real development means the development, the growth, of people.[48]

This, he argues, is not to suggest living exactly like the masses, but of patiently and thoroughly working to raise them to the level of their own capacity to know and liberate themselves and their society.

Finally, Toure stresses again that no social class or stratum is above the people and that once the people have attained a certain level of consciousness and political capacity, they will guard their power and win the liberation struggle. As he states, "no social strata, no group of workers, no proletarian category can pretend to be more revolutionary than the people, because the people are highly conscious of their needs and aspirations, determined to transform the conditions of their existence, jealous of their sovereignty and resolved to effect their complete emancipation."[49] Congratulating the peoples of Africa for their heroic liberation struggles, he tells them: "People of Africa, from now on you are reborn in history, because you mobilize yourself in the struggle and because the struggle before you restores to your own eyes and renders to you, justice in the eyes of the world."[50]

Gramsci sums up the dialectics between intellectual and mass development when he states:

The process of development is tied to a dialectic between the intellectuals and the masses. The intellectual stratum develops both quantitatively and qualitatively, but every leap forward towards a new breadth and complexity of the intellectual stratum is tied to an analogous movement on the part of the mass of the "simple," who raise themselves to higher levels of culture and at the same time extend their circle of influence towards the stratum of specialised intellectuals, producing outstanding individuals and groups of greater or less importance.[51]

MAULANA KARENGA

But he warns that "the process of creating intellectuals is long, difficult, full of contradictions, advances and retreats, dispersals and regrouping, in which the loyalty of the masses is often sorely tried." Certainly, as Fanon observed, "The future will have no pity for those men who, possessing the exceptional privilege of being able to speak words of truth to their oppressors, have taken refuge in an attitude of passivity, of mute indifference, and sometimes cold complicity."[52] But in reality, it is the masses who are the makers of history and forgers of the future and it is they, who having become self-conscious agents of their own liberation, must and will defend their gains—even against those who claim class suicide and similarity and attempt to speak in their name.

NOTES

1. Amilcar Cabral, *Revolution in Guinea* (New York: Monthly Review Press, 1969), pp. 12–17; W.E.B. Du Bois, "The Talented Tenth", in *The Negro Problem: Articles by Representative American Negroes of Today*, ed. Ulysses Lee (New York: Arno Press and the New York Times, 1969), pp. 31–76; Frantz Fanon, *The Wretched of the Earth* (New York: Grove Press, 1968); Harold Cruse, *The Crisis of the Negro Intellectual* (New York: William Morrow and Company, 1967); E. Franklin Frazier, "The Failure of the Negro Intellectual," in *The Death of White Sociology*, ed. Joyce A. Ladner (New York: Vintage Books, 1973), pp. 52–66.

2. V. I. Lenin, *What Is to Be Done?* (New York: International Publishers, 1921).

3. Antonio Gramsci, *Selections from the Prison Notebooks of Antonio Gramsci* (New York: International Publishers, 1971), pp. 2–35.

4. Cabral, *Revolution in Guinea*, pp. 32–107, 109.

5. Ibid., p. 109.

6. Ibid., p. 110.

7. Ibid.

8. Ibid., p. 95.

9. Karl Marx, *The Communist Manifesto* (London: Allen and Unwin, 1948).

10. Samuel P. Huntington, *Political Order in Changing Societies* (New Haven, Conn.: Yale University Press, 1978), p. 298.

11. Ibid., p. 290.

12. Frazier, "The Failure of the Negro Intellectual," p. 60.

13. Ibid., p. 66.

14. Cruse, *The Crisis of the Negro Intellectual*, p. 475.

15. Ibid., p. 453.

16. Ibid., p. 455.

17. Ibid., p. 475.

18. Du Bois, "The Talented Tenth", pp. 31–76.

19. Ibid., p. 75.

20. Ibid., p. 45.

21. W.E.B. Du Bois, *Dusk of Dawn: An Essay Toward an Autobiography of a Race Concept* (New York: Harcourt, Brace and Company, 1940), p. 217.

22. Fanon, *The Wretched of the Earth*, p. 150.

23. Ibid., p. 149.

24. Julius Nyerere, *Freedom and Development* (New York, Oxford University Press, 1974), p. 28.

25. Ibid., p. 25.

26. Ibid., p. 27.

27. Sekou Toure, "The African Elite in the Anti-Colonial Struggle" *The Black Scholar*, vol.3, no.5, (January 1972), p. 2.

28. Ibid., p. 6.

29. Quoted from Kwame Nkrumah, *Class Struggle in Africa* (New York: International Publishers, 1970), pp. 38–39.

30. Ibid., p. 39.

31. Milton M. Gordon, *Human Nature, Class and Ethnicity* (New York: Oxford University Press, 1978), p. 244.

32. Ibid.

33. Huntington, *Political Order in Changing Societies*, p. 289.

34. Lenin, *What Should Be Done?*

35. Karl Marx, *German Ideology* (New York: International Publishers, 1976), p. 121.

36. Huntington, *Political Order in Changing Societies*, p. 337.

37. Ibid.

38. Gramsci, *Selections from the Prison Notebooks of Antonio Gramsci*, p. 6.

39. Toure, "The African Elite in the Anti-Colonial Struggle," p. 12.

40. Irving L. Markovitz, *Power and Class in Africa: An Introduction to Change and Conflict in African Politics* (Englewood Cliffs, N.J.: Prentice-Hall, 1977), p. 196.

41. Cabral, *Revolution in Guinea*, p. 44.

42. Amilcar Cabral, *Return to the Source* (New York: African Information Service and PAIGC, 1973), pp. 53–54, emphasis added.

43. Ibid.

44. Ibid.

45. Fanon, *The Wretched of the Earth*, p. 197.

46. Frantz Fanon, *Toward the African Revolution* (New York: Grove Press, 1967), pp. 102–3.

47. Nyerere, *Freedom and Development*, p. 25.

48. Ibid.

49. Sekou Toure, "Unionism and Revolution," *The Black Scholar*, vol.3, no.9 (May 1972), p. 12.

50. Sekou Toure, "The Permanent Struggle," *The Black Scholar*, vol.2, no.7 (March 1971), p. 9.

51. Gramsci, *Selections From the Prison Notebooks of Antonio Gramsci*, pp. 334–35.

52. Fanon, *Toward the African Revolution*, p. 117.

Part **III**

CONCEPTS OF CULTURAL VALUE

7

AFRICAN TRADITIONAL EDUCATION: A TOOL FOR INTERGENERATIONAL COMMUNICATION

FELIX BOATENG

The increasing interdependence among nations of the world and the influence of modern technology and Western education on human development have brought growth for some countries but have raised serious problems and questions for others. In Africa, the introduction of Western formal education has oftentimes served as an obstacle to the process of cultural transmission and intergenerational communication, which are viewed culturally as some of the functions of the school. It is an accepted fact in educational circles that the school must participate in the process of passing on to the young the nation's heritage and in developing the skills needed for its upkeep. Unfortunately, as an indispensable agent of colonialism in Africa, Western formal education did not consider cultural transmission as a goal of the educative process for Africans. Needless to say, the increasing deterioration of intergenerational communication in Africa has been attributed to systems of education introduced by Western colonial powers.

The traditional role of African cultural education—bridging the gap between the adult generation and youth—is gradually giving way to the development of the so-called creative individual who is completely removed from his tradition, thanks to Western education. Many have called for a return to more traditional education in Africa. However, there is wide disagreement as to what the values of traditional African education can do and cannot do today and whether the essence of this educative process has any implications for Africa's development. Some even favor a complete rejection of the past and advocate a total concentration on and exploitation of modern opportunities to ensure the acquisition of optional benefits for Africa and her people. But as David Scanlon points out in *Traditions of African Education*, in education "tradition is inescapable, whether one reaffirms it or repudiates it."[1] In Africa's continuous search for the decolonization of her societies, it may be necessary to recall the caution in Ralph Perry's dictum: "The past as embodied in contemporary adults is both the bed of reactionaries and the springboard of innovations. It provides a man's working capital whether he squanders it, lives on the interest, or invests it in new enterprises."[2] Africa's heritage in education is what has come to be referred to as traditional African education. It is the education of the African before the coming of the European—an informal education that prepared youth for their responsibilities as adults in the community.

The primary purpose of this chapter is to analyze the philosophical foundations of traditional African education in an attempt to illustrate its inherent effectiveness as a vehicle for intergenerational communication. Today's Western (nontraditional) educational system has failed to achieve this objective. Although traditional African education is today weakened by the pressures of Westernization, the study should contribute toward the recognition of traditional and informal education as a springboard for innovations in contemporary African education.

Traditional education in Africa has been defined in several ways by researchers like K. A. Busia, Willie Abraham, and David Scanlon. A close study of these definitions and those given by the elders of the various communities in Africa simply shows that traditional African education, unlike the formal systems introduced by the colonialists, was inseparable from other segments of life. Traditional African education was there not only to be acquired but also to be lived. Children acquired education by participating in sociopolitical and religious institutions that ensured effective means of communication between generations.

Intergenerational communication refers to the smooth transmission and continuous preservation of the values and traditions of a society from one generation to the other. Intergenerational communication ensures a peaceful transition from youth to adulthood and creates an understanding of the proper roles of each generation in society. A breakdown in intergenerational communication may contribute to the development of conflicting values in a society and the emergence of rebellious youth. In traditional Africa, intergenerational communication was achieved through a network of traditional institutions and a set of norms, mores, and folkways which produced common understandings, an essential element in cultural growth and stability.

An analysis of the role of traditional oral literature, secret societies, and other religious practices in the education of youth will show how this system of education ensured intergenerational communication. While the focus is on the continent of Africa, examples will be taken mostly from societies in West Africa. The writer is familiar with problems that arise when one generalizes the traditions of one or two communities in Africa as "African culture." However, very often understanding is gained by moving from the smaller to the greater—and from the particular to the general. The experience of one African community may contribute, by comparison and contrast, to the understanding of the larger concept of traditional education.

ORAL LITERATURE

One area which served as an important educational vehicle for the youth in traditional Africa and still does is the area of oral literature. Oral literature encompasses fables, folktales, legends, myths, and proverbs.

Fables

Fables in the form of trickster stories conveyed moral lessons and, according to Willie Abraham, were more of "pedagogic devices rather than literary pieces."[3] Many of these tales were carefully constructed to inculcate the values of the societies into children without necessarily and formally telling them what to do and how to do it. In most of these stories, a catalogue of likely tricks are set out in story forms and successful countermoves to them are described. They are sometimes used to insist on justice and resist arbitrariness while maintaining courtesy.[4] One device was to put impossible conditions on impossible demands.

In one fable taken from the Ashantis of Ghana, a person is ordered by a ruthless ruler to make a human being. For raw materials, the victim asks for a thousand loads of charcoal made of human hair and a hundred pots of tears. In another instance from the Cameroons, the tortoise is asked to fetch water in a basket. After being given the order, the tortoise politely but firmly asks for a carrying strap of smoke. In these two fables, respect for authority is easily combined with the integrity of justice. The merit lies in the avoidance of openly personalized conflict with constituted authority. Instead of a blunt refusal and disobedience, authority is presented with seeming cooperation which is in many ways destructive of the purpose of the given task.

Among the Akan of Ghana, Anansi (the spider) a main character in their folktales, has a similar method for dealing with impertinence. A story is told about a tyrant who could not bear to be contradicted. He put to death all those who could not satisfy his idiotic requests. One day Anansi visited him and withstood all provocations. Anansi then invited the tyrant back to his (Anansi's) place, but Anansi hid himself after having told his children how to handle the tyrant. The tyrant arrived at Anansi's place, and, after having waited for a while, asked for a drink of water from the cooler pot. He was told that the top layer of the water belonged to Anansi who was away, the middle part to an aunt who would be furious if her portion were disturbed, and only the bottom portion to the children who could not reach it without disturbing the other portions. Upon asking for the whereabouts of Anansi, the tyrant was told that in trying to pluck a fruit from a tree with his penis, Anansi had broken his penis in several places and he had gone to fetch medicine. Anansi's excuse for being absent is ridiculous, but it is enough to teach the tyrant a lesson.

As Abraham points out, some of these fables were designed to emphasize the superiority of brilliance over steadiness.[5] For example, the African tortoise is said to have won his race against the hare not by toiling upward in the night while his companion slept, but by planting several tortoises like him in the shrubs along the route, the last of whom stirred himself to the tape at the right time. The unity of the clan and the value of cooperative effort are major African values which are brought out in such a story.

Many stories reveal the merits in group solidarity and the dangers in individualism. Many West African societies tell the story about the spider (Anansi) who set out to collect all wisdom in the world into a pot and hide it on a tree so that he will be the only wise creature on earth. After collecting what he thought was all the wisdom on earth, Anansi called on his son to accompany him to the forest to hide the pot in a big tree. In the forest the spider began to climb the tree with the pot tied to his stomach. Of course this arrangement presented difficulties.

His son, who was supposed to have lost all his senses, advised Anansi to tie the pot on his back so that he could climb. Anansi then gave up the whole idea because he realized that he had failed since there was some wisdom left in the brain of his own son. Selfishness, individualism, and blind ambition are some of the vices exposed in the story.

It must be noted that most of these fables, which also served as sources of entertainment, were told during moonlit nights, and children would go to bed with most of the lessons vividly in their minds. All attempts were made to make the storytelling interesting and entertaining. Storytelling was often characterized by periodic group singing led by the storyteller which kept listeners awake, interested, and involved. Values were thus communicated to children in the most informal, serene, and unruffled way. It is quite safe to compare the impact that these stories had on the African youth with the impact that the modern cinema has on the minds of youth today. In modern cinematography, lessons that reflect what is good (or who is the good guy) and what is bad (or the bad guy) in the society are communicated to the youth through the presentation of stories on the screen. The communicative power of the cinema is thus comparable with that of the African fable. The only difference is that, whereas the modern cinema puts the images before the child, the African child had to imagine and develop his own mental pictures. It is this exercise in imagination that left the deepest impression on the African child. Today the African child who is exposed to Western movies experiences problems in value identification especially if the child is raised in rural areas where traditional forms of education still prevail vis-à-vis formal education.

Myths and Legends

Closely connected with fables were the myths and legends which were told about various African communities. Myths played an active part in the African's everyday life and were a vital social force. Ladislas Segy aptly remarks in his study of traditional African societies that myths and legends not only supplied accounts of the group's origin but related precedents to present-day beliefs, actions, and codes of behavior.[6] It was taken for granted that beliefs and practices had existed unchanged since their adoption. Consequently, the reference to a precedent codified and in many ways sanctified the beliefs and placed them beyond question or change. According to many African myths and legends, certain religious actions produced results for *the forefather*; therefore, it is assumed these actions are still effective.

Mythology, which even today forms an important aspect of traditional education in the Akan communities of Ghana, is a collection of sacred stories about the people. Some of these myths and legends relate to creation, divine or supernatural beings, family ancestry, and activities. They are often connected with the worship of the gods and are told to explain festive ceremonies and forms of religious images or what are referred to today as African art-pieces. Myths in the Akan communities are sacred but, in the words of Peter Sarpong, "they may be taken for history."[7] In traditional African education, history may merge with myth. This merger is often employed to enshrine the peoples' beliefs about their remote and sometimes recent past. The myth about the old woman with the pestle is well known in the Akan communities in Ghana. Its variations are found in many other African societies. It is said that God was once very near to the earth. But each time an old woman was pounding her *fufu*, or corn, the pestle hit him. God protested several times, but he realized it was all to no avail so he decided to withdraw to the skies.

A careful analysis of this myth will show that God did not become angry and punish the woman. He only left her to herself. The lesson from this myth is clear. God wants to be with man, but man's disobedience does not allow Him to do this. It is the fault of humankind that there is suffering. The myth also explains that even though God is so far from humans, he takes a keen interest in human affairs.

The Akan concept of the composition of man provides another lesson to children about the Akan social system. According to an Akan myth, a man is supposed to derive his blood from his mother, one soul from God, another soul or spirit from his father, and his breath of life from God. This myth is an attempt, if a very unconscious one, to rationalize the matrilineal social structure of the Akan. If the mother gave the blood to the child, then the child is closer to her than anyone else. It is therefore reasonable that the child should belong to her clan and so practice matriliny. Since all members of the clan derive their blood ultimately from the same ancestress and so have the same blood, it is again reasonable that they should refrain from marrying among themselves. The myth therefore vindicates matrilineal customs and exogamy. Furthermore, if the father gives the spirit to the child, then it follows that the child should not offend him. If he does, he injures the spirit of the father and hence hurts his own spirit and as a result dies or falls sick. Also, the child may not marry his father's brother's daughter because they possess the same spirit. The myth clearly explains the social system. From the Akans' idea about human composition, or nature, the child builds up and internalizes his community's theology, system of lineages, filial affection, and rules of marriage. Common understandings develop between the child and the adult about what their society stands for, and thus intergenerational communication is enhanced through the lessons that the youth draw from myths and legends.

It must be pointed out that in many societies in Africa, though myths may not refer to "what actually took place," like all myths they are not wholly untrue. As Peter Sarpong remarks in his study of the Ghanaian society, "They are at times only exaggerated history in the same way as what is supposed to be history may only be a mythicized event."[8] In other words, in African societies, much history contains myth, and many myths contain historical truths. Sarpong concludes that in traditional African education: "All myths are true. They all have a teaching and a message to give. This message corresponds to some generalized experience of humanity or section of humanity. The symbol used may be fiction or it may be historical but this fact is irrelevant to the function of myth."[9]

Apart from supporting authority, myths often sustain morality, ritual, law, and sanctions against offenders. Perhaps the most famous myth that contains a lot of historical truths, and that is usually told to Ashanti children, is the one about the heavenly origins of the Golden Stool of Ashanti. According to this historical and mythical account, there was no Ashanti nation before the second half of the seventeenth century. Kumasi was only one of the several chiefdoms of what is now Ashanti. All were independent of one another, but under the hegemony of the state of Denkyira. Osei Tutu, chief of Kumasi in the early part of the eighteenth century, took the initiative in challenging the authority of the chief of the Denkyira. Osei Tutu, however, could not have achieved the feat without the indispensable assistance of his trusted friend and fetish priest Okomfo Anokye. Anokye is said to have called an assembly of all the chiefs of the other paramountcies in Kumasi on a Friday afternoon. After what is described by historians as an inspirational speech on the dangers inherent in a subsidiary position, he collected clippings of the nails and hair of the different chiefs and queens present, set some of them afire and in the midst of the smoke brought down the

Golden Stool from the heavens. After that he mixed the rest of the clippings into a concoction and smeared the stool with the resultant substance. He then gave the rest of the mixture to the chiefs to drink and told them that from then on their souls were in the stool. The destruction of the stool would mean the destruction of them all as a people. This was how the Ashanti confederacy is supposed to have started. After this demonstration of the importance of unity, the new Ashanti nation went to war and defeated the Denkyiras.[10]

The heavenly origins of the stool may be a myth. But this is a myth with tremendous practical consequences. If the soul of the nation is contained in the stool, then it must be more important than any one person or group of persons, even the king. It follows that the custodian of this repository of the nation's soul is the most important person. Since Anokye made Osei Tutu the guardian of the stool, it is no wonder that he emerged as the greatest of the Ashanti kings with all the power, fame, and pomp that have been commonly associated with Ashanti kings ever since.

The strength of the myth and the communicative power it has developed between different generations of the Ashanti people are borne out by the attitude of the Ashantis toward the stool in the course of history. In 1896, the Ashantis allowed their king, Prempeh I, to be deported by the British rather than risk the loss of the Golden Stool by fighting to defend him. In 1900, after the British had overcome Ashanti resistance to colonial rule, the British governor went to Kumasi and demanded the surrender of the Golden Stool so that he could sit on it as the representative of Queen Victoria. His speech, which Ashantis felt was nonsensical, is a classical example of the Europeans' ignorance of and insolence toward African beliefs. The governor obviously mistook the stool for a kind of throne instead of what the myth had made it—the shrine of the Ashanti nation. According to the myth, even the Ashanti king does not sit on it; a white man cannot touch the stool; and, moreover, one does not ask for the Golden Stool at a mere woman's request. The Ashantis listened to the speech in complete silence, dispersed, and prepared for war against the British. Ashantis fought and won the war only to defend the Golden Stool and thus succeeded in preventing it from becoming one of the exhibits in the British Museum. The educative value of this myth was so strong that it even upheld the communication link between Ashantis of the 1700s and Ashantis of 1900s. The belief in the power of the stool is still strong, and it is clear from contemporary feelings that Ashantis would still do anything to defend it.

It can be seen from the foregoing that myths may explain the origins of the existing social and political system by reference to the ruling line's divine origin, to the magical powers of its progenitors, and to its achievements in the past. By ensuring common understandings which facilitate intergenerational communication, myths justify the existing order, to show that it is right for the rulers to rule and for the ruled to be ruled. Subjects find subjection less irksome and rulers rule with more assurance and confidence when all are convinced that the existing order is divinely inspired.

Proverbs

Another means by which traditional education promoted intergenerational communication was through proverbial sayings. Proverbial sayings are widespread in Africa, and their themes bear strong similarity to one another. The educative and communicative power of proverbs in traditional Africa lies in their use as validators of traditional procedures and beliefs. Children are raised to believe strongly that proverbial sayings have been laid down and their validity tested by their forefathers. Like other aspects of traditional African culture, proverbs are inextricably linked with the ancestral spirits and other forms of the magico-religious life. Among the Fante and Asante of Ghana, correct procedure in interpersonal relations is stressed through the large number of proverbs which outline patterns of accepted behavior. There is a pronounced tendency on the parts of adults to moralize and to communicate their values indirectly to children by the use of proverbs. Proverbs, dealing with the respect due to elders, obligations to kinsmen, or the proper attitude toward chiefs are used to indoctrinate children with regard to the acceptable standards of social behavior. Proverbial sayings are always preceded by credits to the revered ancestors. "It is our ancestors who said that . . . " is a clause that precedes proverbial sayings to affirm that the messages from the proverbs began with the very genesis of the community.

"A wise child is talked to in proverbs" is a Twi maxim that is widely observed, for this maxim is commonly used to admonish the child who misbehaves as well as to praise the obedient one. "The male cat is not one man's pet" is a proverb usually told to a child who complains that too many adults are sending him or her on errands or requesting his or her services. Further examples of child-oriented proverbs include: "The child who provokes his mother and father eats food without salt", and "If the foreleg is larger than the thigh, then there is an illness." These proverbs teach the child that he should not consider himself superior to his parents. Finally, "When a child behaves as an adult, he sees what an adult sees", that is, he is punished as an adult. Hundreds of such maxims can be cited from other societies in Africa, but it will suffice now to point out that the lessons drawn from proverbial sayings help the child and the adult to see the world from the same viewpoint. Through such informal instructional devices, the African child comes to respect the values of his society without ever feeling that he is bombarded with instructions on proper standards of social behavior.

SECRET SOCIETIES

Folktales, legends, myths, and proverbs could not achieve their maximum efficiency as educational and communicative tools without the proper orientation of boys and girls in their traditional roles in the societies. As was pointed out earlier, traditional education was there not only to be acquired but also to be lived. The act of living the education was accomplished partly through the proper identification, allocation, and playing of roles by adults and children of the various societies. One area in which the process of living the education becomes pronounced can be found in the role of secret societies. Scanlon refers to them as principal educational agents.[11] Briefly, secret societies were formally charged with the responsibility of overseeing the initiation ceremonies of boys and girls.

In Western cultures, social scientists agree that the transition from youth to adult with its sexual ripening, is accompanied with prolonged conflicts marked by varying degrees of frustration, guilt, and at times a total break in intergenerational communication. In traditional African societies, secret societies or initiation ceremonies helped the African youth to avoid this break in communication and all the attendant negative reactions. R. S. Rattray, Peter Sarpong, Elliot Skinner, and most anthropologists agree that the most important and most widespread role of the secret society was the separate education of the adolescent boy and the adolescent girl and the final admission of each into an adult society. There were a variety of secret societies which were organized communally; what prevailed in each depended upon the beliefs and practices of the particular community. Generally, to undergo the initiation into adulthood, the boy, after having reached puberty at about age eleven, entered the male secret society. The long and complicated ritual that ensued was a form of intensified education which formally opened the gates of adulthood to him. The boy's instruction generally included complicated ritual dances, secret languages, sacred myths, religion, and magic. Among the tests of endurance he underwent included circumcision, prolonged silence, and hunting. Boys were also trained to work collectively, giving a hand where needed. Girls went through a comparable course of initiation. This has been mostly studied in connection with the feminine secret societies called Sande in Sierra Leone and among the Bijago on the Bissagos Islands.[12] Peter Sarpong remarks in his studies of Ghanaian initiation ceremonies that in all secret societies the mode of adult behavior is signified particularly. Sarpong concludes that after the performance of one's initiation ceremony, "one has the right, and at times is bound, to perform certain acts that were formerly out of bounds to him or her."[13] In some societies, after a girl has been initiated, she is entitled to be referred to by all who have not been initiated as "mother." The point to note here is that all the ceremonies were of communal interest and are mostly marked by tests of endurance that immediately pushed childhood behavior and frivolities behind the new initiate.

The educational importance and the intergenerational communicative value of initiation ceremonies are clear. The African father did not evade the issue of the coming manhood of his son. It was, however, made easier for him by having the responsibility for it assumed communally by the assembly of all fathers. Since children of the same age entered the secret societies at the same time, and, since all activities were supervised by all adults in the community (masks were sometimes worn by the adults to hide their identity), the child's psychic resentment against the father was lessened or avoided. It may be worth noting that it is such psychic resentment that sometimes inhibits a boy's sexual development in many Western cultures.[14]

The problem of the boy's relationship to his mother was also dealt with through these initiation ceremonies which helped to cut the psychic "umbilical cord." In these initiation rites, the youth was born anew into his community, and his manhood or womanhood was clearly defined for him or her. The African youth thus appears to have been spared the agonies and fears that so often overshadow adolescence in Western cultures. In modern scientific terminology, the African initiation ceremony was the African way of attempting to prevent mother fixations. The circumcision ceremony and other activities had the effect of making the boy feel assured of potency and of helping him to avoid the self-doubts that harass many adolescents and adults in other cultures. No amount of formal sex education today could be as effective as these initiation ceremonies.

The initiation ceremonies also helped to preserve the traditions handed down by the myths which could be described as the foundation of social unity and intergenerational communication in Africa. The youth underwent fear, privation, and physical pain; for the rest of his life he carried the scars of these ceremonial mutilations. These dramatic rituals impressed the traditions of his community deep into his consciousness. The communication between the adult society and the youth was therefore reinforced and facilitated by the unquestioned acceptance of roles by both groups.

CONCLUSION

Under traditional African education, children's beliefs in and acceptance of morals, lessons, and roles drawn from legends, proverbs, and initiation ceremonies were reinforced by practical examples in adult life relative to the norms of the societies. For example, social norms like group solidarity and respect for authority were given practical interpretation by adults through activities like *nnoboa* (men gathering on different days to help each other on the farms) and adults removing their sandals before talking to a chief or a king. To a large extent there was no conflict between what children were expected to do and what was happening in their immediate environment. What was real was not different from what was taught. Consequently, children's acceptance and appreciation of the mores and norms of the societies facilitated communication between them and adults even in the practical lessons the children received in hunting, farming, and other socioeconomic activities. In a nutshell, custom and example were heavily relied upon as the principal educational agents. A variety of formal observances, in addition to the experiences of daily living, impressed upon the youth his place in the society—a society in which religion, politics, economics, and social relationships were invariably interwoven. This was traditional education.

Today, critics argue that traditional African societies could afford such social harmony and intergenerational communication because traditional African societies did not have open to them the different occupations and specializations that European science and technology have made available. They argue that in contemporary Africa training the young to earn their living is discussed in terms of facilities for producing technologists, scientists, engineers, doctors, economists, and other specialists. This is true, but is must be noted that all this is basically an extension of the traditional concept of imparting to the young the skills necessary for coping with their environment. What is different is that today most of the training given to youth prepares them for an environment which is to a large extent alien to their own.

While a wholesale revival of the past is unrealistic and unacceptable, educational planners should note that a total rejection of the African heritage will leave African societies in a vacuum that can only be filled with confusion, loss of identity, and a total break in intergenerational communication. Anthropologists now believe that people in different cultures and environments not only learn different things but also "learn to learn" differently. The learning process is greatly influenced by tradition. Consequently, a recognition and consideration of traditional educational philosophy and process is bound to give more meaning to what is being done today. One cannot help but conclude that the essential goals and methods of traditional African education are still admirable and remain challenging.

NOTES

1. David G. Scanlon, *Traditions of African Education* (New York: Columbia University Press, 1964), p. v.

2. Ibid., p. vi.

3. W. E. Abraham, *The Mind of Africa* (London: Weidenfeld and Nicolson, 1962), p. 94.

4. Ibid., p. 95.

5. Ibid.

6. Ladislas Segy, *African Sculpture Speaks* (New York: De Capo Press, 1975), p. 25.

7. Peter Sarpong, *Ghana in Retrospect* (Accra: Ghana Publishing Co., 1974), p. 125.

8. Ibid.

9. Ibid., p. 132.

10. Adu Boahen, *Topics in West African History* (London: Longmans, 1966), p. 75.

11. Scanlon, *Traditions*, p. 4.

12. Segy, *African Sculpture*, p. 38.

13. Sarpong, *Ghana*, p. 75.

14. Segy, *African Sculpture*, p. 40.

8

TIME IN AFRICAN CULTURE

DORTHY L. PENNINGTON

Every culture has a concept of time, and no study of a culture is complete without attention being given to the way in which it marks time, both conceptually and behaviorally. Such an understanding is fundamental, but it is obscured by the fact that time-binding is so well integrated into the other activities within a culture that the ability to isolate this phenomenon may prove difficult. Few people consciously ponder their concept of time; it often goes unarticulated. Therefore, many cross-cultural judgments are made out of an ignorance not only of the rules governing the temporal behavior of the other culture, but also out of an ignorance of one's own culture and of the foundations of temporality, in general. The subject of temporality is, many times, outside the boundaries of conscious awareness.

The aim of this discussion is to illuminate the African concept of, attitude toward, and use of time. This will be undertaken from the basic thesis of the cultural determinism of time-concepts. In order to establish perspective, time-binding will be treated as a cultural phenomenon, and those features of culture which help to determine its time-binding will be specified. These principles will be applied to the African culture with the realization that the diversity among African peoples makes rigid generalizations untenable. Likewise, caution is urged against strict use of the term "cultural determinism," in the sense of making one-to-one causal attributions. It is safer, rather, to think in terms of tendencies. This discussion assumes that, while describing African temporal behavior may be informative, it will be more instructive, at the same time, to foster an understanding of the principles which govern temporal behavior in general.

TIME-BINDING AS A CULTURAL PHENOMENON

Although time-binding is a culturally determined phenomenon, culture must be viewed as dynamic, thus indicating that the process nature of culture helps to shape its time-binding behavior. The nature of the process, then, is a transactional one rather than one in which the mind is reduced to a passive observer. At the same time, however, one can abstract some general principles about time-binding and note the ways in which these principles operate according to the specific circumstances of each culture. Mary Sturt sums up this posture:

No psychologist can accept time as something real and unchanging, since such a view reduces the experiencing mind to a mere observer, and the variations which are so noticeable a feature of the time-experience become just so many errors and failures in observation. Merely to catalog the mind's lapses is a dispiriting task. The natural assumption is that time is a concept which is built up through individual and racial experience. It is then possible to trace the development of this concept and to note the different forms it takes under different conditions. Divergencies from the normal are not errors, but rather curious adaptations to special circumstances.[1]

Since time-binding is regarded as a cultural phenomenon, more insight is provided by specifying those features of a culture believed to influence its time-binding.

One explanation holds that a culture's religious and philosophical doctrines provide the basis for its time-binding. More specifically, the parts of religious doctrines seen as relevant are, first, those which define the relation of humans to a supreme being, to other humans, and to other forces, including nature. For example, one may ask what are the beliefs in the supernatural or in a supreme being and in the ability of humans to control it? What degree of control is exercised by the supernatural? In what contexts is the supernatural appealed to? Is this done through rituals, prayers, or other ceremonies, such as sacrificial offerings? Do humans perceive themselves to have control over their fate and destiny, or are other forces seen as having ultimate control?

To what extent does a group rationalize its fate by postulating mysterious forces and beings in nature and mysterious powers among their fellows or higher forces? What are seen as the causal factors linking events to which everything may be ultimately attributed? It is safe to say that the more a group perceives itself as being in control of its fate and destiny, the more time-conscious it will be. On the other hand, those who perceive that there is a higher force in charge will likely be less time-conscious, reasoning that no matter how conscientiously humans plan their lives, they are not the final determinants of events. Likewise, do humans seek to gain dominion over nature, to integrate themselves harmoniously with it, or to subdue themselves to it? Those humans who seek to gain dominion over nature are those who tend to regard themselves as having control over their existence, leading them to be conscious of how they mark their time. At the same time, if humans believe that the supreme being is an omnipotent, omnipresent one who intervenes into their affairs to adjudicate, they are likely to emphasize compassion and regard for their fellows, believing, again, that the supreme being is in ultimate control. Second are those religious doctrines which pertain to the question of existence and being, to the soul, to the ego, and to the place of humans in the world. One may ask, for example, do the religious doctrines of a culture teach that the soul extends its existence infinitely into the future or do they teach that the soul does not extend beyond the present? And likewise, is the ego seen as extending into the future, following a unilinear progression, or does the ego refer to the past for its completion? The philosophy of the soul and ego-extension determines the attitudes of a culture in terms of its having a past, present, or futuristic orientation. Those with a futuristic ego-extension tend to emphasize youth and planning for an abstract "tomorrow," thus reckoning time in isolation of other events. On the other hand, those whose egos extend into the past for a sense of completion emphasize the importance of the ancestors or those of the past who are believed to give meaning to one's present existence. This view may be likened unto a helix in which, while there is a sense of movement, the helix, at the same time, turns back upon itself and depends upon the past from which its springs to guide and determine its nature; the past is an indispensable part of the present which participates in it, enlightens it, and gives it meaning.

In a related sense, one may ask what is a group's perception of its existence in terms of linearity and circularity. How is this symbolized?

If a culture's existence presupposes change during time, made in a linear progression, those persons will tend to have a greater consciousness of time than those whose existence does not presuppose significant change over time; the latter group may perceive its existence in a circular or cyclical motion.[2]

There is an alternative explanation to that of religious doctrines providing the basis for a culture's temporality. The alternative explanation attributes time-binding to the effects of the nature of the activities in which a group is engaged and to its location. In commercialized and technological societies, for instance, time-binding tends to be more commercial and standardized. On the other hand, in traditional, agrarian cultures where daily life is rather flexible and relatively unhurried and where travel is slow, accurately measuring time to the second is not of great concern. Additionally, technology, commercialization, and the resulting social habits are divisive forces which separate humans from natural rhythms. In nontechnological, communal cultures, the relationship of humans to time and destiny is more group-directed, and the sense of continuity belongs more to the collectivity and less to the individual; in communal cultures, many acts are ritualistically prescribed throughout the life of the inhabitants.[3]

There are other determinants of how time will be measured. Joost Meerloo provides four categories of determinants: (1) the biological sense of time or one's individual rhythm; (2) the estimation of time span; (3) the historical or gnostic sense of time in which one files events as they happen; and (4) the sense of continuity, the conscious experience of time emerging into an occurrence directed at a future goal.[4] Although this is a model of individual rather than cultural time-binding, the divisions pertaining to the historical or gnostic sense of time and to a sense of time having continuity are relevant to the cultural perceptions influencing the way in which time is conceived and used by that group.

Because of the complexities involved in the concept and use of time, caution must be urged to avoid simplistically dichotomizing time-binding in existence as being either circular or linear, for there are indications that humans may function in several dimensions simultaneously. Thinking, therefore, rushes "back and forth in time. The future goal we want to reach directs our course right now while at the same time, unconscious ancient patterns are acted out."[5] Meerloo discusses a "dual temporal determinism" of both conscious and unconscious intentions, pointing to a complicated relationship.[6] Furthermore, time is not completely unilinear, but four-dimensional, wherein everyone lives along his or her own subjective time dimension (individual growth) which interacts with and intersects the three other dimensions of past, present, and future.[7]

Although there are variations among individuals and a consciousness of time precipitated by an awareness of constantly changing events (day and night, seasonal variations, physiological changes, the interactions of the dimensions), authorities agree that culture greatly influences time-binding.[8]

THE AFRICAN CONCEPT OF TIME

It was indicated earlier that the religious doctrines of a culture help to determine its concept of time, and, while it is convenient to make generalizations about the religious philosophy of Africa, on many issues, the diversity of African peoples makes such generalizations untenable. Of religious beliefs and ontology, however, certain commonalities are observed among African peoples. In addition to the religious philosophy, other factors impinging upon African temporality can be shown, as well as some of the means used to symbolize the concept of time.

Religion permeates all aspects of African life, and one can better understand African religion by outlining the hierarchy of religious ontology. According to Mbiti, there are five divisions of the ontology, ranked in the order of descending importance: (1) God, (2) spirits, (3) man, (4) animals and plants, and (5) inanimate objects.[9] The ontology is anthropocentric in that attention is focused upon man (humans) as the center, but Mbiti quickly points out that humans are acutely aware of their position in relation to other forms of existence since a balance must be maintained at all times and since all modes must keep their proper place and distance from each other. Unity and interdependence are crucial since an upset in one of the categories upsets the whole order. God is believed to be the creator, the sustainer, and the ultimate controller of life; Africans thus have little difficulty reconciling His intervention into the affairs of humans, even though the spirits are believed to be His emissaries. Darryl Forde further describes this relationship: "God, spirits, and magical forces beyond the community, together, with witches and sorcerers within it, are postulated in explanation of the workings of the universe, of the incidence of benefits and misfortune, and of the strains of life in society."[10]

It is not surprising, therefore, that one can find the relationship of God to African peoples described as that of an "owner to his slaves. He orders them, protects them, sets their affairs straight, and avenges injustice."[11] This belief in God's intervention and ultimate control of the affairs of humans can account for an apparent resignation to fate or to higher forces observed on the part of traditional African peoples.

Because, however, the concept of fatalism can be easily misunderstood by Westerners who stereotypically assign it to Africans, further explanation is necessary. Ethel Albert indicates that the stereotype of fatalism held by Westerners is "only about half-true," and she provides further information about this concept as it relates to Africans.[12] She concurs that fatalism is a world view in which it is believed that humans do not have the power to cause events and that their intellects are not such that they can understand or predict the future with any degree of confidence. In some measure, then, fatalism can be called a "self-fulfilling prophecy" and a "self-correcting mechanism," so that accidents and failures may be assigned to suprahuman forces; Albert however, distinguishes between fatalism and a sense of complete futility:

Far from teaching men to sit back and do nothing (as is often believed), fatalism teaches dignity in the face of adversity and humility in the event of prosperity. Intellectual resources are not expended on the natural world but are reserved for the serious business of navigating the individual's destiny in a world characterized by risk and uncertainty. Regularities—the stock and trade of science— are not interesting. Ingenuity is needed to devise ways to appeal to the causes of events, and appeals are phrased in ways to please or to move the higher powers.[13]

Therefore the dichotomy often mentioned between fatalistic and doing-oriented societies is, in part, a false one, since fatalists are also activists. The distinction is one of orientation regarding the degree of control exercised by humans vis-à-vis external forces. Although fatalists believe that humans can and must act, the view is "steadfastly maintained and daily verified that no matter how conscientiously a man may perform his duties, he may fail or suffer, whereas some men who are worthless or evil may prosper."[14] This partially explains the belief of Africans that humans exercise relatively little control over their destiny.

In the face of the perceived incontrollability, uncertainty, risk, and unpredictability of life, appeals are made to the cause of events. While in the view of outsiders, virtuousness may be ascribed to establishing regularity and to planning, in the eyes of Africans, these traits would not be efficacious, since the very nature of the external controlling force is, itself, unpredictable. Helen Green provides further insight into the belief of Africans that the destiny of humans is controlled by an external force, and she deems the understanding of this "life-force," along with two other principles, as necessary to any examination of the African concept of time.

First, the life force is considered the essence of being, and its movements vary in an irregular pattern. Since time is seen as inseparable from the life force, the rhythm of time is not constant or measurable in a quantifiable sense, as in Western tradition. Time, rather, is dependent upon the unpredictable rhythm of the life force and moves accordingly.[15]

Another principle is that dual unity, wherein complementary opposites (such as day and night, male and female, subject and object, comedy and tragedy, concrete and abstract, work and rest, organic and mechanical, old and young) form a "dual identity in their function. These opposites function reciprocally, not dichotomously, and serve to unify the actual with the illusory, the dead with the living, the personal with the communal, and the individual psyche with the individual soma."[16] Green points out that many of these polarities underlie African thought about time.

Yet another principle is that of the dynamism between the two complementary dualities which gives a beat to the life force: "While one opposite surges, the other lapses, so that there is always an equipose which is, at the same time, unstable. Alternation of this instability creates the rhythm." The unpredictability of the life force particularly affects the attitude toward the future. Because of the mysteries and uncertainties involved in the life force, there is always a "fearful concern," about the feasibility of long-range planning, for the supposition is that "since the present will soon be the past of the future, the next phase of living will not be very different" from the present one.[17]

The life force is seen as having the ability to be omnipresent, wherein its presence can inhabit not only the present generation but dead ancestors, as well. Procreation is therefore given primordial importance in African culture because it is believed that this is a way of passing on the life force to one's offspring. At the same time, this should not be interpreted as a belief in a linear process wherein something is passed from the present to the future. The value given to procreation must be viewed in a different sense, as establishing continuity among generations and as allowing the individual to participate in a larger process of unity. The existence of individuals therefore is not thought to be complete until they have procreated, thus establishing themselves as links in a continuous chain. In this way, "personal immortality is externalized in the physical continuation of the individual through procreation, so that the children bear the traits of their parents or progenitors. Procreation is the absolute way of insuring that a person is not cut off from personal immortality."[18] In this view, the ancestors can have a close relationship to the present, the now. This reflects a communal linkage among kin, the living and the dead, throughout the clan or tribe so that all individuals are a part of a common origin. This spirit of communalism and caring for the welfare of others takes priority over a concern with the time which may be required to do so. Individuals are thus linked to one another in time, by time, and through time.

A more specific explanation of these beliefs and principles is found in the African concept of time divisions; according to Mbiti, the concept of the future for African peoples is virtually nonexistent. Rather than including a linear concept of the future, African time is two-dimensional, with a long past and the present. Mbiti says further:

The linear concept of time in Western thought, with an indefinite past, present, and infinite future is practically foreign to African thinking. The future is virtually absent because events which lie in it have not taken place, they have not been realized, and cannot, therefore, constitute time.[19]

However, those events pertaining to the rhythm of nature which extend into the immediate future, such as pregnancy or the growing of crops, constitute "potential" time, rather than "actual" time: "Actual time is therefore what is present and what is past. It moves 'backward' rather than 'forward' and people set their minds not on future things, but chiefly on what has taken place."[20] One can note immediately that the idea of time as moving with an emphasis on the past is in direct contrast to the Western notion of time as following a linear, irreversible progression toward the future. Pursuing this line of reasoning, one finds that "African peoples have no 'belief' in progress," the idea that the development of human activities and achievements moves from a low to a higher degree. The people neither plan for the distant future nor "build castles in the air."[21] This is unlike the Western tradition in which individuals want to leave an imprint for the future, as described by Marion Smith.[22]

Furthermore, time for Africans does not exist in a vacuum as an entity which can be conceptually isolated. Time is conceived only as it is related to events, and it must be experienced in order to make sense or to become real. The mathematical division of time observed by Westerners has little relevance for Africans, for to them, in reckoning the time length of a month or year, the events which occur within that time period are more important than the actual number of days comprised. Thus, an African month may last from twenty-five to thirty-five days, depending upon the nature of the activity engaged in, such as hunting or the planting of the crops. Likewise, one year may have 350 days, while another may have 390 days, since the actual number is of secondary importance.[23] An example of such time measurement is cited not only by Mbiti but also by Gunter Wagner who conducted research with a specific African group, the Logoli. According to his findings, this group distinguishes the different times of the day by the various activities which they must perform.[24] Whereas for Westerners time is a commodity by which humans are often enslaved, for Africans, "man is not a slave of time; instead, he 'makes' as much time as he wants."[25] It is not uncommon, therefore, to find Africans spending the day by conversing among friends, which may be regarded by Westerners as idleness. For Africans, however, the event is the essence; the feeling of communal participation is the essence; time, therefore, is of less consequence.

Because religion and the belief in God as the Supreme Being permeates all aspects of African life, the African view of existence in time is rooted in their conception of God as immortal. He is described as an eternal, infinite and immutable spirit who endures for ever and ever. His eternal nature is believed to make him impervious to change and limitation. Just as the lives of African peoples are anchored in the past, God is seen as being in and beyond the past.[26] Just as God is believed to exist eternally, humans are also seen as sharing this immortality, for "without exception, African peoples believe that death does not annihilate life and that the departed continue to exist in the hereafter."[27] (As pointed out earlier, both the living and the deceased can have the life force.) Once persons have departed this life, they become what is referred to as the "living dead," which means that their spirits live on, often returning in reincarnated or transmigrated forms. In Mbiti's words:

In some cases it is definitely said that the spirits of the departed are imperishable. It seems as if the living-dead move on beyond the horizon of human memory, and merge into the group of spirits, some of which were once human beings and others of which have other origins. Perhaps we could describe these concepts as indicating a belief in some form of immortality.[28]

Because of the facility with which African beliefs in resurrection, reincarnation, and transmigration can be construed as corrolating a belief in the future, Mbiti hastens to arrest this propensity:

The concept of resurrection lingers on among many peoples, in stories and myths describing what happened, or what men should have inherited, but not as a possibility for the future. As far as evidence goes, African peoples do not expect any form of individual or collective resurrection after death. Man has neither the hope nor promise to rise again; he lost that gift in the primeval period.[29]

Therefore, the apparently irreconcilable paradox is best accommodated by stating that, though African peoples believe in reincarnation and transmigration of the departed, immortality is placed in the perspective of the past, rather than in the future. As Mbiti indicates, all African myths (of creation, the first humans, the coming of death, the birth of nations, etc.) look toward the past; there are no myths about the future.[30] Likewise, the idea of the soul or the ego extending infinitely into the future does not seem to be a real one for African peoples. While the concept of time can be described as helical, the emphasis of the helix lies heavily on the past.

Though religion permeates all aspects of African life and influences Africans' view of their existence in time, mention must also be made of the role played by other factors upon the traditional African view of time: (1) isolation and the absence of machine technology and (2) a well-defined social structure.

Because traditional Africa lacked both machines and applied science, it was largely dependent upon the physical environment for its survival and livelihood. For example, growing food was not a commercial activity, but a means of survival which Africans repeated year after year, noting the cycle established by this necessary activity. Unlike those societies in which mechanical technology and science have reduced the dependence of people upon the inconsistencies of the natural environment, traditional Africans have established a relationship with nature wherein they easily note its vagaries and unpredictability. The cyclicity of survival activities became a custom strengthened by tradition, and these traditions and values have been transmitted virtually intact. According to George Dalton, African children lead much the same life as did their parents. He adds:

Cultural and physical isolation means the absence of knowledge of real alternatives; whether in child-rearing practices or techniques for growing crops, the traditional African community did not have much knowledge of different, alternative ways . . . . To deviate from traditional practice, moreover, was risky. To experiment with new crops or new techniques of production was to risk hunger if the innovation failed.[31]

Therefore, patterned behavior for traditional Africans resulted, in part, from attempts to satisfy functional needs, based upon the development of the environment in which they lived.

The fact that African children lead essentially the same lives as did their parents may also result from rigidly defined social stratification practiced by some African groups. Some of the bases for stratification were occupation and ascribed heredity inheritance.[32] Social stratification also contributed to the repetitive customs and cycles of behavior just as did the growing of crops every year, for "where social rank was sharply defined, for the lowly farmer to be too ambitious or too successful was to risk punishment by social superiors for attempting to rise above his station and thereby to threaten more highly placed persons."[33]

By being in close relationship with nature through agriculture, therefore, Africans were made to know how unpredictable it was, since the life-force could also move in nature. By the same token, any control of nature was thought to be out of their hands. By invoking other powers and by establishing harmony with the natural forces, traditional Africans hoped that they would achieve the desired results. When coupled with the rigid social stratification, the absence of machine technology could have instilled in Africans with regard to the concept of time a sense of uncertainty, of dependency, of cyclicity, and a clear sense of hierarchical order which was not to be upset.

SYMBOLIC REPRESENTATIONS OF THE CONCEPT OF TIME

A consideration of the forms used to express or represent the African view of time should contribute to its being further understood, since in any society the development of symbols often insipiently reflects the nature of its beliefs and orientation. Though controversy exists on the issue of whether or not symbols and that which they symbolize are reversible, it is generally agreed that there is some correspondence or suggestion between life-symbols, ideas, and referents. According to Suzanne Langer, life symbols are at the root of a society's ideas as reflected in its myths: "While religion grows from the blind worship of life and magic, 'aversion' of Death to a definite totem-cult or other sacramentalism, another sort of 'life-symbol' develops in its own way, starting also in quite unintentional processes, and culminating in permanent significant forms. This medium is myth."[34]

Ernst Cassirer extends the relationship among a society's myths, symbols, and reality by asserting, unlike other philosophers on language, that symbols are not merely representations of reality, but, rather, that they create a reality of their own. He says that, though a culture's myths, art, and science appear as symbols, they are not symbols "in the sense of mere figures which refer to some given reality by means of suggestion and allegorical renderings, but in the sense of forces, each of which produces and posits a world of its own." Because of the inward dialectical determinism involved, "the special symbolic forms are not imitations, but organs of reality," since it is solely through their agency that anything real becomes intellectually apprehensible and visible.[35] Hence, the ability of a culture's myths and symbols to serve as ideational vehicles is acknowledged as an extension of, rather than a preclusion of, their mere representational nature, and with an allusion to the suggested roles played by these symbolic forms, the African attitude toward time can be further considered.

That African time in view of existence is not linearly conceived is confirmed by the symbol of the serpent in much of the art and mythology. The snake is seen as possessing a fecundating power in African culture, and much of African mythology originates around the life-giving force of the snake as a symbol:

A Dahomian clay modeling shows a snake with its tail in its mouth forming a complete circle or sphere and is designated The Snake of Eternity. A Yoruba

panel from Nigeria pictures a coiled snake, which again in Dahomian mythology, suggests that the coils represent the supportive structure of the earth: 3500
coils above, and 3500 below .... And the Baga of Guinea have wooden
sculptures of snakes carved from a single piece of wood, six feet tall, that is
the subject of a myth that all water on earth was still until the snake came and
traced the course for the rivers, thereby bringing life to the world.[36]

The serpent, which in Christian philosophy is linked to original sin,
is positively regarded among Africans. And because of its eternal, life-
giving ability, the snake is accorded different roles in African legends,
from a belief that it embodies the spirit of the deceased kin, back to
visit the loved ones, to a belief in its being a manifestation of God
Himself.[37] Snakes, therefore, particularly pythons, are not killed, but
are kept and nourished on milk, meat, beer or other forms of libation.

The eternal nature of the snake and its fecundating power appear in
many African myths, one of which indicates how the chameleon (linked
to death in African mythology) cursed humans by making them mortal
and at the same time bestowed upon the snake the gift of immortality.
The Vugusu provide an example of one such myth:

According to the Vugusu version of the story, the chameleon came one day to
the homestead of one of the sons of Maina, the eldest son of the tribal ancestor.
He was sitting in front of his hut eating his evening meal. The chameleon
begged him for food, but Maina's son refused. It kept on begging until he
became impatient and drove the chameleon away. Before leaving, the chameleon
uttered the following curse: "I am leaving, now, but you all shall die." Then
the people started to breathe the air, get ill and die. Later the chameleon visited
the snake and begged it for food as well. The snake willingly gave the chameleon
what it had asked for, and as a reward the chameleon uttered a blessing, saying
that the snake should live on for ever. So, when it gets old, it merely casts its
skin, but does not die unless it is killed by force.[38]

It is not surprising therefore that the snake, the symbol of life, re-
juvenation, and immortality, is used as a cure for barrenness in women,
in those conditions where the inability to conceive prevails. The procedure is a part of a sacrificial ritual in which a fowl or a chicken is
given to a snake, and one group which engages in this ritual is the
Gimiri-Maji, Gisu.[39]

Regarding the snake as a life-symbol, it is highly significant to note
that it is often pictured in a circular, continuous position, as opposed

to a straight, linear one. The apparent indication is that African peoples do not view their existence in terms of a straight, irreversible progression toward the future, but, rather, as one which relies heavily on the past. In this regard, to see other African symbols, in addition to the life-giving one, with a distinct emphasis on the past should not be surprising. In the Sank∂fas's symbols, the concept of time relies significantly on the past to inform the present and usually shows a bird whose beak is turned backward, rather than forward.

In these examples, a culture's symbols serve a communicative function in their ability to not only edify and instruct, but also to serve as a repository of values and customs strengthened by tradition. Symbols are, therefore, tools of perception which not only reflect values but, as shown, create a reality of their own. Their appeal is one of dynamism in which the observer must become a creative participant in the meaning exuded. The venerative power generated by such African symbols as that of the serpent or the bird with its beak turned backward, therefore, is not withstanding. Nor is the symbolized view of time in existence a coincidental one, for the religious and philosophical doctrines, the ontology, and other factors influencing the African concept of time have been described.

SUMMARY

It has been asserted that every culture has a concept of time, although the concept often goes unarticulated by the people within that culture. The African concept of time is determined, among other things, by the religious and philosophical doctrines, by the view of the progression and links of existence, and by the nature of the activities engaged in at a particular time. The religious doctrines teach that there is a Supreme Being, God, who ultimately controls and intervenes into the affairs of humans. God is seen as an immortal and noncontingent Being. Although He is thought to exercise final control over the fate and destiny of humans, they do not resign themselves into a sense of complete futility. Instead, with an acute awareness of the power of the Supreme Being, they seek to fashion their activities so as to please and achieve harmony with the Supreme Being, with the life force, and with nature. Hopefully, the life force can be supplicated to meet the needs of the people. The Supreme Being is invoked through various rituals and ceremonies as a sine qua non. What might occur in time is viewed as not being predictable with any degree of confidence because the life force or the causal factor, itself, is unpredictable. Since control is viewed as being out of the hands of humans, the reasoning is why should humans observe rigid time consciousness or future planning?

The nature of the traditional activities in terms of an agrarian culture without machines aided traditional Africans in establishing a relationship with nature whose vagaries were, again, unpredictable, being governed by the life force. At the same time, the nature of an agrarian existence allowed a sense of cyclicity or déjà vu to be established. A sense of linear progression to their existence, devoid of bringing along the past, was difficult to fathom. This fact, however, should not be interpreted as implying stagnation, but rather, as the paradox involved in saying that, while there was some familiarity afforded by cyclicity, the unpredictable vagaries required constant creativity and ingenuity in order to be negotiated. The past and the ancestors were indispensible in giving meaning to one's present existence.In regard to the historical or gnostic sense of time, events were filed as they happened, and, although initiative was shown on the part of the people in negotiating events, there was always a conscious awareness and respect for the causal factors linking events among traditional Africans. Time, as continuity, was directed from the perspective of the past, rather than toward a future goal.

There was an organic view that the whole order was related in a dynamic sense. Tampering with one part was believed to affect the whole. All parts had to be in rhythm and harmony with one another, leading to a sense of connectedness for the cosmos.

Time, in traditional African culture, has been viewed as a central phenomenon. The world view has had a religious base and has emphasized an external locus of control and the need for humans to temporally harmonize themselves with the forces of control and with the forces around them. Time has been used in establishing a complexity of balanced relationships; one, time as used to establish a relationship with the Supreme Being; two, to establish a relationship of continuity between the present and past generations; three, to establish a relationship with nature and the forces of one's environment (nature); and four, to create group harmony and participation among the living. This sense of temporal synchronization and group connectedness can be seen in the performing arts of Africans, such as dance and drumming. Time for traditional Africans, has been organic, rather than mechanical.

NOTES

1. Mary Sturt, *The Psychology of Time* (New York: Harcourt, Brace, 1925), p. 134.

2. Jules Henry, "White People's Time, Colored People's Time," *Transaction* (March-April, 1965), p. 33.

3. Joost A. Meerloo, *Along the Fourth Dimension: Man's Sense of Time and History* (New York: John Day, 1970), p. 160.

4. Ibid., pp. 62–97.

5. Ibid., p. 201.

6. Ibid.

7. Ibid., p. 197.

8. Ibid.; Harry H. Turney-High, *Man and System* (New York: Appleton-Century-Crofts, 1968), p.28; Thomas Kochman, *Rappin and Stylin' Out* (Chicago: University of Chicago Press, 1972), p. 19.

9. John S. Mbiti, *African Religions and Philosophy* (New York: Doubleday, 1970), p. 20.

10. Darryl Forde, ed., *African Worlds* (London: Oxford University Press, 1954), p. x.

11. Mary Douglas, "The Lele of Kasai," in *African Worlds*, ed. Darryl Forde (London: Oxford University Press, 1954), p. 8.

12. Ethel M. Albert, "Conceptual Systems in Africa," in *The African Experience*, ed. John N. Paden and Edward W. Soja, vol. 1 (Evanston, Ill.: Northwestern University Press, 1970), p. 106.

13. Ibid.

14. Ibid.

15. Helen B. Green, "Temporal Attitudes in Four Negro Subcultures," in *The Study of Time*, ed. J. T. Fraser, F. C. Haber, and G. H. Muller (New York: Springer-Verlag, 1972), pp. 402–15.

16. Ibid., p. 406.

17. Ibid., pp. 406, 407.

18. Mbiti, *African Religions and Philosophy*, pp. 32–33.

19. Ibid., pp. 21–23.

20. Ibid., p. 23.

21. Ibid., p. 30.

22. Marian Smith, "Different Cultural Concepts of Past, Present, and Future," *Psychiatry*, vol. 15, no. 4 (November 1952), pp. 24–25.

23. Mbiti, *African Religions*, pp. 24–25.

24. Gunter Wagner, "The Abaluyia of Kavirondo," in Forde, *African Worlds*, p.30.

25. Mbiti, *African Religions*, pp. 24–25.

26. John S. Mbiti, *Concepts of God in Africa* (London: C. Tinling and Company, 1970), p. 27.

27. Ibid., p. 264.

28. Ibid., p. 265.

29. Ibid.

30. Ibid., p. 12.

31. George Dalton, "Traditional Economic Systems," *The African Experience*, ed. Paden and Soja, p. 70.

32. Pierre L. Van Den Berghe, "Major Themes in Social Change," in *The African Experience*, ed. Paden and Soja, p. 269.

33. Dalton, "Traditional Economic Systems" in *The African Experience*, ed. Paden and Soja, p. 70.

34. Suzanne K. Langer, *Philosophy in a New Key* (New York: New American Library, 1951), p. 148.

35. Ernst Cassirer, *Language and Myth* (New York: Dover Publications Inc., 1946), p. 8.

36. Paul C. Harrison, *The Drama of Nommo* (New York: Grove Press, 1972), p. 97.

37. Mbiti, *Concepts of God in Africa*, p. 100.

38. Wagner, "The Abaluyia ..." in Forde, *African Worlds*, pp. 43–44.

39. Mbiti, *Concepts of God in Africa*, p. 191.

9

SOCIALISM IN THE AFRICAN CULTURAL CONTEXT

EGHOSA OSAGIE

Socialism is one of the most influential and important political ideas ever introduced by philosophers. Since its formal introduction in the nineteenth century as a logical reaction to the extreme individualism engendered by laissez-faire capitalism, socialist adherents have been persecuted in several parts of the world. In a number of countries, socialists have either seized power or been voted democratically into power. This powerful social doctrine has attained the status of a secular religion in countries following the socialist path, especially among some of the most brilliant scholars and students.

My purpose is rather straightforward. Concretely, it calls for the relation of the socialist ideal to the social and cultural reality of the African continent, not only of the past or present, but more importantly of the future. In tackling this intellectual problem, it is necessary to introduce and explain carefully the concept of socialism, its origins, and the prospects of socialism as a vehicle or instrument of development in Africa and to specify an alternative to socialism based on assumptions derived from African culture.

But first, a discussion of some terms is necessary because misunderstanding regarding their meanings more often than not confuses and mystifies rational ideological analysis. For example, the terms *socialism* and *communism* tend to be confused in the popular press. To avoid confusion, it is necessary to note that central to the idea of socialism is the community's ownership and control of the means of production (land, labor, and capital), whose use should be directed to satisfying the interest of all in society. Indeed, it has been asserted that the essence of socialism is not equality, but the "idea of community . . . in the doctrine that men can realize their full potential and achieve human emancipation in community."[1] To Marx, socialism is a transition phenomenon preparing the way for the eventual emergence of communism, "the undefined realm of man's freedom." In communist society classes are abolished, a situation which is yet to be attained anywhere in the world, although political parties, regimes, and nation-states refer to themselves as communist. This leaves communism within the realm of ideals, utopia, and wishful thinking.

The terms *socialism* and *Marxism* are often used interchangeably as if one were synonymous with the other. But these terms are not congruent. Socialism, as we shall see later, has different schools of thought, the most dominant among which is the Marxian school. In the twentieth century, due to the voluminous labors of Marx and Engels and the academic elaboration of, and commentaries on, their work by scholars in such fields as philosophy, politics, economics, and sociology, Marxian studies have developed into an important field for academic research and writing. Socialist thought and research are only a part of the interests of Marxian scholars.

An additional pair of phrases should occupy our attention before we proceed: *African socialism*, and *socialism in Africa*. African socialism refers to a modified version of scientific socialism to suit the African circumstance, while socialism in Africa refers to the role of any of the competing versions of socialism on the African scene.

ORIGINS OF EUROPEAN SOCIALISM

As a formal body of thought, as opposed to practice, socialism may regard the nineteenth century as its century of birth and Western Europe as its labor ward. But if we carry our research far into centuries before Christ and particularly into the era of the great Greek philosophers, we may rightly argue that some aspects of socialism may have had their intellectual ancestry in the work of Plato, who studied in Egypt and, hence, the idea may have had roots in ancient Africa.[2] In more recent times, elements of socialist thought can rightly be traced to the radical theological teachings of the Anabaptists in the sixteenth century, and the Levellers and Diggers in the seventeenth century.[3] Similarly, certain aspects of socialism were foreshadowed in the work of the eighteenth-century philosopher Rousseau.

Let me give a brief overview of the works of the utopian socialists (Saint-Simon, Fourier, J. S. Mill) and Marx. The utopians were a remarkable, in some cases eccentric, dedicated group of thinkers who, I would say, have not been given enough credit for their work. Among them was Robert Owen, an originator of the cooperative movement. Owen exemplifies this group of socialists with innovative ideas about how the affairs of society may be reordered to the benefit of the European oppressed, but with limited ability to carry through their suggestions in the practical world of affairs. A remarkable feature of these socialists was their "relative deprivation." Saint-Simon, though claiming to be a descendant of Charlemagne, was imprisoned during the French Revolution and died a poor man. Marx was hounded out of Germany and France by apprehensive governments scared by his revolutionary writings; while taking refuge in London where he wrote copiously, he depended on the generosity of Engels. Perhaps, if they had been less deprived, they may not have felt as strongly as they did, and the world of ideas would definitely have been the poorer for it.

There is some slight disagreement regarding when and where the word "socialist" was first used. The French claim that *socialistes* was first used in the magazine *Globe* issue of February 13,1832, in reference to the followers of Saint-Simon.[4] The English, on their part, claim precedence in the use of the word as "socialist" is used in the *London Cooperative Magazine* in 1826, though several years expired before the followers of Robert Owen started refering to themselves as socialists.[5] If we follow the view that what matters is not when the word socialist first appeared in the popular press, but its use to refer to followers of one of the founding fathers of socialist thought, then France claims the credit for inventing the word socialist.

It may be necessary to be informed about the life and ideas of Saint-Simon whose followers were first called Socialists. Claude Henri de Saint-Simon, who has been referred to as "the last gentleman and the first socialist of France," was praised by Engels, who, while noting the "genius" and "breadth of view" of his work remarked that "it contained the seeds of all the ideas of later socialists which are not strictly economic."[6] This remarkable man, born in 1760 into an aristocratic family, was as a young man awakened each morning by his valet thus:

"Arise, Monsieur le Comte, you have great things to do today."[7] He fought in the American Revolution; he also had a mystical experience which radically changed the course of the remaining part of his remarkable life. In his words:

During the cruelest period of the Revolution, and during a night of my imprisonment in Luxembourg, Charlemagne appeared to me and said: "Since the beginning of the world, no family had enjoyed the honour of producing both a hero and philosopher of first rank. This honor was reserved for my house. My son, your success as a philosopher will equal those which I achieved as a warrior and politician."[8]

After this vision, he spent most of his fortune in an unrelenting pursuit of knowledge, married on a three-year contract though the union collapsed after one year, and did most of his writing in poverty. He once remarked: "Remember that in order to do great things, one must be impassioned."[9]

Saint-Simon's doctrine was that for man to share in the fruit of production he must work. He argued that workers deserve more reward than those who do not work, but he noted that invariably, the nonlaboring classes were better remunerated. Some of his followers even went so far as to demand the abolition of private property, but unfortunately Saint-Simon himself and his followers failed to specify how their idea of a better society was to be implemented.

Charles Fourier, another utopian socialist, fervently believed that the world was disorganized and needed restructuring.[10] He came up with detailed proposals including the ideas of workers sharing in their production and communal profits. His ideas caught on for some time in the United States.

John Stuart Mill, himself a classical economist, disagreed with the view of Ricardo that there were objective economic "laws" regulating the distribution of society's wealth. Rather, he believed, distribution depended on the laws and customs of society. If these conventions of society were just and equitable, so too would be the distribution of wealth and vice versa.

Karl Marx was the most influential of the European socialist founding fathers, not only when assessed by the rigor, perception, and breadth of scope of his work, but also by the effectiveness of his followers in countries ruled by his ideas. His philosophy was *dialectical materialism*.

It is dialectical because it incorporates the Hegelian process of the dialectic, the idea of "inherent change," in which the challenge of a thesis by its opposite, its antithesis, leads to a synthesis, which thus becomes the new thesis, which in time is challenged by a new antithesis. This philosophical interpretation of the world was, however, reviewed by Marx in his analysis of dialectical materialism. "Marx found conflict in the world itself, and the ideas sprang from conflict instead of causing it."[11] The word materialism points to the fact that the philosophy is based on social and physical circumstances. For each society, said Marx, there exists an economic base to which is affixed a superstructure of social institutions governing property ownership, the legal system, political institutions, etc. The dialectic providing for social change creates new classes which displace formerly dominant ones.

Eventually, class struggle leads to revolution. Marx found that there existed a serious incompatibility between the technical economic base of capitalism and its superstructure represented by private property. The technical base in the form of industrial production is interdependent and well organized, but private property is individualistic, and wealth owners hostile to industrial planning by a central coordinating authority. The result, following the iron logic of Marx's analysis, is that capitalism would destroy itself through planlessness leading to economic instability and business failures. Not only would capitalism self-destruct, but also it would provide a fertile soil for its successor (socialism) by establishing mass production as the technical base for socialism and by creating the proletariat which, in Marx's vision, was destined to displace the bourgeoisie. Indeed, Marx envisaged a two-stage development in industrial countries.[12] A democratic revolution was to occur, resulting in the victory of the middle classes at the expense of the feudal aristocracy, culminating in the development of capitalist production, and the securing of political rights for all. A social revolution was to lead to the economic victory of the proletariat who were destined to become the owners of capital, the means of production.

How and when shall the proletariat take over? Marx constructs a model of pure capitalism without the weaknesses of the real system. He then sets in motion an analysis, showing how this perfect capitalist model eventually collapses, arguing that if the perfect model collapses, the real imperfect model would collapse even more quickly and more readily. His "laws of motion of a capitalist system" are employed to demonstrate the inevitability of capitalist self-destruction. The analysis assumes the labor theory of value, that the value of a commodity is measured by the value of labor employed in its production. Each commodity is sold at its value. Similarly, labor is paid a wage equal to the amount of the labor that it takes to produce labor power or the value of the resources that it takes for the laborer to remain alive. In effect, this is the subsistence wage. If the value of the product of a worker is more than the subsistence wage that he receives, the difference, known as *surplus value*, provides the basis for profitmaking by the capitalist who has a monopoly of access to capital. As capitalists in their competition expand their scale of production and accumulate more capital, the demand for labor increases, leading to higher wages and consequently lower surplus value. To restore profits to their previous higher levels, capitalists introduce labor-saving devices which result in the firing of some workers and lowering wages to the subsistence level. As machines cannot be exploited (the capitalist pays a price for a machine equal to its value), the profit base is narrowed. The ratio of labor (and hence surplus value) to total output falls, production is no longer profitable, consumption falls, bankruptcies and business failures of small firms occur. At this juncture, the larger capitalists buy up machinery of failing firms at bargain prices, employ labor at lower wages, and surplus value appears once again. This cycle of expansion and collapse repeats itself, with each successive collapse being more serious than the previous one. At last, when conditions become unbearable, the working class revolts, taking over the ownership of capital. The "expropriators are expropriated."

This powerful analysis of a process of transformation from capitalism to socialism has been vindicated in many parts of the world. There have been business failures, corporations have become larger, and even in some Western countries, workers share in the ownership of enterprises. In some socialist countries like Yugoslavia, workers' committees manage factories, but in others like the USSR where centralized planning is the accepted orthodoxy, the government, not the proletariat, has replaced the capitalist.

Marx's analysis suggested that the industrial countries of Western Europe would be the first to experience the transition from capitalism to socialism. But the Bolshevik Revolution in Russia, which was far less industrialized than Western Europe, proved him wrong. There, will power and Lenin's modifications to the basic Marxist theory made possible the triumph of socialist forces. After the Second World War, more modifications were made. Highly centralized economies were liberalized to provide for the market mechanism and profits. Dogmatic adherence to rigid ideological positions was replaced by economic pragmatism in Yugoslavia, Poland, Romania, and to some extent in the Soviet Union. This movement is known as revisionism.

Events in the Third World have largely confounded Marx's predictions. He had dismissed peasants as reactionary, small-minded because of a preoccupation with private property, and used the phrase "rural idiocy" to describe their general consciousness.[13] But it was these peasants under revolutionary leadership in China (Mao Tse-Tung), Cuba (Fidel Castro), and Mozambique (Samora Michel), not the proletariat, that overthrew capitalism or colonialism in their respective countries which may now be considered as among the vanguard of advancing world socialism.

SOCIALISM IN AFRICA

When we apply Marxist analysis and conclusions to Africa, we come face to face with a number of difficulties. Is it appropriate to apply results derived from an analysis of industrial societies to others which are not only unindustrialized but also characterized by a form of capitalism which can be characterized as peripheral and client to the major capitalist centers of the West? How would dialectical materialism fit into such a milieu? Can we seriously talk of classes and class antagonism of the scale foreshadowed in Marx's analysis? Indeed, the situation is made more complex by the existence of such factors as competing ethnic groups and religious factors which did not loom large in Marxian analysis, but which are crucial in several African countries. The problem of liberating the masses in Africa does not so much require their liberation from exploitation by capitalists (indeed the African industrial sector is relatively small, and industrial workers form an insignificant segment of African populations) as their effective involvement in ownership, production, and distribution in *all* sectors of the national economy aided by deliberate governmental, financial, material, and organizational support. There is the need to reassure the people that government represents their interest and not the selfish interest of those temporarily in power, as well as those of their foreign business supporters. Regarding the application of Marxism to Third World countries, it has been aptly remarked: "The social structures of these areas are vastly different from those of Europe, and it is difficult to see where Marxist categories could be applied.''[14]

In spite of this difficulty, most African leaders who have ventured to reveal a preference in the great worldwide ideological struggle have proclaimed themselves ''socialist'' even when they were pursuing capitalist goals with capitalist methods. This preference for socialism may be due to the desire to identify with a historical-progressive movement, to create an identity transcending ethnic and religious boundaries, and to concentrate power in the hands of the ruling elite, providing for the nationalization of industries and the replacement of foreign capitalists by local bureaucrats. Other factors responsible for the socialist preference include the African experience during the anticolonial struggle when the nationalists had the support of socialists at home and abroad; intellectual contacts with European socialist academics and political parties established by local academicians and labor leaders; and the examples of the USSR and China, which are often regarded as models of modernization in most Third World countries. As the major goals of these societies are modernization and industrialization, socialism is often seen as the instrument for attaining these objectives.

The question to which African leaders have directed their attention was whether Marxist socialism could be applied to the African context, and what modifications were deemed desirable. If the economic base is so radically different from the European one, would it not have been desirable to abandon the Marxist analysis or paradigm and construct a new model in which the economic base and the superstructure are suited to Africans themselves? From what follows, we find that most African political leaders have chosen to place their ideas within a Marxist straightjacket even when these ideas do not conform to orthodox Marxism. One of the writings on ideology by two African collaborators who are not political leaders has openly suggested an alternative model.[15] Four brands of socialism in Africa have been recognized by Fenner Brockway. These are (a) Communism or Marxist-Leninism, (b) African Socialism, (c) African Pragmatic Socialism, (3) African Democratic Socialism. We shall discuss each brand briefly.[16]

Communism or Marxism-Leninism posits that socialism is scientific and universal in its applicability. Supporters tend to be restricted to the campuses and the trade unions. They tend to be rigid in their adherence to ideological purity but they have been more effective in opposition and as pamphleteers.

African Marxists adapt scientific socialism to African conditions. The leading exponents of this brand of socialism are Nkrumah, Sekou Toure, and Nyerere. They are more flexible and less doctrinaire than supporters of Marxism-Leninism; they are also more religious, do not believe in inevitable class war, but believe a classless society can be brought about through state control of the factors of production. They also believe in the one-party system.

The leading exponent of African Pragmatic Socialism is Leopold Senghor, who is perhaps "the leading African exponent of Marxist theory."[17] He rejects "the class struggle, dictatorship of the proletariat, dialectical materialism, atheism and . . . Marx's dehumanized humanism," considers it a betrayal of Marx "to superimpose his method on to Negro African, West African realities." Calling for an autonomous African socialism he makes this passionate plea:

Our African socialism, then, will be elaborated not in the dependence but in the autonomy of our thoughts, and it will choose the most scientific, up-to-date, and above all, the most efficient methods and institutions and techniques of the Western World and elsewhere. But in the final analysis, they will be efficient only if adapted to the African situation . . . . Our separation in this way from the Marxist theory after it has been assimilated is all the more necessary as Marx and Engels were not anti-colonialists. The latter defended slavery in ancient times and the former British colonialism in India in the name of history.

Senghor argues that "socialism exists for man and not man for socialism."[18] Senghor's socialist thought, though Marxian in language and ideas, is anchored in traditional African values.

African Democratic Socialists are the least influenced by Marx. They reject the substance of Marxist philosophy and seek to marry democratic principles in politics to some socialist economic ideas. The leading exponents are the ruling KANU in Kenya and Chief Obafemi Awolowo in Nigeria. KANU considers socialism as an ideal, not an ideology, as it plunges headlong into the building and consolidation of peripheral capitalism in Kenya. Chief Awolowo's position is entirely different from communism and the Marxian concept of socialism. In his view, the economic forces at work must be brought under complete control, coordinated, and humanized for the benefit of all.[19]

It is evidently difficult to assess these competing brands of socialism in Africa. What comes out clearly is the impression that attempts by political leaders in Africa to modify socialism to suit local conditions lack the theoretical elegance associated with the work of Marx. In fact, these African leaders reject so much that is basic to Marx's analysis that one wonders why they even bother to force their ideas into a Marxist mold. One wonders why these leaders fail to call their systems something other than socialist. Senghor's call for an autonomous African socialism that suits African conditions is really a call for a genuinely African ideology, though this predisposition is obscured by his admiration for Marx's abstract philosophy. The brand that is called African democratic socialism should, in all honesty, not be considered as socialist. A careful reading of the position of their exponents, particularly Awolowo's, shows that they consider equality more important than community ownership of productive resources, a point of view at variance with the tenets of all socialist schools of thought. Awolowo is surprisingly cautious regarding state ownership of "all the means of production," a step which he advises should be taken "subject to the dictates of prudence and pragmatism." While the first socialist, Saint-Simon, argues that man should work before sharing in society's produce, Awolowo seems to reverse this as he lays more emphasis on the provision of "free" social amenities to citizens than their organization to increase the national cake. We can therefore conclude that Awolowo is more welfarist than socialist, and, since he appears to reject the philosophical position of utopian and Marxist Socialists, the impression cannot be entirely wrong that he, so far as the twentieth century is concerned, has his sympathies for the mixed economy which in itself has strong doses of capitalism.

What emerges from the foregoing exposition of African modifications of socialism is the fact that, though claiming to be socialist, African leaders have come up with models which are not essentially socialist. Lacking theoretical rigor and foundation, African versions of socialism are nothing but "pure rhetorics, a language to impress, to intimidate, rather than a set of guidelines for specific action."[20]

THE ALTERNATIVE

We have demonstrated that since African societies are not industrial and have operating within them several factors such as ethnicity, foreign economic domination, inefficiency in production and religious fundamentalism, factors which have no place in Marx's analysis, Marxist socialism cannot easily and reasonably be applied to Africa. Moreover, the irrelevance of class antagonism, dictatorship of the proletariat, and the rejection by most Africans of atheism calls for the construction of an ideological alternative to socialism. Such an alternative cannot be capitalism or its closely related cousin, the mixed economy, because the weaknesses of such systems (unjustifiable inequalities in the distribution of wealth, exploitation of workers, domination by multinational corporations, and corruption) are so well known as to discourage their adoption.[21] The relevant and appropriate alternative is one which recognizes as important inputs into the analysis aspects of the African environment and employs a logical methodology designed to yield consistent conclusions.

The alternative model put forward in *An Ideology for Social Development: Ending the Capitalist-Socialist Struggle*, co-authored in 1977 by S. O. Wey and Eghosa Osagie accepts two ideas from Marxian theory. These are that "the spark plug of conflict and change is economics," and that "ideas and the values underpinning them are ultimately meaningful and significant only when squarely put in their contextual social setting."[22] Thus, the base of society is economic, while the superstructure must fit that base if the system is to survive and remain stable. Though employing these Marxian principles, the originators of this approach arrive at non-Marxist conclusions about the ideal economic system.

This school of thought considers the different stages through which African society has progressed. First was the precolonial system where the base was functional self-sufficiency in production and the superstructure was communal ownership. International trade brought a segment of the precolonial system into contact with Europe; a new merchant class and a professional military class, finding their interest lay more with Europeans, joined forces with them to overthrow the precolonial system. Thus the protectorate was born. In the protectorate, the base was individualistic and haphazard production, and the superstructure was private property. Thus was breached the African's communalism. The operation of the protectorate, in turn, encouraged the germination of new social forces which eventually destroyed the protectorate system. A crop of educated youths who could not rise to the top of their professions or were not admitted into the civil service because of the rigid racial barriers to professional advancement of Africans founded nationalist movements to oppose the colonial ruling class of white administrators. Nationalist agitation led to independence. But in effect, independence changed nothing significantly, as the economic base and the superstructure remained the same. What changed was the composition of the ruling class, as the nationalist leader simply replaced the European administrator. The newly independent economy could still be manipulated by the former colonial power by economic influence exercised through multinational corporations and some of the former nationalist leaders. This is today's era of neocolonialism. In some countries, where nationalistic policies have indigenized the officer corps of the military, and nationalistic economic policies made millionaires of commission agents, a new ruling elite soon emerged (military officers and business tycoons) after military coups. Even under the military, the economic base remains inefficient and production haphazard and the superstructure remains one of private property. It is at this point that most African Marxists want to jump Marx's queue. They want a socialist society without the prior development of an industrial base. But, given the structure of most African countries, a significant industrial sector can be developed only within the framework of economic communities involving many nations. It is only after the successful establishment of an African economic community that socialism in the sense of Marx is possible and indeed conceivable.

This school of thought, which for lack of a better term has chosen to call its system *integratism*, argues that there is no point in going through all the stages outlined above to arrive at a better organization of society. Instead of following Marx to have mass production, as base of the socialist system, the integratists prefer to have as their economic base production by the masses. Once that is achieved, the integratists believe that true democracy is finally attained; the representatives of the masses now organized for socially beneficial production also become the political leaders. There would be no room for political parties which are vehicles for securing the class interests of the educated and monied elite. Other features of integratism include emphasis on production for social use, the elimination of unjustifiable inequality in the distribution of income, the utilization of technology for human convenience, an educational system that provides required workerpower suited to the chosen technology, and the mutually beneficial coexistence of religion and ideology. Another feature of integratism is its opposition to particularism. Unlike socialism, which champions the interests of the proletariat against those of the bourgeoisie, integratism "does not favour a group or groups in society against the interest of other groups. Rather it seeks to identify the common interests that cut across the totality of society . . . social cooperation, rather than confrontation is emphasized.''[23] Moreover, integratism does not see present national borders as final lines of demarcation separating countries. Rather it strives to achieve an international regrouping of nations which does not subjugate some countries to more powerful countries, but balances regions and guarantees the equality of communities around the world.

THE FUTURE

So far, no independent African country has introduced a truly socialist economic system. Mozambique has had problems in her efforts at becoming a socialist economy, and has had to call for cooperation from neighboring capitalist economies. Guinea has had to depend on capitalist Americans to run her mines. Soon after winning the preindependence elections in Zimbabwe, the "Marxist" Robert Mugabe suddenly became friendly with capitalist Western powers and readily accepted a non-Marxist Nigerian economist as the United Nations Development Program Representative. The closing years of the twentieth century call for level-headedness and the rejection of emotional attachments to extant ideologies. So far as Africa is concerned, the prevailing ideological signpost points in one direction—in the direction of integratism. All other directions lead to ideological blind alleys.

NOTES

1. *International Encyclopedia of the Social Sciences*, vol. 14 (New York: MacMillan and Free Press, 1968), p. 507.
2. George James, *Stolen Legacy* (San Francisco: Richardson, 1956).
3. *International Encyclopedia*, vol. 14, p. 506.
4. Ibid.
5. Ibid.
6. Ibid.
7. Robert L. Heilbroner, *The Worldly Philosophers* (New York: Simon and Schuster, 1961), p. 90.
8. Ibid., p. 98.
9. Ibid., p. 99.
10. Ibid., pp. 101–3.

11. A.J.P. Taylor, "Introduction," *The Communist Manifesto* (Harmondsworth, England: Penguin, 1967), p. 9.

12. *International Encyclopedia*, vol. 14, p. 507.

13. Ibid., pp. 508, 526.

14. Ibid.

15. S. O. Wey and Eghosa Osagie, *An Ideology for Social Development: Ending the Capitalist-Socialist Struggle* (Lagos: Ogiso, 1977).

16. H.M.A. Onitiri, *Karl Marx and African Thought on Economic and Social Development* (Ibadan: University of Ibadan Press, 1977), pp. 383–96.

17. Ibid., pp. 388–89.

18. Ibid., p. 390.

19. Obafemi Awolowo, *The Problem of Africa* (London: Macmillan, 1977), pp. 3–27.

20. *International Encyclopedia*, p. 528.

21. Eghosa Osagie, "Social and Economic Development in Nigeria: Bottlenecks and Solutions," unpublished paper presented to Nigerian Youth Service Corp., July/August 1978.

22. Wey and Osagie, *An Ideology for Social Development*, p. 24.

23. Ibid., p. 34.

Part IV

CULTURAL CONTINUA

10

AFRICAN-AMERICAN HISTORIANS AND THE RECLAIMING OF AFRICAN HISTORY

JOHN HENRIK CLARKE

The Africans who came to the United States as slaves started their attempts to reclaim their lost African heritage soon after they arrived in this country. They were searching for the lost identity that the slave system had destroyed. Concurrent with the black man's search for an identity in America has been his search for an identity in the world, which means, in essence, his identity as a human being with a history, before and after slavery, that can command respect.[1]

The Afro-American connection with Africa is not new. In fact, this connection was never completely broken. "Africa-consciousness," in varying degrees, good and bad, has always been a part of the psyche of the African people, in forced exile in South America, the Caribbean Islands, and in the United States. There has always been a conflict within the Black American's "Africa-consciousness." This conflict was created early and was extended beyond all reasonable proportions by the mass media of the twentieth century through jungle movies, elementary textbooks on geography and history, and travel books written to glorify all people of European extraction—in essence, white people. These distorted images have created both a rejection of Africa and a deep longing for the Africa of our imagination, the Africa that was our home and the first home of what man has referred to as "a civilization."[2]

Contrary to a still prevailing opinion, most of the literate Africans in forced exile have always had a positive image of Africa. They have rejected the image of Africa as a backward and barbarous land. To the extent that the information was available, the early black writers and thinkers made every attempt to locate Africa on the map of human geography. They soon discovered that Africa and her people had a history older than the history of their oppressors. They also learned how and why the Europeans came to Africa in the first place, and the circumstances, in Africa and in Europe, that set the slave trade in motion. They learned why the Christian church had to read the Africans out of the respectful commentary of human history. While the pretense was that Africans were being civilized and Christianized, this was really the beginning of what Walter Rodney has called "The Under-development of Africa." In his book on the subject, Rodney analyzes the first European impressions of the people and cultures on the west coast of Africa. "Several historians of Africa," he pointed out, "after surveying the developed areas of the continent in the 15th century, and those within Europe at the same time, find the difference between the two in no way to Africa's discredit."[3]

He quotes a Dutch account of the city of Benin in west Africa to prove that, at first, the Europeans compared African cities and cultures favorably to their own:

The town seems to be very great. When you enter into it, you go into a great broad street, not paved, which seems to be seven or eight times broader than the Warmoes Street in Amsterdam.

The King's palace is a collection of buildings which occupy as much space as the two of Harlem, and which is enclosed with walls. There are numerous apartments for the Prince's ministers and fine galleries, most of which are as big as those of the Exchange at Amsterdam. They are supported by wooden pillars encased with copper, where their victories are depicted, and which are carefully kept very clean.

The Town is composed of 30 main streets, very straight and two hundred and twenty feet wide, apart from an infinity of small intersecting streets. The houses are close to one another, arranged in good order. These people are in no way inferior to the Dutch as regards cleanliness; they wash and scrub their houses so well that they are polished and shining like a looking glass.[4]

In his essay, "The African Roots of the War," written for the *Atlantic Monthly*, May 1915, the great Afro-American scholar, W.E.B. Du Bois, decried the fact that:

There are those who would write world history and leave out this most marvelous of continents. Particularly today most men assume that Africa lies far afield from the center of our burning social problems and especially from our present problem of world war.

Yet in a very real sense, Africa is a prime cause of this terrible overturning of civilization . . . . In Africa are the hidden roots, not simply of war today but of the menace of war tomorrow.

Always Africa is giving us something new or some metempsychosis of a world-old thing. On its black bosom arose one of the earliest if not the earliest, of self-protecting civilizations, and grew so mightily that it still furnishes superlatives to thinking and speaking men. Out of its darker and more remote forest vastnesses came, if we may credit many recent scientists, the first welding of iron, and we know that agriculture and trade flourished there when Europe was a wilderness.

Nearly every human empire that has arisen in the world, material and spiritual, has found some of its greatest crises on this continent of Africa, from Greece to Great Britain. As Mommsen says: 'It was through Africa that Christianity became the religion of the world.' In Africa the last flood of Germanic invasions spent itself within hearing of the last gasp of Byzantium, and it was again in Africa that Islam came to play its great role of conqueror and civilizer.[5]

In the reestablishment of the connection with Africa and in the search for a more enlightened image of that continent and its people, the early black writers in the United States soon learned that Africa was an important factor in world history, and that in the great human drama of the rise and fall of nations, Africans had played every role from saint to buffoon.

These writers, preachers and self-educated men of affairs, referred to themselves mainly as Africans—not "coloreds," nor "Negroes" nor "blacks," but as Africans. Nearly all their organizations bore the name "African," and they thought of themselves as African people. This small group of black freedmen and escaped slaves began to develop during the latter half of the eighteenth century. By the end of that century, their presence was being felt as petitioners, antislavery speakers, and pamphleteers. Their writings and their place in history is well recorded in *Early Negro Writing 1760–1837*, by Dorothy Porter, giving the following information.[6]

The first literary talent of Afro-Americans began to develop in the years between 1760 and 1837, concurrently with mutual benefit organizations expressing their social consciousness. In most cases these organizations bore African names and their leaders referred to Africa as their homeland. Mrs. Porter tells us:

This early disposition to associate together for mutual improvement provided a training ground for the half-educated as well as for the educated and ambitious among the sons of Africa in the United States. The very titles of these orga- nizations suggest that they were directed in the main to the improvement of the social and political status of Blacks.[7]

The Free African Society was organized by the black Methodists in 1787. This society under the leadership of Richard Allen and Absalom Jones brought into being the first independent black church in the United States—the African Methodist Episcopal Church. The early black churches were more than religious organizations. They performed the services of social agencies, publishers, community centers, and occa- sionally hiding places for escaped slaves. The first historical protest and literary writings of the black freedmen in the New England states found an outlet in the church or organizations affiliated with the church. In the *Essay on Freedom with Observations on the Origins of Slavery*, written by a member of the Sons of Africa Society that was formed in 1798, the writer outlines some of the difficulties blacks were encoun- tering in seeking freedom and expresses appreciation to the people of the city of Salem, Massachusetts, for showing signs of "approbation of the Africans' freedom." These pamphlets, broadsheets, and mono- graphs continued to appear throughout the first half of the nineteenth century, and their writers helped to establish the early black press in the United States. Some of these writers became editors of such papers as *Freedom's Journal*, *The North Star* and *The Anglo-African Magazine*.

The spiritual and cultural return to Africa is reflected in the names of early black institutions, especially in the churches. In his book, *The Redemption of Africa and Black Religion*, St. Clair Drake draws this picture of the black church during its formative years:

Black people under slavery turned to the Bible to "prove" that Black people, Ethiopians, were so powerful and respected when white men in Europe were barbarians. Ethiopia came to symbolize all of Africa; and throughout the 19th century, the redemption of Africa became one important focus of meaningful activity for leaders among New World Negroes. "Ethiopianism" became an energizing myth in both the New World and in Africa itself for those pre- political movements that arose while the powerless were gathering their strength for realistic and rewarding political activity. Its force is now almost spent, but "Ethiopianism" left an enduring legacy to the people who fought for Black Power in the 20th century, and some of its development needs to be understood.[8]

In the closing years of the nineteenth century, the Africans in the Caribbean Islands, South America, and in the United States continued to object to the distorted pictures of Africans in elementary school books, geographies, travel books, and histories. As far back as 1881, the renowned Dr. Edward Wilmot Blyden, on the occasion of his inauguration as president of Liberia College, sounded the note that called for a new approach to the teaching of African history and culture. Dr. Blyden is the best known of the Caribbean scholars who returned to Africa. Of his many books, *Christianity, Islam and the Negro Race*, first published in 1887 and reprinted in 1967, is an enduring classic.[9]

In the United States, W.E.B. Du Bois continued some of the work of Dr. Blyden and carried it into the twentieth century. The unity and liberation of all Africa was the main mission of the life of W.E.B.DuBois. He did not pursue this mission in isolation, and he sought allies wherever he could find them. His interest in Africa began during his student days at Harvard University. As a result of this interest, he wrote his first major work, *The Suppression of the African Slave Trade to the United States* (1896). This interest was continued in two other works, *The Souls of Black Folks* (1903) and *The Gift of Black Folks* (1924). During his editorship of the *Crisis Magazine*, 1910-1934, he introduced Africa as a subject of concern for Black Americans. *The Negro*, published in 1915, was his first attempt to write a survey history of the African world. His little-known, yet important essay, *The African Roots of the War*, was published the same year. In this essay, he dared to deal with the imperialist origins of the First World War and Africa in general.

After World War I new men and movements rose to challenge the old social order and to ask for a new one. The best-known movement of this period was the Universal Negro Improvement Association (UNIA). The best-known personality was its dynamic founder, Marcus Garvey. Concurrent with the rise of the Garvey movement a literary and cultural awakening called the Harlem Renaissance brought more attention to the world's most famous ethnic community. The Harlem Renaissance, in its own way, was an African-consciousness movement, accentuated by Marcus Garvey and his program that asked Black Americans to consider a return to their motherland.[10]

Among black writers, artists, and thinkers like W.E.B. Du Bois, James Weldon Johnson, J. A. Rogers, Arthur A.Schomburg, and William Leo Hansberry, the period of the Harlem Renaissance was a time of African rediscovery. In their writings these scholars affirmed that Africans were great storytellers long before their first appearance in Jamestown, Virginia, in 1619. The rich and colorful history, art, and folklore of West Africa, the ancestral home of most Afro-Americans, present evidence of this, and more.

Contrary to a misconception which still prevails, the Africans were familiar with literature and art for many years before their contact with the Western World. Before the breaking up of the social structure of the West African states of Ghana, Melle (Mali), and Songhay, and the internal strife and chaos that made the slave trade possible, the forefathers of the Africans who eventually became slaves in the United States lived in a society where university life was fairly common and scholars were beheld with reverence.

There were in this ancestry rulers who expanded their kingdoms into empires, great and magnificent armies whose physical dimensions dwarfed entire nations into submission, generals who advanced the technique of military science, scholars whose vision of life showed foresight and wisdom, and priests who told of gods that were strong and kind. To understand fully any aspect of Afro-American life, one must realize that the Black Americans are not without a cultural past, though they were many generations removed from it before their achievements in American literature and art commanded any appreciable attention. I have been referring to the African origin of Afro-American literature and history. This preface is essential to every meaningful discussion of the role of the Afro-American in every major aspect of American life, past and present. I want to make it clear that the African people did not come to the United States culturally empty-handed.

I will elaborate very briefly on my statement that the forefathers of the Africans who eventually became slaves in the United States once lived in a society where university life was fairly common and scholars were beheld with reverence. During the period in West African history—from the early part of the fourteenth century to the time of the Moroccan invasion in 1591, the city of Timbuctoo and the University of Sankore in the Songhay Empire was the intellectual center of Africa. Black scholars enjoyed a renaissance that was known and respected throughout most of Africa and in parts of Europe. At this period in African history, the University of Sankore, at Timbuctoo, was the educational capitol of the Western Sudan. In Lady Lugard's "A Tropical Dependency," there is a fitting description of ancient Timbuctoo:

The scholars of Timbuctoo yielded in nothing to the saints in their sojourns in the foreign universities of Fez, Tunis and Cairo. They astounded the most learned men of Islam by their erudition. That these Negroes were on a level with the Arabian Savants is proved by the fact that they were installed as professors in Morocco and Egypt. In contrast to this, we find that the Arabs were not always equal to the requirements of Sankore.[11]

I will speak of one of the great black scholars of ancient Timbuctoo. Ahmed Baba was the last chancellor of the University of Sankore. He was one of the greatest African scholars of the late sixteenth century. His life is a brilliant example of the range and depth of West African intellectual activity before the colonial era. Ahmed Baba was the author of more than forty books, nearly every one of which had a different theme. He was in Timbuctoo when it was invaded by the Moroccans in 1591, and he was one of the first citizens to protest the occupation of his beloved home town. Ahmed Baba, along with other scholars, was imprisoned and eventually exiled to Morocco. During his expatriation from Timbuctoo, his collection of 1,600 books, one of the richest libraries of his day, was lost.

Now, West Africa entered a sad period of decline. During the Moroccan occupation, wreck and ruin became the order of the day. When the Europeans arrived in this part of Africa and saw these conditions, they assumed that nothing of order and value had ever existed in these countries. This mistaken impression, too often repeated, has influenced the interpretation of African and Afro-American life in history for over 400 years.[12]

The essence of the African-consciousness of the writers who were a part of the Harlem Renaissance is contained in the book, *The New Negro*, edited by Alain Locke. Essays like "The Mind of the Negro Reaches Out," by W.E.B. Du Bois, "The Legacy of the Ancestral Arts," by Alain Locke, and "The Negro Digs Up His Past," by Arthur A. Schomburg, show a creative concern for Africa.[13] When the book, *The New Negro*, was published in 1925, the Association for the Study of Negro Life and History, under the leadership of its founder, Carter G. Woodson, was ending the first decade of its existence. In 1926 he founded what we now know as Afro-American or Black History Week.

The terms, Black History Week or Afro-American History Week, taken at face value or without serious thought, appear to be incongruous. At the time, the question did arise, why is there a need for a Black History Week when there is no similar week for the other minority groups in the United States? The history of the United States in total consists of the collective histories of minority groups. What we call "American civilization" is no more than the sum of their contributions. The Afro-Americans are the least integrated and the most neglected of these groups in the historical interpretation of the American experience. This neglect has made Black History Week a necessity.[14]

Most of the large ethnic groups in the United States have had, and still have, their historical associations. Some predate the founding of the Association for the Study of Negro Life and History (1915). Dr. Charles H. Wesley tells us, "Historical societies were organized in the United States with the special purpose in view of preserving and maintaining the heritage of the American nation."[15] In 1944 there were a total of 904 ethnic historical societies in the United States and Canada, an increase of 46 percent over the number listed in 1936, 583. Among these societies were those representing groups whose origins were German, Irish, French, Jewish, Dutch, Spanish, Russian, Norwegian, Scandinavian, Swedish, Swiss, and Finnish. The leaders of these historical societies were of the opinion that the history of the United States could not be written from the point of view of "adaptation and assimilation," but that the "cultural riches brought to the Western world, in what has been termed the elements composing the national whole, must be studied and appraised before a complete understanding of American history and American civilization is possible."[16]

In "Racial Historical Societies and the American Tradition," included in his book, *Neglected History* (1965), the Afro-American historian, Charles H. Wesley, describes the work of ethnic historical societies in this manner: "They must gather up precious records and interpret them. Both in language and in that subtle understanding which they have absorbed by natural circumstances of the way of life of their own folk, they possess keys to unlock doors that bar the way to a full comprehension of the social history of America."[17]

Within the framework of these historical societies, many ethnic groups, black as well as white, keep alive their beliefs in themselves and their past as a part of their hopes for the future. For Black Americans, Carter G. Woodson led the way and used what was then called "Negro History

Week" to call attention to his people's contribution to every aspect of world history. Dr. Woodson, then Director of the Association for the Study of Negro Life and History, conceived this special week as a time when public attention should be focused on the achievements of America's citizens of African descent. Black History Week comes each year about the second Sunday in February, the objective being to select the week which will include both February 12, the birthdate of Abraham Lincoln, and February 14, the date Frederick Douglass calculated must have been his natal day. Sometimes the celebration can include only one day, in which case the Douglass date gets preference. The aim is not to enter upon one week's study of black people's place in history. Rather, the celebration should represent the culmination of a systematic study of black people throughout the year. Initially, the observance consisted of public exercises emphasizing the salient facts brought to light by the researchers and publications of the association during the first eleven years of its existence. The observance was widely supported among Black Americans in schools, churches and clubs. Gradually the movement found support among other ethnic groups and institutions in America and abroad.

The acceptance of the facts of black history and the black historian as a legitimate part of the academic community did not come easily. Slavery ended but left its false images of black people intact. In his article, "What the Historian Owes the Negro," the noted Afro-American historian, Benjamin Quarles says:

The Founding Fathers, revered by historians for over a century and a half, did not conceive of the Negro as part of the body politic. Theoretically, these men believed in freedom for everyone, but actually they found it hard to imagine a society where Negroes were of equal status to whites. Thomas Jefferson, third President of the United States, who was far more liberal than the run of his contemporaries, was nevertheless certain that "the two races, equally free, cannot live in the same government."[18]

Early white American historians did not accord African people anywhere a respectful place in their commentaries on the history of man. In the closing years of the nineteenth century, black historians began to look at their people's history from their vantage point and point of view. "As early as 1883 this desire to bring to public attention the untapped material on the Negro prompted George Washington Williams to publish his two-volume *History of the Negro Race in America.*"[19]

The first formally trained Afro-American historian was W.E.B. Du Bois, whose doctoral dissertation, published in 1895, *The Suppression of the African Slave Trade to the United States 1638-1870*, became the first title to be published in the Harvard Historical Studies. Carter G. Woodson, another Harvard Ph.D., advanced African world history and became a defender who could document his claims. Woodson was convinced that unless something were done to rescue black people from history's oversight, they would become "a negligible factor in the thought of the world." Woodson in 1915 founded the Association for the Study of Negro Life and History. During the preceding twenty years, an American Negro Academy had been founded in Washington, D.C., and a Negro Society for Historical Research had appeared in New York. These organizations were short-lived because they lacked a historian of Woodson's ability, someone who was also a leader of men and an organizational administrator.

Carter G. Woodson was born of former slaves, Annie and James Woodson, in 1875 at New Canton, Virginia. He suffered all the hardships of poverty while growing up. Only a five-month district school was available to him, and he was unable to attend it on a regular basis. He studied at home while working on the family's farm. Already he had established a lifetime habit—studying at home. In his early years he was mostly self-taught. He mastered all the fundamentals of common school subjects by the time he was seventeen, then went to Huntington, West Virginia, where he worked in the coal mines. He later entered Douglass High School and earned a teaching certificate in less than two years; pursued further education at Berea College in Kentucky, where he received the Litt. B. degree. He continued his education at the University of Chicago, where he was awarded the B.A. and M.A. degrees. His travels in Europe and Asia and graduate studies at the Sorbonne in Paris enriched his cultural background and prepared him for graduate work at Harvard University, where he was awarded the Ph.D. in 1912. After Harvard he had an extensive career as an educator: principal of Douglass High School, teacher of languages and history in high schools of Washington, D.C., dean of the School of Liberal Arts, Howard University, and supervisor of schools in the Philippines. This varied experience made Carter G. Woodson see the need for a special time each year to call attention to his people's contribution to the history and culture of this country and the world. Thus, Black History Week.

After serving many years as a teacher in public schools, Woodson

became convinced that the role of his people in American history and
in the history of other cultures was being either ignored or misrepre-
sented. The Association for the Study of Negro Life and History was
founded to conduct research into the history of African people all over
the world. The next year he began publication of the *Journal of Negro
History*, which has never missed an issue.

A chronicle of Woodson's far-reaching activities must include the
organization in 1921 of the Associated Publishers, Inc., which had as
one of its purposes the publication of books on African people not
usually accepted by most publishers; the establishment of Negro History
Week in 1926; the initial subsidizing of research on Black history; and
the writing of many articles and books on Afro-American and American
life and history.

Woodson believed that there was no such thing as "Negro history."
He said what was called "Negro history" was only a missing segment
of world history. He devoted the greater portion of his life to restoring
this segment. He also realized that once this segment was integrated
into school textbooks and taught with respect and understanding, there
would no longer be a need for a Negro History Week.[20]

In the U.S. Civil War blacks fought bravely and died in great numbers
for their own freedom. The idea that the black man played an insignificant role while white men fought and died to set him free is not
supported by official records. Materials related to the Black Americans
are available in official Civil War records, but unfortunately are completely omitted in most school textbooks.

Africa came into the Mediterranean world mainly through Greece,
which had been under African influence; and then Africa was cut off
from the melting pot by the turmoil among the Europeans and the
religious conquests incident to the rise of Islam. Africa prior to these
events had developed its history and civilization, indigenous to its people
and lands. Africa came back into the general picture of history through
the penetration of North Africa, West Africa, and the Sudan by the
Arabs. European and American slave traders next ravaged the continent.
The imperialist colonizers and missionaries finally entered the scene
and prevailed until the recent reemergence of independent African nations.

Africans are, of course, closely connected to the history of both North
and South America. The Afro-American's role in the social, economic,
and political development of the American states is an important foundation upon which to build racial understanding, especially in areas in

which false generalizations and stereotypes have been developed to separate peoples rather than to unite them.

The spiritual and intellectual journey to Africa was continued by many black scholars other than Carter G. Woodson. At Howard University, William Leo Hansberry, considered to be the greatest Africanist to emerge from the Black American community, trained a generation of students to learn and respect African history. His articles, monographs, and conference papers on the subject appeared in leading journals throughout the world.

In the period of the Italian-Ethiopian War, the streets of Harlem were an open forum, presided over by master speakers like Arthur Reed and his protege, Ira Kemp. Young Carlos Cook, founder of the Garvey-oriented African Pioneer Movement, was on the scene, also bringing a nightly message to his street fellows. Part of every message was about Africa.

The Blyden Society, the Ethiopian World Federation, and other organizations attracted a number of African supporters, some of them students like Nkrumah. The American black press improved its coverage of news about Africa. In reporting on the Italian-Ethiopian War, this press was fortunate in having in its service at least two reporters who had been well schooled in African history in general. The reporters were J. A. Rogers, a historian and journalist, and Willis N. Huggins, historian, teacher, and community activist. In his dispatches from Ethiopia, J. A. Rogers gave an astute analysis of the war to the *Pittsburgh Courier*. He was the only reporter on the scene who was looking at the Italian-Ethiopian conflict from a black point of view. Rogers also commented on the political intrigues in Europe that led to this conflict. Later, in a small book, *The Real Facts About Ethiopia*, he digested his reports and produced the most revealing document about the Italian-Ethiopian War that has so far appeared in print. Willis N. Huggins, a high school history teacher and founder of the Blyden Society for the Study of African History, went to Geneva and reported on the League of Nations meetings concerning the war for the *Chicago Defender*. Dr. Huggins had already written two books on Africa: *A Guide to Studies in African History*, and *Introduction to African Civilizations*.[21]

In the collective talent of Rogers and Huggins, the Afro-American press was fortunate enough to have observers who could see through the subterfuge and pretenses of European powers and their frantic schemes to keep their African colonies. Both Rogers and Huggins saw behind and beyond the headlines and foretold the future repercussions of Ethiopia's betrayal. Their reports were a high-water mark in Black American journalism.

A revolution in thinking about Africa occurred after World War II. The revolution was most widespread among Black Americans, who are the most estranged and alienated African people in all the world.

In 1947, J. A. Rogers published his most outstanding work, *World's Great Men of Color*, in two volumes. This is the enduring masterpiece in African world biography. Before his death in 1966, at the age of eighty-five, he had devoted at least fifty years of his life to researching the lives of great African personalities and the roles they had played in the development of nations, civilizations, and cultures.[22]

In 1958, the American Society of African Culture published the book, *Africa As Seen by American Negroes*. The editors of this book had creatively compiled some of the best essays that Black American scholars had written on Africa during the preceding ten years.[23]

In 1964, *Ebony* Magazine published a series of articles on the ancient and medieval history of Africa by William Leo Hansberry. This was the most extensive series of this nature ever to appear in a black publication. The articles were extracted from a projected four-volume history of Africa that Hansberry had been writing for nearly a generation. Unfortunately, this larger work was not finished before he died in 1965. However, two of his books, edited by Joseph E. Harris, head of the History Department of Howard University, were published in 1974 and 1977: *Pillars in Ethiopian History* and *Africa and Africans as Seen by Classical Writers*.[24]

During the Civil Rights movement, called the "American Black Revolution," interest in Africa led to a massive demand for black studies, mostly by black students at predominantly white universities. A number of books by Black American scholars, helped to place Africa in proper historical focus during this period. In my opinion, some of the most important of these books are: *The African Presence in Asia* by Joseph E. Harris (1971), *Introduction to African Civilizations* by John G. Jackson (1974), *The Destruction of Black Civilization: Great Issues of a Race From 4500 B.C. to 2000 A.D.* by Chancellor Williams, and three books by Yosef Ben-Jochannan, *Black Man of the Nile* (1970), *Africa: Mother of Western Civilization* (1970), and *African Origins of the Major Western Religions* (1971).[25]

Afro-American and Afro-Caribbean scholars from the early part of the nineteenth century to the present made a personal mission out of the effort to reclaim African history. They repudiated the often repeated charge that Africans have no history.

They found that we cannot place African humanity and history in proper perspective until we deal with the distortions of African history. The hard fact is that what we call "world history," in most cases, is only the history of Europe and its relationship to non-European people. The Western academic community, in general, is not yet willing to acknowledge that the world did not wait in darkness for European people to bring the light. The history of Africa was already old when Europe was born.

NOTES

1. John Henrik Clarke, *In the Absence of a Curriculum: Creative Approaches to the Teaching of African and African American History* (New York: Hunter College, Department of Black and Puerto Rican Studies, 1978), p. 3.

2. John Henrik Clarke, "The Afro-American Image of Africa," *Black World* (February 1974), p. 4.

3. Walter Rodney, *How Europe Underdeveloped Africa* (London: Bogle-L'Ouverture Publications, 1972), p. 69.

4. Ibid.

5. W.E.B. Du Bois, *The African Roots of War (1915) in W.E.B. Du Bois', A Reader*, ed. Meyer Weinberg (New York: Harper and Row, 1970), pp. 360–71.

6. Dorothy Porter, *Early Negro Writing, 1760-1837* (Boston: Beacon Press, 1971) pp. 1–86.

7. Ibid., pp. 1–2.

8. St. Clair Drake, *The Redemption of African and Black Religion* (Chicago: Third World Press, 1971), pp. 11–15.

9. Edward Wilmot Blyden, *Christianity, Islam and the Negro Race* (1887; rpt. Edinburgh: University of Edinburgh Press, 1967).

10. John Henrik Clarke, ed., *Marcus Garvey and the Vision of Africa* (New York: Random House, 1973), pp. 173–97.

11. Lady Lugard, *A Tropical Dependency* (London: Nisbet Ltd., 1906), p. 216.

12. John Henrik Clarke, "The Origin and Growth," pp. 632–33.

13. Alain Locke, ed., *The New Negro* (1925; rpt. New York: Atheneum Publishers, 1969).

14. Charles H. Wesley, "Racial Historical Societies and the American Tra-

dition," in *Neglected History: Essays in Negro American History* (Wilberforce, Ohio: Central State College Press, 1965), pp. 9–22.

15. Ibid., p. 9.

16. Ibid., p. 11.

17. Ibid.

18. Benjamin Quarles, "What the Historian Owes the Negro," *Saturday Review*, 3 September 1966, pp. 10–13.

19. Ibid., p. 12.

20. Carter G. Woodson, *The Negro in Our History* (Washington, D.C.: Associated Publishers, 1922); *Negro Makers of History* (Washington, D.C.): Associated Publishers, 1928); *The Mis-Education of the Negro* (Washington, D.C.: Associated Publishers, 1933); *The Story of the Negro Retold* (Washington, D.C.: Associated Publishers, 1935); *The African Background Outlined* (Washington, D.C.: Associated Publishers); and *African Heroes and Heroines* (Washington, D.C.: Associated Publishers, 1939).

21. Willis N. Huggins, and John Jackson, *A Guide to Studies in African History* (Chicago: privately published, 1934); and Willis Huggins and John Jackson, *Introduction to African Civilizations* (Chicago: privately published 1937).

22. Valerie Standoval, "The Brand of History: A Historiographic Account of the work of J. A. Rogers," *Schomburg Center for Research in Black Culture Journal* (Spring 1978), pp. 11–17.

23. American Society of African Culture, *Africans as Seen by American Negroes* (Paris: Présence Africaine, 1958).

24. William Leo Hansberry, *Pillars in Ethiopian History*, ed. Joseph E. Harris (Washington, D.C.: Howard University Press, 1974); and *Africa and Africans as Seen by Classical Writers*, ed. Joseph E. Harris (Washington, D.C.: Howard University Press, 1977).

25. Joseph E. Harris, *The African Presence in Asia* (Washington, D.C.: Howard University Press, 1971); John G. Jackson, *Introduction to African Civilization* (Secaucus, N.J.: Citadel, 1974); Chancellor Williams, *The Destruction of Black Civilization: Great Issues of a Race from 4500 B.C. to 2000 A.D.* (Chicago: Third World Press, 1974); Yosef Ben-Jochannan, *Black Man of the Nile* (New York: Alkebu-lan Books, 1970), *Africa: Mother of Western Civilization* (New York, Alkebu-lan Books, 1970), and *African Origins of the Major Western Religions* (New York: Alkebu-lan Books, 1971).

11

QUILOMBISMO: THE AFRICAN-BRAZILIAN ROAD TO SOCIALISM

ABDIAS DO NASCIMENTO

Pardon, beloved Lady Motherland, for having arrived so late!
Pardon, brothers and sisters for only now arriving!
Pardon, King Zumbi, for arriving only now to receive the inheritance
   you have left me!—from a letter of Gerardo Mello Mourao

Only now, nearly four centuries later, we, Black Brazilians, were able for the first time collectively to visit the Serra da Barriga, in the Brazilian state of Alagoas, and recapture the historic space where the famous Republic of Palmares existed, founded in the sixteenth century by Africans who rose up against slavery and created a free country, egalitarian, just, and productive. This first visit to our ancestral land took place on the 24th of August 1980, when dozens and dozens of African men and women gathered in Maceio (capital of Alagoas) in order to discuss the creation of a memorial to Zumbi, the Afro-Brazilian king of Palmares—not a park or monument, but a veritable pole of Afro-Brazilian liberation culture.

The feats of that cluster of *quilombos* (military communities) called Palmares were heroic to the point of mingling with legend, and catapulted the republic into history as the Black Troy. Nevertheless, they are not celebrated in Brazilian civic holidays or even remembered—much less studied or taught—in the scholastic curricula on any educational level. This has been the major means of eradicating African memory and history from the scenario of Brazilian life.

But we were there to recapture, celebrate, and reaffirm them in all their content of beauty, myth, and history. With this sentiment, I climbed the impenetrable paths of the Serra's slope, treading the same trail that Zumbi's followers had walked. And from the villagers of Serra da Barriga I heard the oral account (however fragmented) of the histories, legends, and stories that enable us to reconstruct the concrete existence of those 30,000 bronze heroes who wrote, with their lives and blood, the page of history most vibrant with the love of liberty known in American lands. With sweat covering my face from the effort of the climb, I noticed on the third tier, very distant, the great closed forest where people would be lost forever if they took away the fruits of the trees. There was also the belief that buried somewhere in the forest was the hidden treasure of the *quilombolas*; an institution from the United States has even projected excavations to search for Zumbi's gold. Meanwhile, even today many mothers in the area (not of African origin) scare their rambunctious children with the threat: "I'll get Zumbi out here to fix you!" And it is said that one can hear in certain areas and valleys of the Serra, the sounds of chains, the crack of breaking bones, muffled screams of those who leap or are thrown to the abyss.

The *quilombos'* lines of defense, it seems, began with deep trenches almost at the foot of the hills, filled with pointed spears on which attackers would impale themselves—the first palisade. This military defense system was repeated, forming four lines of palisades up to the top. I climbed up to the place where possibly there existed the fourth and last of these. Along the entire path I found reminiscences of what the *quilombolas* of the sixteenth century probably harvested: bamboo, oranges, *jaca*, mangoes, yams, lemons, corn, and sugar cane, and everywhere there were the elegant palms—coconuts of various species. They were the *palmares* that gave the place its name, and there they stood, green and mute, giving witness to so many centuries of Afro-Brazilian history—a history that will be rescued, beginning now, from the distortion and oblivion that the dominant elite has practiced.

UPDATING ANCIENT AFRICAN KNOWLEDGE

Afro-Brazilian memory, much to the contrary of the statements of conventional historians of limited vision and superficial understanding, does not begin with the slave traffic or the dawn of African chattel slavery in the fifteenth century. In Brazil, the ruling class always, particularly after the so-called abolition of slavery (1888), developed and refined innumerable techniques for preventing Black Brazilians from identifying and actively drawing on their ethnic, historical, and cultural roots, cutting them off from the trunk of their African family tree. Except in terms of its recent expansionist economic interests, Brazil's traditional elite has always ignored the African continent. Brazil turned its back on Africa as soon as the slaver elite found itself no longer able to scorn the prohibition of commerce in African flesh imposed by Britain around 1850. A massive immigration of Europeans occurred a few years later, and the ruling elite emphasized its intentions and its actions in order to wrench out of the mind and heart of slaves' descendants any image of Africa as a positive memory of nation, of motherland, or native home. Never in our educational system was there taught a discipline revealing any appreciation or respect for the cultures, arts, languages, political or economic systems, or religions of Africa. And physical contact of Afro-Brazilians with their brothers in the continent and the diaspora was always prevented or made difficult, among other methods, by the denial of economic means permitting black people to move and travel outside the country. But none of these hindrances had the power of obliterating completely, from our spirit and memory, the living presence of Mother Africa. And even in the existential hell we are subjected to now, this rejection of Africa on the part of the dominant classes has functioned as a notably positive factor, helping to maintain the black nation as a community above and beyond difficulties in time and space.

Diversified as are the strategies and devices arrayed against black people's memory, they have recently undergone serious erosion and irreparable discrediting. This is due largely to the dedication and competence of a few Africans preoccupied with the secular destitution the black race has suffered at the hands of European and Euro-American capitalist civilization.[1] This group of Africans, simultaneously scholars, scientists, philosophers, and creators of literature and art, includes persons from the African continent and diaspora. To mention only a few of their names: Cheikh Anta Diop of Senegal; Chancellor Williams, Shawna Maglangbayan Moore, Haki Madhubuti, Molefi K. Asante, and Maulana Ron Karenga of the United States; George G. M. James and Ivan Van Sertima of Guyana; Yosef Ben-Jochannan of Ethiopia; Theophile Obenga, of Congo Brazzaville; Wole Soyinka, Ola Balogun and Wande Abimbola of Nigeria. These figure among the many who are actively producing works fundamental to the contemporary and coming development of Africa. In different fields, with diverse perspectives,

the energies of these eminent Africans channel themselves toward the
exorcism of the falsities, distortions, and negations that Europeans for
so long have been weaving around Africa with the purpose of obscuring
or erasing from our memory the wisdom, scientific and philosophical
knowledge, and realizations of the peoples of Black African origin.
Black Brazilian memory is only a part of this gigantic project of reconstructing the larger past to which all Afro-Brazilians are connected.
To redeem this past is to have a consequent responsibility in the destiny
and future of the Black African nation worldwide, still preserving our
role as edifiers and genuine citizens of Brazil.

It is appropriate here to refer briefly to certain basic texts of Cheikh
Anta Diop, principally his book *The African Origin of Civilization*
(1974), selections translated from *Nation nègre et culture* and *Antériorité des civilizations negres*. Let is be said from the outset that the
volume presents a radical confrontation and unanswerable challenge to
the Western academic world, describing its intellectual arrogance, scientific dishonesty, and ethical vacuum in dealing with the peoples,
civilizations, and cultures produced by Africa. Using Western Europe's
own scientific resources—Diop is a chemist, director of the radiocarbon
laboratory of IFAN, in Dakar, as well as an Egyptologist, historian,
and linguist—this sage reconstructs the significance and value of the
ancient Black African civilizations, far too long obscured by manipulations, lies, distortions, and thefts. These civilizations include ancient
Egypt. The Egyptians were black and not a people of any Aryan (white)
or so-called "dark-red race," as Western scholars have claimed Egyptians to be, with an emphasis as deceitful as it is self-interested. Let us
see how Diop characterizes this situation:

The ancient Egyptians were Negroes. The moral fruit of their civilization is to
be counted among the assets of the Black world. Instead of presenting itself to
history as an insolvent debtor, that Black world is the very initiator of the
"Western" civilization flaunted before our eyes today. Pythagorean mathematics, the theory of the four elements of Thales of Miletus, Epicurean materialism, Platonic idealism, Judaism, Islam and modern sciences are rooted in
Egyptian cosmogony and science. One needs only to meditate on Osiris, the
redeemer-god, who sacrifices himself, dies and is resurrected to save mankind,
a figure essentially identifiable with Christ.[2]

Diop's statments are based on rigorous research, examinations, and
conclusions, leaving no margin for doubt or argument, yet far from

taking on that dogmatism that always characterizes the "scientific" certainties of the Western world. What Diop did was simply to demolish the supposedly definitive structures of "universal" knowledge with respect to Egyptian and Greek antiquity. Like it or not, white Westerners have to swallow truths like this one: "four centuries before the publication of *La Mentalité primitive* [*Primitive Mentality*] by Levy-Bruhl, Black Muslim Africa was commenting on Aristotle's formal logic (which he plagiarized from the Black Egyptians) and was already expert in dialectics."[3] And let us not forget that this was almost five centuries before Hegel or Marx were born.

Diop turns around the entire process of mystification of a Black Egypt turned white by the magical arts of European Egyptologists. He notes how, after the military campaign of Bonaparte in Egypt in 1799, and after the hieroglyphs of the Rosetta stone were deciphered by Champollion in 1822, Egyptologists were dumbfounded before the grandiosity of the revealed discoveries:

They gradually recognized [Egypt] as the most ancient civilization, that had engendered all others. But, imperialism being what it is, it became increasingly "inadmissible" to continue to accept the theory—evident until then—of a Negro Egypt. The birth of Egyptology was thus marked by the need to destroy the memory of a Negro Egypt at any cost and in all minds. Henceforth, the common denominator of all the theses of the Egyptologists, their close relationship and profound affinity, can be characterized as a desperate attempt to refute that opinion. Almost all Egyptologists stress its falsity as a matter of course.[4]

The Eurocentric pretentiousness of this episode is exposed in all its nakedness: the Egyptologists continued obstinately in their vain efforts to prove "scientifically" that this great civilization of Black Egypt had a white origin. Precarious as their theories were in fact, they were accepted by the "civilized" world as a cornerstone in the belief of white supremacy.

Diop, compassionate and humane before the dogmatism of the white Egyptologists, reveals much patience and generosity, explaining what should be obvious to anyone approaching the subject in good faith: that he does not allege racial superiority or any specific black genius in this purely scientific confirmation that the civilization of ancient Egypt was built and governed by black people. The event, explains Diop, resulted from a series of historical factors, climatic conditions, natural resources, and so on, added to other nonracial elements. So much so that even after having expanded through all of Black Africa, to the central and western parts of the continent, the Egyptian civilization, under the impact of other influences and historical situations, later entered into a process of retrogressive disintegration. What is important here is to note some of the factors that contributed to the construction of Egyptian civilization, among which Diop enumerates these: geographical conditioning of the sociopolitical development of the peoples that lived on the banks of the river Nile, such as floods and other natural disasters that forced collective measures of defense and survival; a situation that favored unity and discouraged individual or personal egotism. In this context arose the need for a central coordinating authority over common life and activities. The invention of geometry was born of the imperatives of geographical division, and other advances were attained in the effort to attend to the exigencies of building a viable society.

One detail is particularly important to the memory of Brazilian blacks. Diop mentions ancient Egypt's relationship to Black Africa, specifically the Yoruba people, who constitute an important element of Afro-Brazilian demographic and cultural heritage. It seems that these Egyptian-Yoruba relationships were so intimate that one can ''consider a historical fact the common possession of the same primitive habitat by the Yorubas and the Egyptians.'' Diop raises the hypothesis that the Latinization of the name of Horus, son of Osiris and Isis, resulted in the appellative Orisha. Following this line of comparative study, in the field of linguistics and other disciplines, Diop cites J. Olumide Lucas, of Nigeria. In *The Religion of the Yorubas* (1948) Lucas traces Egyptian links with his people, concluding that all paths lead to the verification of (a) a similarity or identity of language; (b) a similarity or identity of religious beliefs; (c) a similarity or identity of religious ideas and practices; (d) a survival of customs, names of places and persons, objects, etc.[5]

My objective here is simply to call attention to this significant dimension of the antiquity of Afro-Brazilian memory. It is for the Afro-Brazilian and African researchers of the present and future to flesh out the details of such a fundamental aspect of our history, a task too vast to touch upon here.

PRE-COLUMBIAN AFRO-AMERICA

It is not only in ancient Egypt or west Africa that we find the historical antecedents of Afro-Brazilian peoples and culture. Another dimension of our memory lies in the presence of Africans in various parts of ancient America, long before the arrival of Columbus. And this is not a superficial or passing phenomenon, but a presence so deep that it left indelible marks on pre-Colombian civilizations. Various historians and researchers have left evidence of this phenomenon. Among others, we can cite the Mexican colonial historian Orozco y Berra, who by 1862 had already mentioned the intimate relations which ancient Mexicans must have cultivated with African visitors and immigrants.[6] The most important recent contribution in this sense has been that of Ivan Van Sertima, whose book *They Came Before Columbus* (1976) registers in unanswerable and definitive form the African contribution to the pre-Colombian cultures of the Americas, particularly those of Mexico.[7] Nevertheless, other authors of various epochs and origins have also confirmed the same result: R. A. Jairazbhoy, Lopez de Gomara, Alexander von Wuthenau, Leo Weiner, and others, each in their own specialties, have added to the reconstitution of the African presence in America before Columbus.[8]

Elisa Larkin Nascimento has noted linkages with Egyptian and West African symbols and artistic techniques, manifested in the funeral urns and other art of San Agustin and Tierradentro in Colombia, sites of indigenous civilizations dating from more or less a century before Christ.[9] Similar types of comparisons also can be documented with respect to the Taina culture of Puerto Rico and the Olmec, Toltec, Aztec, and Maya of Mexico, as well as the Inca of Bolivia, Ecuador, and Peru.[10] Remarkable portraiture of African faces and figures in ceramics and sculpture, shared mummification techniques, funeral traditions, mythical and artistic themes, symbols such as the feathered serpent, as well as countless linguistic identities, are among the visible witnesses to the active interchange between ancient American and African civilizations. Perhaps most intriguing is the obvious connection in engineering techniques of pyramid construction in Nubia, Egypt, and the Americas.[11] At this point it is well to note, along with Elisa Larkin Nascimento, that the pre-Colombian presence of African civilization in the Americas "in no way underestimates or detracts from the enormous design and engineering capacities of the original American peoples that were the authors and builders of the formidable pre-Columbian urban civilizations."[12]

This African-American interchange, among the original peoples of the respective continents, establishes an extensive and legitimate relationship between African and American indigenous peoples that long predates European chattel slavery of Africans. The true historical basis for solidarity among these peoples is thus much deeper and more authentic than has generally been recognized. As *quilombismo* searches for the best world for Africans in the Americas, it knows that such a struggle cannot be separated from the mutual liberation of the indigenous peoples of these lands, who are also victims of the racism and wanton destructiveness introduced and enforced by the European colonialists and their heirs.

BLACK CONSCIOUSNESS AND QUILOMBIST SENTIMENT

From a narrower perspective, Black Brazilian memory reaches a crucial historical stage in the slavist period, beginning around 1500, just after the territory's "discovery" by the Portuguese and their inaugural acts toward its colonization. Along with the briefly enslaved and then progressively exterminated Indians, Africans were the first and only workers, throughout three and a half centuries, who built the structures of Brazil. I think it necessary to evoke once more the vast lands Africans sowed with their sweat, or to remember again the cane fields; cotton fields; coffee plantations; gold, diamond, and silver mines; and the many other elements in the formation of Brazil which was nourished with the martyred blood of slaves. The black, far from being an upstart or a stranger, is the very body and soul of this country. Yet, despite this undeniable historical fact, Africans and their descendants were never treated as equals by the minority white segments that complement the national demographic tableau, nor are they today. This minority has maintained an exclusive grip on all power, welfare, health, education, and national income.

It is scandalous to note that significant portions of the Euro-Brazilian population began to arrive in Brazil at the end of the nineteenth century as poor and needy immigrants. Immediately they bought into the enjoyment of privileges which the conventional white society conceded them as partners in race and Eurocentric supremacy. These poor immigrants demonstrated neither scruples nor difficulties in assuming the racist mythologies in force in Brazil and Europe; endorsing the consequent contempt, humiliation, and discrimination enforced against blacks; and benefiting from these practices, filling the places in the labor market denied to ex-slaves and their descendants. Blacks were literally expelled from the system of production as the country approached the "abolitionist" date of May 13, 1888.

The contemporary condition of black people is worse than it was then. At the margins of employment, or left in situations of semiemployment and underemployment, black people remain largely excluded from the economy. Residential segregation is imposed on the black community by the double factor of race and poverty, marking off, as black living areas, ghettoes of various denominations: *favelas, alagados, poroes, mocambos, invasoes, conjuntos populares,* or *residenciais.* Permanent police brutality and arbitrary arrests motivated by racism contribute to the reign of terror under which blacks live daily. In such conditions, one comprehends why no conscious black person has the slightest hope that a progressive change can occur spontaneously in white society to the benefit of the Afro-Brazilian community. Slums swarm in all the large cities: Rio de Janeiro, São Paulo, Bahia, Recife, Brasilia, São Luis de Maranhao, Porto Alegre, are a few examples. Statistics on these *favelados* (residents of the slums) express expanding misery in themselves alone. According to the Department of Social Services in São Paulo, published in *O Estado de Sao Paulo* on August 16, 1970, more than 60 percent of that city's enormous population lives in extremely precarious conditions. To be *favelado* means starvation or malnutrition, no health care, no lighting, water lines, public services, or houses—only makeshift shanties of cardboard or sheet metal, perched precariously on steep, muddy hills, or swamps. Yet São Paulo is Brazil's best-served city in terms of water and sewer lines; with this in mind we can get an idea of the impossible living and hygienic conditions in which the Afro-Brazilian vegetates all over this country. In Brasilia, according to the magazine *Veja* (October 8, 1969), 80,000 of 510,000 inhabitants of the federal capital were *favelados.* In Rio de Janeiro, the percentage oscillates between 40 and 50 percent of the population. The vast majority of Brazilian *favelados,* 95 percent or more, are of African origin. Such a situation characterizes irrefutable proof of racial segregation; the converse also holds true, the vast majority of black people in Brazil are *favelados.*

Up to now we have dealt with the urban black population. It is necessary to emphasize that the great majority of African descendants still live in the countryside, slaves in fact: slaves of a feudal seignorial landholding and social system, in a situation of total destitution, as peasants, sharecroppers or migrant workers. One could say that these people do not live a life of human beings.

The urban segment of the Afro-Brazilian population makes up a category which the Annual Statistical Report of the Brazilian Institute of Geography and Statistics calls "service employees," a strange euphemism for the severe underemployment and semiemployment which marks the lives of almost 4.5 million Brazilians.[13] Such a euphemism is ironic, since this classification picks up masses of people "employed" without fixed pay, i.e., odd-jobsmen living the small daily adventure of trying to shine shoes, wash cars, deliver packages or messages, sell fruit or candy on the street, and so on—all for the miserable and unreliable "salary" of pennies.

This is an imperfect sketch of a much graver situation which has been the reality of Afro-Brazilians through the entire course of their history. From this reality is born the urgent necessity of black people to defend their survival and assure their very existence as human beings. *Quilombos* were the results of this vital exigency for enslaved Africans, to recover their liberty and human dignity through escape from captivity, organizing viable free societies in Brazilian territory. The multiplicity in space and time of the *quilombos* made them an authentic, broad, and permanent sociopolitical movement. Apparently a sporadic phenomenon in the beginning, *quilombos* were rapidly transformed from the improvisation of emergency into the methodical and constant life form of the African masses who refused to submit to the exploitation and violence of the slave system. *Quilombismo* was structured in associative forms that could be found in whole independent communities in the depths of forests or in jungles of difficult access, facilitating their defense and protecting their economic, social, and political organization. *Quilombos* could also follow models of organization permitted or tolerated by the authorities, frequently with ostensibly religious (Catholic), recreational, charity, athletic, cultural, or mutual assistance objectives. Whatever their appearances and declared objectives, all of them fulfilled an important social function for the black community, performing a relevant and central role in sustaining African continuity and serving as genuine focal points of physical, as well as cultural, resistance. Objectively, this web of associations, brotherhoods, clubs, *terreiros* (houses of worship of Afro-Brazilian religion), *tendas, afoches*, samba schools, *gafieiras, gremios, confrarias*, were and are *quilombos* legalized by ruling society. On the other side of the law are the underground, secretive *quilombos* we know of. Nevertheless, the "legalized" and the "illegal" form a unity, a unique human, ethnic, and cultural affirmation, at once integrating a practice of liberation and assuming command of their own history. This entire complex of African social phenomena, of Afro-Brazilian *praxis*, I denominate *quilombismo*.

It is important to note that this tradition of *quilombist* struggle has existed throughout centuries and exists throughout the Americas. In Mexico, these societies were called *cimarrones*; in Venezuela, *cumbes*; in Cuba and Colombia, *palenques*; in Jamaica and the United States, maroon societies.[14] They have proliferated throughout the Caribbean and South and Central America. Researching and building upon the history of these free African societies in the Americas, and their cultural, economic, political, and social bases, Afro-Americans throughout the entire hemisphere can consolidate their true heritage of solidarity and struggle. *Quilombismo* and its various equivalents throughout the Americas, expressed in the legacy of *cumbes, palenques, cimarrones* and maroons, constitutes an international alternative for popular black political organization.

Easy confirmation of the enormous number of Black Brazilian organizations that have taken the title, in the past and the present, of *quilombo*, or the name of Palmares (evoking the Republic of Palmares, a huge community of *quilombos* which resisted the armed aggression of the Portuguese and the Dutch for a full century, from 1595–1695), testifies to the significance of the *quilombist* example as a dynamic value in the tactics and strategies of survivial, resistance, and progress of African communities in contemporary Brazil. In effect, *quilombismo* has already revealed itself as a factor capable of mobilizing the black masses in a disciplined manner, because of its deep psychosocial appeal, rooted in the history, culture, and experience of Afro-Brazilians. The Unified Black Movement Against Racism and Racial Discrimination registers its *quilombist* concept in the following definition of Black Consciousness Day, published in a 1978 manifesto:

We, Brazilian Blacks, proud of descending from Zumbi, leader of the Black Republic of Palmares, which existed in the state of Alagoas from 1595 to 1696, defying Portuguese and Dutch dominion, come together, after 283 years, to declare to the Brazilian people our true and effective date: November 20, National Black Consciousness Day!

The day of the death of the great Black national leader Zumbi, responsible for the first and only Brazilian attempt to create a democratic society, free, in which all people—Blacks, Indians, and whites—achieved a great political, economic and social advance. An attempt which was always present in all quilombos.[15]

A continuity of this consciousness of political-social struggle extends through all Brazilian states with a significant population of African origin. The *quilombist* model has remained active as an idea-force, a source of energy-inspiring models of dynamic organization, since the fifteenth century. In this dynamic, almost always heroic process, *quilombismo* is in a constant process of revitalization and remodernization, attending to the needs of the various historical times and geographical environments which imposed upon the *quilombos* certain differences in their organizational forms. But essentially they were alike. They were (and are), in the words of Afro-Brazilian historian Beatriz Nascimento, "a place where liberty was practiced, where ethnic and ancestral ties were reinvigorated." Nascimento shows in her scholarly work that the *quilombo* exercised "a fundamental role in the historical consciousness of the Black people."[16]

One perceives the *quilombist* ideal, diffuse but consistent, permeating all levels of black life, in the most recondite wanderings and folds of Afro-Brazilian personality. It is a strong and dense ideal that remains, as a rule, repressed by the systems of domination; other times it is sublimated through various defense mechanisms furnished by the individual or collective unconscious. It also happens, at times, that black people appropriate certain mechanisms that the dominant society concedes to them, intending them as instruments of control. In this reversal of ends, black people utilize such unconfessed propositions of domestication like an offensive boomerang. Such is the example left us by João Candeia, composer of sambas and a black man intelligently dedicated to the rehabilitation of his people. He organized the Quilombo Samba School, in the poor outlying areas of Rio de Janeiro, with a deep sense of the political/social value of the samba for the collective progress of the black community. (Samba schools are generally a means of diversionary control, relegating black creative energies to white-controlled commercial channels in the context of Carnaval, the great tourist attraction.)

This important member of the *quilombist* family, Candeia, recently passed away, but up to the instant of his death he sustained a lucid vision of the objectives of the entity he founded and presided over, the Quilombo Samba School, in the spirit of the most legitimate interests of the Afro-Brazilian people. For illustrations, it is enough to leaf through the book he authored, along with Isnard, and to read passages like this one:

Quilombo Recreational Group for Black Art (Samba School) . . . was born of the necessity to preserve all the influence of the Afro in Brazilian culture. We intended to call the Brazilian people's attention to the roots of Brazilian Black art. The position of "Quilombo" is, principally, against the importation of readymade cultural products produced abroad.[17]

In this passage the authors touch upon an important point in the *quilombist* tradition: the nationalist character of the movement. Nationalism here must not be translated as xenophobia. *Quilombismo*, an anti-imperialist struggle, identifies itself with Pan-Africanism and sustains a radical solidarity with all peoples of the world who struggle against exploitation, oppression, and poverty, as well as with all inequalities motivated by race, color, religion, or ideology. Black nationalism is universalist and internationalist in itself, in that it sees the national liberation of all peoples and respects their unique cultural and political integrity as an imperative for world liberation. Faceless uniformity in the name of a "unity" or "solidarity," conditioned upon conformity to the dictates of any Western social model, is not in the interests of oppressed non-Western peoples. *Quilombismo*, as a nationalist movement, teaches us that every people's struggle for liberation must be rooted in their own cultural identity and historical experience.

In a pamphlet entitled *Ninety Years of Abolition*, published by the Quilombo Samba School, Candeia registers the fact that "It was through the Quilombo, and not the abolitionist movement, that the struggle of the Black people against slavery was developed."[18] The *quilombist* movement is far from having exhausted its historical role. It is as alive today as in the past, for the situation of the black community remains the same, with small alterations of a superficial character. Candeia goes on to say:

The Quilombos were violently repressed, not only by the forces of the government, but also by individuals interested in the profits they would obtain by returning escapees to their owners. These specialists in hunting escaped slaves earned a name of sad recall: bush captains.[19]

Citation of the bush captains is important. As a rule they were mulattoes, that is, light-skinned blacks assimilated by the white ruling classes and pitted against their African brothers and sisters. We must not allow ourselves today to be divided into adverse categories of "blacks" and "mulattoes," weakening our fundamental identity as Afro-Brazilians, Afro-Americans of all the continent; that is, Africans in the diaspora.

Our Brazil is so vast, so much still unknown and "undiscovered," that we can suppose, without a large margin of error, that there must exist many rural black communities, isolated, without ostensive connection to the small cities and villages, in the interior of the country. These are tiny localities, unlinked to the mainstream of the country's life, maintaining African or quasi-African life styles and habits, under a collective agricultural regimen of subsistence or survival. Many might continue to use their original language brought from Africa, clumsy or transformed, it may be true, but still the same African language, conserved in the species of *quilombismo* in which they live. At times they may even earn special and extensive attention in the press, as has occurred with the community of Cafundo, situated in the area of Salto de Pirapora, in São Paulo state. The members of this African community inherited a plantation from their colonial master; recently their lands have been invaded by surrounding landowners. These white *latifundiarios* (giant landholders), with their slaver mentality, cannot accept the idea that a group of African descendants can possess real property. They are bent on destroying Cafundo. This is not a unique situation, but it is one which has received publicity, mobilizing blacks of the city of São Paulo in their defense. The foremost organization of this nature is ECO (Experiencia Comunitaria), a group that works under the able leadership of Hugo Ferreira da Silva.

In 1975, the first time I visited the town of Conceicão do Mato Dentro, in Minas Gerais state, I had the opportunity of meeting one of the villagers of a black community in that area similar to Cafundo. These Africans had also inherited their property, according to this villager, a black man 104 years old, mentally and physically active and agile. Every day, he would walk a distance of nearly 10 kilometers on foot, and so maintained the contact of his people with the town of Conceicao do Mato Dentro.

The advance of big landowners and real estate speculators onto the lands of black people calls for a broad and intensive investigation. This is happening in the cities as well as in rural areas. It was noted in the magazine *Veja*, for instance:

Since their long-ago appearance in Salvador, almost two centuries ago, the Candomble *terreiros* (houses of worship) have always been harassed by severe police restrictions. And, at least in the last twenty years, the police siege has been considerably strengthened by a powerful ally: real estate expansion, which has extended to areas distant from the center of the city, where drums resounded. Worse yet, at no time has the Mayor's office sketched legal boundaries to protect these strongholds of Afro-Brazilian culture—even though the capital of Bahia extracts fat dividends from exploitation of the tourism fomented by the magic of the Orishas. And never have sanctions been known to be applied to the unscrupulous landlords of plots neighboring the houses of worship, to take over areas of the *terreiros* with impunity. This was how, a few years back, the Saint George of the Old Mill Beneficent Society, or White House Terreiro, ended up losing half of its former area, 7,700 meters square. Even more unlucky, the Saint Bartholemew of the Old Mill Society of the Federation, or Bogum Candomble, impotently watches the rapid reduction of the sacred space where stands the mythical ''tree of Azaudonor''—brought from Africa 150 years ago and periodically attacked by a neighbor who insists upon lopping off its most leafy branches.[20]

With all reason, cinematographer Rubem Confete recently denounced, in a round-table discussion sponsored by the news magazine *Pasquim*:

How much was robbed from the Black people! I know five families who lost all of their land to the government and to the Catholic Church. Jurandir Santos Melo was the owner of land that stretched from the current airport of Salvador to the city. Today he is a simple taxi driver, living on small savings. The family of Ofelia Pittman owned all the area that today is the MacKensie (University in Sao Paulo). This is more serious than is generally thought, because there was a time when Black people had representation and economic strength.[21]

Here we see how ruling society closed in the circle of destitution, hunger, and genocide against African descendants. Even those few individuals, the rare exceptions that by some miracle manage to surpass the implacable frontiers of poverty or religious institutions—those who have occupied a certain space over centuries find their estates invaded and their families usurped from their lands!

QUILOMBISMO: A SCIENTIFIC HISTORICAL-CULTURAL CONCEPT

Conscious of the extent and depth of the problems they confront, black people know that their opposition cannot be exhausted in the attainment of small gains in employment or civil rights, in the context of the dominant capitalist white society and its organized middle class. Black people understand that they will have to defeat all components of the system in force, including its intelligentsia. This segment was and is responsible for the ideological coverup of oppression by way of "scientific" theories of the biosocial inferiority of blacks, and by academic elaboration of the ideology of whitening (socially compulsory miscegenation) or the myth of "racial democracy." This Euro-Brazilian "intelligentsia," along with its European and North-American mentors, fabricated a set of historical or human "sciences" that assisted in the dehumanization of Africans and their descendants, serving the interests of the Eurocentric oppressors. Therefore, European and Euro-Brazilian science is not appropriate to black people's needs. A historical science which does no service to the history of the people it deals with is negating itself.

How can Western human and historical sciences—ethnology, economics, history, anthropology, sociology, etc.—born, cultivated and defined by other peoples, in an alien socioeconomic context, offer useful and effective service to African people worldwide, their existential realization, their problems, aspirations and projects? Can the social sciences elaborated in Europe or in the United States be so universal in their application? Black people know in their very flesh the fallaciousness of the "universalism" and "objectivity" of this Eurocentric "science." Indeed, the idea of an historical science that is pure and universal is now passé, even in European circles.

Black people require a scientific knowledge that allows them to formulate theoretically—in systematic and consistent form—their experience of almost five centuries of oppression, resistance and creative struggle. There will be inevitable errors, perhaps, in our search for systematization of our social values, in our efforts toward self-definition and self-determination of ourselves and our future paths. For centuries we have carried the burden of the crimes and falsities of "scientific" Eurocentrism, its dogmas imposed upon our being as the brands of a definitive, "universal" truth. Now we return to the obstinate "white"

segment of Brazilian society its lies, its ideology of European supremacy, the brainwashing with which it intended to rob us of our humanity,
our national identity, our dignity, our liberty. By proclaiming the demise
of Eurocentric mental colonization, we celebrate the advent of *quilombist* liberation.

Black people have a collective project: the erection of a society
founded on justice, equality, and respect for all human beings; on
freedom; a society whose intrinsic nature makes economic or racial
exploitation impossible; an authentic democracy, founded by the des-
titute and disinherited of the country. We have no interest in the simple
restoration of obsolete types and forms of political, social, and economic
institutions; this would serve only to procrastinate the advent of our
total and definitive emancipation, which can come only with radical
transformation of existing socioeconomic and political structures. We
have no interest in proposing an adaptation or reformation of the models
of capitalist class society. Such a solution is not to be accepted as an
ineluctible mandate. We trust in the mental integrity of the black people,
and we believe in the reinvention of ourselves and our history, a reinvention of Afro-Brazilians whose life is founded on our own historical
experience, built by utilizing critical and inventive knowledge of our
own social and economic institutions, battered as they have been by
colonialism and racism. In sum, to reconstruct in the present a society
directed toward the future, but taking into account what is still useful
and positive in the stores of our past.

An operative conceptual tool must be developed, then, within the
guidelines of the immediate needs of the Black Brazilian people. This
tool must not and cannot be the fruit of arbitrary or abstract cerebral
machinations. Nor can it be a set of imported principles, elaborated
from the starting point of other historical contexts and realities. The
crystallization of our concepts, definitions and principles must express
black collective experience, in culture and in praxis, reincorporating
our integrity as a people in our historic time, enriching and expanding
our capacity for struggle.

Where do we find such experience? In the *quilombos*. *Quilombo* does
not mean escaped slave, as the conventional definitions have indicated.
It means fraternal and free reunion, or encounter; solidarity, living
together, existential communion. *Quilombist* society represents an advanced stage in sociopolitical and human progress in terms of economic
egalitarianism. Known historical precedents confirm this position. As

an economic system, *quilombismo* has meant the adaptation of African traditions of communitarianism and/or Ujamaa to the Brazilian environment. In such a system, relations of production differ basically from those that prevail in the capitalist economy, based on the exploitation and social degradation of work, founded on the concept of profit at any human cost, particularly the cost of the lives of enslaved Africans. *Quilombismo* articulates the diverse levels of collective life whose dialectic interaction proposes complete fulfillment and realization of the creative capacities of the human being. All basic factors and elements of the economy are of collective ownership and use. Work is not defined as a form of punishment, oppression, or exploitation; work is first a form of human liberation, which the citizen enjoys as a right and a social obligation.

The *quilombos* of the sixteenth, seventeenth, eighteenth and nineteenth centuries left us a patrimony of *quilombist* practice. It is for the black people of today to sustain and amplify the Afro-Brazilian culture of resistance and affirmation of our truth. A method of social analysis, comprehension, and definition of a concrete experience, *quilombismo* expresses scientific theory: a scientific theory inextricably welded to our historical practice, that can effectively contribute to black people's liberation from centuries of inexorable extermination.

Condemned to survive surrounded and permeated by hostility, Afro-Brazilian society has nevertheless persisted throughout almost 490 years, under the sign of permanent tension. It is this tension, the tension of struggle—repression and resistance—that embodies the essence and process of *quilombismo*.

To assure the fullest human condition of the Afro-Brazilian masses is the ethical grounding of *quilombismo*, and its most basic concept. *Quilombismo* is a scientific historical philosophy whose pivotal focal point is the human being, as actor and subject (not merely as passive object, as in the Western scientific tradition), within a worldview and a conception of life in which science constitutes one among many other paths to knowledge.

NOTES

1. The terms "America," "Afro-American," and "Euro-American" in this chapter refer to all of the Americas and not to the United States exclusively.

2. Cheikh Anta Diop, *The African Origin of Civilization: Myth or Reality*, trans. Mercer Cook (Westport, Conn.: Lawrence Hill, 1974), p. xiv.

3. Cheikh Anta Diop, *Cultural Unity of Black Africa* (Chicago: Third World Press, 1978) p. 212.

4. Ibid., p. 45.

5. J. Olumide Lucas, *The Religion of the Yorubas* (Lagos: C.M.S. Bookshop, 1948), p. 18; and Diop, *The African Origin of Civilization*, p. 184.

6. Manuel Orozco y Berra, *Historia Antiqua y de la Conquista de Mexico* (Mexico City: G.A. Esteua, 1880).

7. Ivan Van Sertima, *They Came Before Columbus*, (New York: Random House, 1976), pp. 110–62.

8. R. A. Jairazbhoy, *Ancient Egyptians and Chinese in America* (Ottawa: Rowman and Littlefield, 1974); Lopez de Gomara, *Historia de Mexico* (Antwerp: Por I. Bellero, 1554); Alexander Von Wurthenau, *Unexpected Faces in Ancient America* (New York: Crown Publishers, 1975); and Leo Weiner, *Africa and the Discovery of America* (Chicago: Innes and Sons, 1922).

9. Elisa Larkin Nascimento, *Pan-Africanismo e Sul-America: Emergencia de uma Rebelião Negra* (Rio de Janeiro: Editora Vozes, 1980).

10. Sertima, *They Came Before Columbus*, p. 152.

11. Ibid., p. 155.

12. Nascimento, *Pan-Africanismo*, p. 139.

13. Institute of Geography and Statistics, Annual Statistical Report, 1970, in Joao Quartim, *Dictatorship and Armed Struggle in Brazil* (New York: Monthly Review Press, 1971), p. 152.

14. Richard Price, ed., *Maroon Societies: Rebel Slave Communities in the Americas* (Garden City: Anchor Books, 1973); Clovis Moura, *O Negro: de Bom Escravo a Mau Cidadao* (Rio de Janeiro: Editora Conquisto, 1971).

15. *Quilombo Manifesto*, November 1978.

16. Beatrize Nascimento, "O Quilombo do Jabaquara," *Revista de Cultura Vozes* (April 1979), p. 3.

17. João Candeia and V. Isnard, *Escola de Samba-Arvore que esquec a raiz* (Rio de Janeiro: Editora Lidador/SEEC-RJ, 1978), pp. 87–88.

18. Candeia, *Ninety Years of Abolition* (Rio de Janeiro: Quilombo Samba School, 1978), p. 7.

19. Ibid., p. 5a.

20. *Veja*, Urban Section (December 10, 1975), p. 52.

21. *Pasquim* (September 14, 1979), p. 4.

12

THE CONCEPT OF AFRICAN PERSONALITY: SOCIOLOGICAL IMPLICATIONS

MWIZENGE S. TEMBO

The publication of Alex Quaison-Sackey's *Africa Unbound* in 1963, J. A. Sofola's *African Culture and the African Personality* in 1973, and Molefi Asante's *Afrocentricity* in 1980, are testaments to the abiding intellectual concern with the African personality. The concept generally refers to the manifestations of cultural uniqueness among Africans as reflected in their behavior, social norms, customs, values, beliefs, religious zeal, attitudes, explanations of the cosmos and the supernatural, social and political systems historically or in contemporary times.

The concept of the African personality has been addressed by many past and present Africans and Afro-Americans. It has been defined differently when used to designate all the black people with an African heritage—mainly those of the Caribbean Islands and the United States of America. Let us examine a few of these definitions, some of which do not precisely define the African Personality but merely seek to describe and explain the personality and cultural uniqueness of Africans. Kenneth Kaunda explains:

Possibly "Psychology" is not the appropriate word, but I do believe that there is a distinctively African way of looking at things, of problem solving and indeed of thinking—we have our own logic-system which makes sense to us, however, confusing it might be to the Westerner. If we were, from my own observation, to try to summarize the difference between African and Western psychology. . . I would say that the Westerner has a problem solving mind whilst the African has a situation experiencing mind.[1]

In the words of D. Chisiza:

There is a tendency in the West, whether the Westerners themselves know it or not, for people to assume that man lives to work. We believe that man works to live. This view of life gives rise to our high preference for leisure. With us, life has always meant the pursuit of happiness rather than the pursuit of beauty or truth. We pursue happiness by rejecting isolationism, individualism, negative emotions, and tensions, on the one hand; and by encouraging positive emotions and habitual relaxation, and by restricting our desires on the other.[2]

Or, Cedric X (Clark) et al. feel that:

African psychology is the recognition and practice of a body of knowledge which is fundamentally different in origin, content, and direction than that recognized and practiced by Euro-American psychologists. . . . The differences between African psychology and Euro-American psychology reflect the differences between Black people and white people or, in terms of basic culture, between Africans and Europeans.[3]

In an article published in the *Présence Africaine*, N'daw explains: "The conception of man is different [among Africans] and, unlike that of Cartesian Europe, is never dualistic or dichotomic. There is never the separation between body and soul found elsewhere."[4] These quotations constitute only a small fraction of the numerous black and African definitions of what can be conceived as the "African personality."

Certain themes prevail in these works. For example, one fundamental assumption is that Africans live in communities with little or no emphasis on the individualism prevalent in Western society. Another is that the African lives by natural rhythms, hence establishing a primordial attachment to the universe and the cosmos. Because the African is immersed in the totality of the social life and because of his strong belief in nature and the ancestral spirits, the African finds it difficult to tear social phenomenon into small bits for purposes of abstract analysis and philosophy. This is, for example, what Kaunda implies when he describes the African as having a "situation experiencing mind," and the Westerner as having "a problem-solving mind."

The argument about the African personality arises mainly from two schools of thought. One is the Western and Western-oriented scholars who express the view that the African needs to exhibit Western traits of thought and culture in order to be considered advanced. This position is argued by European and some African writers with a Western orientation. It is of interest that no African-American has taken this position. The other school of thought maintains that the African behaves, thinks, and lives as he does because he is unique. It holds that Western education and culture should be used by the African so as to further enhance his uniqueness. A few of the views from these two opposing schools of thought will be briefly reviewed. The former will be termed the anti-African personality, the latter the pro-African personality.

ANTI-AFRICAN PERSONALITY SCHOOL

Barnett Potter quotes an incident in which an African appeared before a chief justice in the then Nyasaland (Malawi). The African was charged with murder. During the trial the African's defense was that he had been changed by magic into a crocodile. The chief justice's three African assessors, who had apparently been chosen for their intelligence and sobriety, agreed with the charged man's claim. "The Westerner may find this inconceivable but it is quite consistent with African's obsession with the supernatural."[5] Potter follows a line of argument seen in the writings of numerous racist thinkers who have been inclined to emphasize one type of consciousness over another. For example, Potter reports all of the stereotypes of blacks that the whites in southern Africa have ever created without analysis or judicious comment. On Africans and politics he writes:

I think it was Lessing who wrote that when Africans are educated they are deprived of all subjects of conversation between themselves except politics. Any two Europeans will discuss sports, weather, women, money, wisecracks, the theatre, cinema, clothes, even books and will perhaps mention politics in passing. Two educated Africans will discuss politics for hours on end and when they have finished talking about politics have nothing more to say to each other.[6]

A Nigerian author who has been roundly criticized for his lack of historical knowledge has stated that the African personality is a negative one in the contemporary world context. Arele Oyebola contends that the African society must initiate a revolution of the mind.

It is a revolution of the mind. It is the conquest of the right to think and admit that in all the crises of man's history, our race has always been the underdog. Ours is the only race that has never made it anywhere in the world. We have for too long remained a poor imitator of the other races.[7]

Oyebola dismisses historical records which claim the greatness of Africa's past in Egypt, Ethiopia, Nubia, and Mali as keeping us from progress. Discussing the African's pride in the virtues of African communal life, life by rhythm, and strong belief in the supernatural, Oyebola declares these charactistics insufficient and claims that there is no significant way in which they can contribute to an advancement in technology.

As peoples who are just emerging from centuries of backwardness, foreign domination and dehumanization, the concept of African personality is a constructive force for the Blacks. But the idea that black man's past, his religious and spiritual life, his respect for elders and communal spirit are more important than his technology is inimical to our progress.[8]

The anti-African personality school attacks the African past as retrogressive and reactionary. This school of thought does not entertain at length any questions about why Africans behave and think as they do. Implicitly, this school of thought emphasizes Westernization as the "solution" to Africa's lag in electronic technology without recognizing Africa's superiority in spiritual and cultural sectors.

With an identical orientation, R.A. LeVine goes into further detail.[9] He states that evidence indicates that the African society is distinguishable from societies elsewhere. LeVine further says that there are certain characteristics which are distinctively African and that prevail with dominant frequency in Africa: subsistence agriculture, polygamous marriages, strong and wide family and kinship relationships, and bride price (dowry) as a marriage custom. He suggests seven other characteristics which he claims are widely shared by all Africans on the continent; social distance between persons differing in age and sex, age-sex hierarchy, emphasis on material transactions in interpersonal relations, functional diffuseness of authority relations; a tendency to blame and fear others under stress, a relative absence of separation anxiety and related effects, and, finally, concreteness of thought. Some of these characteristics which LeVine ascribes to most Africans are, at best, highly subjective value judgments of the African society, by a person who has hardly lived within it, and they implicitly assume that Western social values should prevail in Africa.

His assertion that there is an emphasis on material transactions in interpersonal relations among Africans is vastly exaggerated. How many material goods do Africans have which could generate a reliance on their exchange, of the magnitude that LeVine suggests? A few cattle, a couple of chickens, several goats perhaps. He claims that Westerners put emotional involvement in a relationship first and that material aspects are only incidental but expresses ignorance as to whether this is hypothetical or genuine among Westerners. Consider the volume of material goods that are exchanged among Westerners to express "love." They would likely far exceed the volume exchanged by Africans in personal relationships.

In the same vein, LeVine identifies food and feeding as one of the most important ways of expressing interpersonal relationships among Africans. "In many domains of behavior that do not involve actual feeding or oral activity—economics, sexuality, political succession—linguistic idioms, metaphors, and imagery derived from eating are widely used."[10] This is hardly surprising in a harsh environment where members of the society can easily be struck by famine and constantly experience seasonal food shortages. Since the African society does not have an excessive availability of food in restaurants at every bush corner, survival dictates the development of norms of this nature. On second thought, it might seem that LeVine's point is entirely missed since he contends that he is only making "objective" academic observations.[11] The alarming fact is that, when such a statement is made by a Westerner, it has hidden implications and meaning. For example, the issue of material goods and food being of central significance in relationships among Africans is often regarded as further clarification and speculation. Perhaps the reason why Africans overemphasize food might be the same reason Westerners overemphasize overt "love" in speech and behavior to other human beings, pets, and plants. Perhaps genuine love is diminishing.

Another point related to this one is LeVine's assertion that the Westerner desires intimacy in social relationships. He says this is evident in the hugging, kissing, and kind treatment of animals. Whereas, the African lacks intimacy in relationships. For this reason he suggests that there is a relative absence of separation anxiety and its related effects when two apparently intimate Africans are separated.

The formality of primary group relationships and the relative absence of separation anxiety make physical separation of husband and wives, parents and children, less painful and disruptive to the individual than in our culture and the emphasis on material obligation makes it possible to maintain relationships during prolonged absences.[12]

This observation, which is obviously made by an individual external to the entire African social experience, is erroneous. Hugging and kissing are not only inadequate as criteria for exhibiting affection or intimacy, but in this instance endorse cultural values for another society whose standards for expression of love and intimacy are different. This observation has elements of ethnocentricism.

It is one thing for an individual to leave his home voluntarily and spend ten years away from his wife, children, and relatives without any "separation anxiety." It is another thing for individuals to be torn apart from wives and relatives through extraneous conditions of slavery, colonialism, and present underdeveloped economies under neocolonialism. An African intellectual who has known how the Africans feel and perhaps express their loneliness in the absence of spouses and relatives would not agree with such a blatantly biased view. To add insult to injury, LeVine asserts that so long as the husband provides his wife with kids, a pregnancy every two years, he can be away for long periods of time, and the relationship will still be the same. These are the kinds of arguments used by pro-apartheidists to justify labor migration which results in the separation of black families in South Africa.

PRO-AFRICAN PERSONALITY SCHOOL

The pro-African personality school of thought is sympathetic toward the African and seeks to analyze the personality issue as a genuine and authentic subject of social inquiry. The proponents of this school of thought generally maintain that the African social consciousness owes its origins to the rapid and mostly destructive effects of slavery, colonialism, and, in contemporary times, neocolonialism. The African social consciousness has been described as a unique and genuine system of social thought and character arising from environmental conditions and historical experiences which are predominantly different from those of Asia, Europe, and the United States. Scholars who offer more abstract theories of African personality are Senghor, Mbiti, Cesaire, and Sofola.

Molefi Asante's Afrocentricity is also finding intellectual currency among writers.

Negritude, as one form of expression, older than Afrocentricity, seeks to define the African's personality in terms of his total response to the environment: emotions, responses to nature, speech, communal existence, explanations of the cosmos and beliefs in the supernatural. "Quite simply, negritude is the sum total of the values of the civilization of the African world."[13]

Senghor explains the characteristics and virtues of the African culture and the significance of articulating and defining them. He establishes the uniqueness of the African culture by discussing in detail African metaphysics, emotions, religion, conception, and apprehension of reality and democracy. He contrasts the African approach with the Western approach toward social phenomena in order to illustrate the difference.

For example, he explains the differences in the African and Western apprehension of reality. Senghor says that the European distinguishes the object from himself, "a pitiless factual analysis."[14] The European uses an object he killed or fixed for practical ends and, apart from mere scientific analysis, destroys it in the process. Whereas,

the African is, as it were, shut up inside his black skin. He lives in primordial night. He does not begin by distinguishing himself from the object, the tree or stone, the man or animal or social event. He does not keep it at a distance. He does not analyze it. Once he has come under its influence, he takes it like a blind man, still living, into his hands. He does not fix it or kill it.[15]

Senghor further mentions that Africans react more naturally to stimuli because of rhythm. The African has direct reactions to sensations which give rise to memory, language, and art. Africans live in symbiosis with others in the communal society. As Senghor puts it, "Subject and object are dialectically confronted in the very act of knowing one another."[16]

The concept of negritude is said to have been the reaction of black intellectuals to the effects of colonialism, including the cumulative effects of the slavery, such as a racial inferiority complex. It was a literal and ideological movement of French-speaking black intellectuals in Africa in conjunction with black people in America and the West Indies. The movement sought to fight what they saw as a subjection of black people to the political, social, and moral domination of the West. "Negritude as we had then began to conceive and define it was a weapon of defense and attack and inspiration rather than an instrument of construction."[17]

Senghor further describes the nature of negritude and seeks to pick out strands of behavior in the African consciousness which are said to reflect characteristics or dominant traits of negritude. For example, "emotive disposition" represents a being of emotion. It is further claimed that even the physical constitution of the African predisposes him to respond to the external world in such a way that it becomes an engulfing experience in which the whole of the self is involved, and, by implication, no distinction is made between the physical and psychic self on the one hand and the external natural environment on the other. This assertion is confirmed by the author's own observation. Most Americans, it seems, cannot perceive a social experience such as a beautiful sunset, a meal, or the like unless they mention in advance that it is beautiful, nice, or looks good. It seems essential and an integral part of the experience to know and mention that one is experiencing enjoyment before he can perceive the enjoyment of ecstasy inherent in nature. My argument (which is in slight contradiction with some elements of negritude) is not that one or the other is better but that both should be regarded as genuine and legitimate perceptions of the social and natural environment.

In Abiola's words "Senghor derives from his exposition of the distinctive psychology of Negro-African, what one might call a theory of knowledge implicit in the African's attitude to the world, a black epistemology."[18]

From what has transpired, it is evident that knowledge becomes discovery through emotion. It is this sensuous grasp of reality that Senghor refers to as intuition. He states that an African is not moved by the outward appearance of an object. One example which he cites to illustrate this point is that, "what moves him in water is not that it flows, is liquid and blue, but that is washes and purifies."[19] Physical appearance, therefore, is of less significance than function. This exposition seems to imply that the African looks at objects in terms of their utility in the dynamics of society and in their seeming existence in the continuation of the life cycle in nature.

Some critics like Abiola have denounced negritude.[20] Abiola maintains that the theoretical formulation of negritude is poor and that its practical implications are insignificant. Abiola claims that the theory of negritude seems to bear some racist connotations and, therefore, is not suitable as a basis for practical action.[21] Abiola's criticism, however, is an emotional reaction to some very hard questions raised by Senghor and others. Negritude can be challenged, to be sure, but it cannot be dismissed.

Senghor disagrees with these views. To support his assertions, he maintains rightly that there are some young African intellectuals who have read Marx carelessly and are also not cured of the inferiority complex taught by colonialism. These intellectuals consequently blame him for reducing the African "mode of knowledge to pure emotion."[22] They accuse him of denying that there is an African rationality and an African technology. Senghor refutes these notions and emphasizes that there is a white European civilization and a black African civilization, and according to him their significance is to explain the reasons for prevailing differences. He says that, contrary to popular belief, emotion is not failure of consciousness but rather "the accession to a higher state of consciousness."[23] It is the emotive attitude toward the world that explains African cultural values.

What is the relevance of negritude to the concept of African personality? Negritude bears a major positive and relevant element because it draws attention to the reality and existence of African cultural values and philosophy of life which were assumed not to exist in a dark and backward continent. Beyond this point, direct relevance to contemporary African thinking needs further serious searching.

Another pro-African personality proponent explains the African's social consciousness and its uniqueness in the modern world in terms of the traditional concept of time in Africa and how this has changed radically under modern conditions.[24] This change did not occur under normal and usual circumstances where creativity, assimilation, and accomodation were possible. On the contrary, colonialism and racial myths that Africa has essentially neither a culture nor a history because of technological backwardness made the African society adopt a modern Western concept of time in such a way that it has produced perverted features in Africans.

Mbiti says that the conception of time in African society was in terms of *sasa* which meant now, and *zamani* which meant the past. Events receded into *zamani* when they were over, and this included human beings after death, except that man joined his ancestors after death. African society did not have the concept of future in the Western mathematical sense. Mbiti asserts that the rapid changes brought by modernization have hardly been harmonious or creative for most Africans. He says: "Modern change has imported into Africa a future dimension of time. This is perhaps the most dynamic and dangerous discovery of the African peoples in the Twentieth Century."[25]

Finally, there is an observation that Mbiti makes which seems to be in direct opposition to the anti-African personality school of thought. Potter claims that educated Africans converse about politics exclusively. This might rightly be an aberration.[26] However, he provides only a weak and unconvincing explanation for this disposition.

On the other hand, Mbiti claims that Africans are obsessed with politics because they have only recently been released from the shackles of colonialism, when open political discussion was forbidden among Africans. In his words,

the spirit which ignited the fires of nationalism during the colonial days has not lost its power; it has ignited more fires since independence returned to the majority of African states; and it will continue to do so until its energy is harnessed and channeled in other directions. The political pot in Africa is still bubbling, and great is the man who can still it without getting smeared or even scorched.[27]

The sociologist Vernon Dixon, expresses views which bear some relevance to discussion of the pro-African personality school of thought.[28] Dixon states that the assumptions made in certain research often rule out explanation. He cites as an example the assumption that the nuclear family is the only valid form of marital organization. Accordingly, pathologies arise when there is no male head in a black family. This perspective is said to be determined by the orientation of the knowers. Hence, different world views lead to different research methodologies.

Dixon examines African and Euro-American differences in axiology (values which one holds), epistemology (how one knows) and logic (organization of what one knows). He quotes a variety of examples to illustrate the differences between the two societies. Under axiology he cites the "pure" Euro-American emphasis on the future which is anticipated to be bigger and better. Among Westerners, nobody wants to be old fashioned, and few are rarely satisfied with the present. Time is transformed into an object—sold, bought, and utilized as in the popular Western saying, "Time is money." Individuals with this disposition inherently, "function more effectively when activities are preplanned 'progress'

and time scheduled. Clock-time rules the day when the phenomenal world (object) is separated from self."[29] This is not the case in the African orientation in which time has to be experienced. That is why Mbiti says it is experienced as events which have occurred, those which are to take place, and those immediately to occur. Events which have not occurred, and those which have no likelihood of occurring, are in "no-time." Time has to be experienced in order to become real. Proceeding from this statement, the future is not real. Dixon says: "Since Africanized time orientation is governed by the dimensions of past and present, the drive for investment of the future-oriented Euro-American time becomes substantially less important."[30] Dixon suggests that the African orientation provides a way of knowing reality that is an alternative to the European way. The implication of Dixon's thesis is that the African orientation of thought vis-à-vis the African personality can be regarded as a positive alternative in modern intellectual orientation and social thought.

CONCLUSION

The implications of the African personality's theoretical model are that it provides a more contemporary and relevant approach to the sociological study of the African society. The approach promises possibilities of dismissing the popular traditional portrayal of the Africans as being a mere fertile ground for anthropological studies of exotic culture. About 75 percent of the African countries are today independent and sovereign. Generations of Africans are developing and emerging that will never have experienced explicit colonialism, and racial prejudice in their societies. These Africans cannot be defined exclusively in terms of Western-oriented metropolitans.

In considering the dominant social philosophies of the Western world today, it is clear that capitalism, Marxism, the Christian doctrine, and Cartesian dualism are concepts which evolved in line with the spirit of the times in the societies. These philosophies gained ground and recognizance because there was nothing better in existence to explain social phenomenon in the Western world. These views were often imposed on Africa during colonialism.

However, this is not the case in this day and age. The espousing of a philosophy per se is not enough. An imported philosophy has the disadvantage of attempting to change the status quo and a traditional way of thinking. This is the context in which the concept of the African personality should be viewed. The notion of the African personality should establish the point that African social consciousness is neither superior nor inferior to any other but certainly different.

There is an erroneous tendency to judge societies according to how much technological advancement they have made and then put them on a scale, with everything else becoming irrelevant. This is not very healthy as there is much more in societies than mere technology, although technology obviously makes life easier and more comfortable.

One of the serious shortcomings of the theories about African personality prior to African independence was that they emerged out of protest against racial injustice and colonialism, for example, negritude, pan-Africanism, and Biko's black consciousness, although the latter occurred in a society not yet free but within the context of continental freedom. When independence was achieved, charges were made around intellectual circles that these theories were either inadequate or no longer applicable to new African social aspirations and Africa's changing image. Critics like Abiola have charged mistakenly that negritude is racist and therefore negative.[31] Because of the rapidly changing image of the African society, the African personality theory should be expanded and integrated into an Afrocentric economic, social, and political theory where and whenever possible. This would serve two purposes: clarifying practical matters relating to economic development and further developing African intellectual theory.

From a practical perspective, the principles of African personality theory could be used for better planning, understanding, and implementation of policies relating to development programs in the African society because the theory will help to identify the limitations and possibilities in pursuing certain development policies. With regard to intellectual theory, a concerted effort on the part of African intellectuals to conduct research in different parts of Africa would yield a legitimate basis for the articulation of the theory so that it can relate to villagers on the one hand, and capture and explain the rapidly changing cultural values of African youth on the other hand. This is a complicated task. But it can be done.[32]

NOTES

1. Kenneth D. Kaunda, *A Humanist in Africa* (Lusaka: Veritas, 1966), p. 26.

2. Dunduza Chisiza. "The Outlook for Contemporary Africa," in *Two Centuries of African English*, ed. L. Brown (London: Heinemann Educational Books, 1973), p. 98.

3. Cedric X (Clark), D. Phillip McGee, Wade Nobles and Nàim Akbar, *Voodoo or I.Q.: An Introduction to African Psychology* (Chicago: Institute of Positive Education, 1976), p. 1. [Also in *The Journal of Black Psychology*, vol. 1, no. 2 (February, 1975).]

4. A. Nd'aw, "Is It Possible to Speak about an African Way of Thought?" .Présence Africaine, vol. 30, no. 58 (1966), p. 38.

5. Barnett Potter, *The Fault, Black Man* (Capetown: Howard Timmins, 1970), p. 23.

6. Ibid., p. 38.

7. Arele Oyebola, *Black Man's Dilemma* (Lagos: Sketch Publishing, 1976), p. 13.

8. Ibid., p. 15.

9. R. A. LeVine, "Patterns of Personality in Africa," in *Responses to Change: Society, Culture and Personality* (New York: D. Van Nostrand, 1976).

10. Ibid., p. 121.

11. Ibid., p. 116.

12. Ibid., p. 132.

13. Leopold Sedar Senghor, *Prose and Poetry*, ed. and trans. John Reed and Clive Wake (London: Heinemann Educational Books, 1965), p. 99.

14. Ibid., p. 29.

15. Ibid., p. 26.

16. Ibid., p. 32.

17. Ibid., p. 99.

18. Irele Abiola, "Negritude: Philosophy of African Being," *Nigeria Magazine*, FESTAC ed. nos. 122–23 (1977), p. 6.

19. Senghor, *Prose and Poetry*, 35.

20. Irele Abiola, "Negritude," pp. 1–13.

21. Ibid., p. 11.

22. Senghor, *Prose and Poetry*, p. 33.

23. Ibid., p. 35.

24. John S. Mbiti, *African Religions and Philosophy* (New York: Anchor Books, 1970).

25. Ibid., pp. 288–89.

26. Potter, *The Fault, Black Man*, pp. 15–37.

27. Mbiti, *African Religions*, pp. 286–87.

28. Vernon J. Dixon. "African-oriented and Euro-American Oriented World Views: Research Methodologies and Economics," *Review of Black Political Economy*, vol. 7, no. 2 (Winter 1971), pp. 119–56.

29. Ibid., p. 125.

30. Ibid., p. 130.

31. Irele Abiola, "Negritude" p. 11.

32. Chinua Achebe, "The Chi in Ibo Cosmology," in *Morning Yet on Creation Day* (London: Heinemann, 1975), pp. 131–45.

13

THE IMPLICATIONS OF AFRICAN-AMERICAN SPIRITUALITY

DONA RICHARDS

Throughout their sojourn in America Africans have been taught the separateness of themselves from Africa and Africans. The teaching has been so ingrained that even in those communities which are "most African" there is the greatest scandal of "being African."

PROBLEMS AND TERMS

I shall maintain that Africa survived the middle passage, the slave experience, and other trials in America because of the depth and strength of African spirituality and humanism. This spirituality allowed the survival of African-Americans as a distinctive cultural entity in New Europe. Furthermore, I shall contend in this chapter that it is our spirituality and vitality which defines our responses to Western culture and that response is universally African.

The argument of the Europeans is all too easy for us to accept. We look around us and, while in the Caribbean and in the black communities of South America, African retentions are often quite visible, black existence in North America is problematical. "How are we Africa?" we blacks ask. We do not know where to look for likeness? Not knowing ourselves, we have not known how to recognize manifestations of our heritage.

If we look deep enough, we will find that our deepest beliefs are shared beliefs, and that deep within we are one people.

Because it is much more difficult, and the evidence is less obvious, I will concentrate on the African-American experience in North America. Retentions in other areas are fascinating and point to the strength and resilience of African culture; but many of these retentions have already been well examined and they do not help to explain how all of us are African. The attempt to understand our experience in North America, however, has something critical to teach us about ourselves throughout the diaspora.

An understanding of our experience in North America necessitates the use of two concepts. They are *ethos* and *world view*—useful cultural concepts which refer to essential aspects of collective human experience. Ethos is intimately related to culture, both influencing it and being influenced by it. Ethos refers in part to the emotional substance of a cultural group; to their collective "emotional tone."[1] By using the term ethos we are accepting the idea that, when a group of people share a common heritage, a common set of experiences, and a common culture, an emotional bond is created between them. The fact that a people's experiences and historical circumstances are shared over long periods of time in the setting of the culture makes them one, and their oneness creates a common spirit. The idea of *spirit* is especially important for an appreciation of the African-American experience. Spirit is, of course, not a rationalistic concept. It cannot be quantified, measured, explained by or reduced to neat, rational, conceptual categories as Western thought demands. Spirit is ethereal. It is neither touched nor moved, seen nor felt in the way that physical entities are touched, moved, seen and felt. These characteristics make it ill-suited to the analytical mode most favored by European academics. We experience our spirituality often, but the translation of that experience into an intellectual language can never be accurate. The attempt results in reductionism.

Our spirit symbolizes our uniqueness as a people, or we could say that the African-American ethos is spiritual. The ethos of a people is related to special characteristics which identify them as a group, setting them apart from other groups. Our ethos refers to our emotional responses and reactions. It does not refer to consciousness or to self-conscious responses and reactions. It has to do with the way in which certain things make us feel good and others displease us. It is the bedrock of our aesthetic. It has to do with the things in life which excite us and those about which we share laughter. It helps to explain why we tend to ignore some things and why others make us cry. That is how ethos functions. It is not a psychological term. It does not refer to individual or idiosyncratic experience or response. Ethos, like culture, is understood to refer to shared reaction and response. The African-American ethos refers to our unique spirit and spiritual being. It is a result of our shared cultural history and is derived from Africa.

Ethos and world view are intimately related; both are byproducts of culture, and both help to create culture. One of the things that culture does for its members is to present them with a systematic way of ordering their experiences, these experiences together making up their phenomenal world. World view refers to the way in which a people make sense of their surroundings, of life, and of the universe. When we have difficulty making sense of life's circumstances and vicissitudes, we usually turn to religion. The term world view does not include our rituals, but it explains why they are necessary. Human beings cannot function in chaos; out of the chaos of life they create an ordered existence. The dominant theme or character of that order (world view) will be a function of their collective ethos.

Culture is ordered behavior. It is not created individually. All groups of people who have been historically related over long periods of time share a way of viewing the world and realities with which it presents them. A world view results from a shared cultural experience, just as it helps to form that experience. It presents us with a systematic set of ideas about many things. Its significance is profound, and it has far reaching effects on those who share it. It affects our perceptions of nature, of ourselves as human beings, of each other, and our relationship to all being. A world view helps to inject meaning into life and to determine which experiences and events are meaningful and which are not. It encompasses Metaphysic. We speak of the African metaphysic (cosmology, epistemology, ontology), indicating our conceptions of the structure of the universe, the relationship and origin of nature, truth and knowledge, reality and the nature of being.

A people's world view affects and determines behavior. A universe understood totally in materialistic or rationalistic terms will discourage spirituality. An ethos characterized by a will-to-power, by the need to control, will derive pleasure from a technical order, from conflict (war), from winning (destroying), and exploitation. African-Americans are forced to ask and to answer the question: "What happens when a people are forced to live (survive) within a culture based on a world view which is oppressive to their ethos?''

Once we understand the nature of the traditional African world view, we will see that it explains the African-American ethos and response to Western European culture and the experiences forced on us by the culture in its New European setting. We must begin, therefore, with an explanation of the traditional African world view, for this knowledge will enable us to recognize its expressions and manifestations in African-American life and culture.

UTARATIBU WA KUTIZAMA DUNIA: AFRICAN PHILOSOPHY AND WORLD VIEW

The African universe is conceived as a unified spiritual totality. We speak of the universe as *cosmos*, and we mean that all being is organically interrelated and interdependent. The Swahili speak of *utaratibu wa kutizama dunia* (the way of the world). The Western/European materialized universe does not yield cosmos. The essence of the African cosmos is spiritual reality; that is its fundamental nature, its primary essence. But realities are not conceived as being in irreconcilable opposition, as they are in the West, and spirit is not separate from matter. Both spiritual and material being are necessary in order for there to be a meaningful reality. While spiritual being gives force and energy to matter, material being gives form to spirit. Enlightenment and the acquisition of wisdom and knowledge depends to a significant degree on being able to apprehend spirit in matter. This crucial difference in European and African thought helps to explain the specialness of African-American spirituality. The mode of determining structure of the Western metaphysic is that of power, control, and destruction. Realities are split into pairs of opposing parts. Conventionally, one of these becomes valued, while its converse is understood as lacking value. One is good and the other is bad. It then becomes necessary (valued behavior) to attempt to destroy one (the bad), while the other ascends to supremacy. The human response to the universe, for instance, is separated into reason and emotion. Reason then becomes the valued aspect of humanity. It must be used to control or deny emotion in order for us to be properly human. Other opposing pairs, in the European view, are knowledge/opinion, objective/subjective, science/religion, mind/body, male/female, man/boy, white/black, and so forth.

To the African, on the other hand, the universe is made up of complementary pairs. These pairs are elements or principles of reality which are interdependent and necessary to each other, in a unified system. The divine being for instance, is androgynous and therefore able to reproduce itself. It does so in the form of male and female twins which then pair in order to reproduce.[2] The determining mode of the African world view is harmony. The goal is to discover the point of harmonious interaction, so that interferences become neutralized, allowing constructive energy to flow and to be received. In the African world view the human and the divine are not hopelessly separated, as they are in Western theology where the divine is defined as the negation of all that is human. It requires a miracle for them to interact. In Africa the human is divine, and the demonstration of this joining is the height of religious experience, as the spirits manifest themselves in us (spirit possession). To the African the sacred and the profane are close and can be experienced as unity. All of this is so because of the multidimensional nature of the African universe. Phenomena and events are understood on many different levels at once. The African universe is alive and rich, filled with myriad possibilities. It is a phenomenal universe.

The African world view is religious in that spiritual truths are thought to contain the essence of things. When Africans use the term religion here, they mean that which concerns itself with spirit. The spiritual is the foundation of all being because the universe is sacred. The universe was created (is continually recreated) by a divine act. We participate in that act as we perform rituals in imitation of the Creator and aspects of the Creator (Oludumare and Orisha, Onyame, and the Abosom, and so forth). Through association with this sacred universe, divinely created, life itself becomes sacred and a most precious gift to be cherished, preserved, passed on, and revitalized. Life is to be lived to its fullest. According to Leonard Barrett, the supreme value in terms of the African world view is "to live robustly."[3] That is, to live life with as much energy and as forcefully as we can. Much of African religious activity, therefore, involves the attempt to strengthen our *force vitale* or life force. It is the spirits (aspects of the deity), and the ancestors, who have the spiritual power to strengthen our *force vitale*, and so through sacrifice, offering, and ritual we ask them to help us in this way.

Sacrifice is a symbolic statement of the reciprocal nature of cosmic relationship. All beings within the cosmos are affected and they affect others. We take from the spirits, and so we must give to them. This conception, so essential in African religious thought, is radically different from Western theology. Through sacrifice we honor, and therefore strengthen the spirits and the ancestors. We keep them strong so that they will continue to be able to keep us strong. The relationship between the human and the divine, the heavenly and earthly spheres, is one of interdependence. The spirits need us, just as we need them; just as spirit needs matter to give form, and matter needs spirit to give it force, being, and reality.

Life, events, and phenomena derive meaning, value, and significance through relationship to an organic whole. The family or community is understood as just such a whole. And, since nothing of significance is merely physical, the community itself becomes a metaphysical reality. We say that the African family includes the dead, the living, and the yet unborn. Its significance is multidimensional; ancestor communion and its wholeness gives meaning and definition to the family members. In addition, the philosophical conception of ancestor communion helps to explain the African concept of sacred time. Spiritual realities are timeless, that is, they are not limited by ordinary categories of time and space. Through its association with spirit, matter becomes ontologically related to the eternal. Sacred time is not perceived lineally, but cyclically, and so categories and perceptions of past, present, and future are eliminated in religious life. These are terms applicable only within the profane, mundane, or secular world. John S. Mbiti is mistaken when he implies that reverence for the *zamani* means "looking towards the past."[4] Through sacred time, life and time are continually regenerated, space is expanded; the eternal is achieved! What is called past, present, and future in lineal terms, are not separated but are joined together in a phenomenal and spatial unity. This is made possible through the extraordinary mechanism of ritual drama.

Spirit does not die. If we continually make that religious and philosophical statement through ritual and if we remember, then the physically deceased members of the family continue to be a part of that family, and we are assured of immortality. For the family to be healthy, its continuity and wholeness must be continually experienced. It is through ancestors that we keep in touch with our sacred origins. We must perform the ritual of ancestor communion daily, ritual of spiritual union and communication. The continued spiritual existence of the physically deceased also manifests itself materially. The spirits of the ancestors take physical form in the new babies which are born to the community. Babies are therefore not new, but represent the timeless regeneration of man. The elders of the community do not die but upon physical death are reborn into the spiritual realm as ancestors.

African life is replete with ritual. It depicts interrelationships among beings in the universe. The principles of interdependence and reciprocity are symbolized in ritual sacrifice. It is through ritual that the unexplainable is understood, that chaos is made to be ordered within the logic of tradition. It is through ritual that trauma is avoided, crises dealt with and overcome, and difficult transitions perceived as passages between stages of normal growth and development.[5] Universally, in ritual the African combines life with artistic expression. Ritual is, in a sense, the ultimate philosophic expression of the African world view, for it is the modality within which the unity of the human and the divine is expressed, in which the unity of spirit and matter is perceived, and in which the eternal moment is achieved. When we perform rituals as our ancestors did, we become our ancestors and so transcend the boundaries of ordinary space and time and the limitations of separation which they impose. When we call the spirits and they enter our bodies, we symbolize in our being the joining of, and therefore communication between, two spheres of the universe: heaven and earth.

The theme of death and rebirth symbolized in our relationship to ancestors contributes to the philosophy which presents us with the eternal cycle of life. This theme is inherent in all ritual drama. It is this philosophy which remains the indomitable strength of a people long plagued by political powerlessness. In ritual drama we die and are reborn just as youth die and are reborn as adults, and as elders die and are reborn as ancestors, or as ancestors are given new life as they become new members of the group. In ritual we are energized and revitalized. Values and beliefs are redefined, reaffirmed, and reinterpreted, at once giving them added viability and sacralizing their new form.

African conceptions are expressed symbolically, and African culture is filled with symbols and symbolic behavior which reflect a "religious" world view. If these symbols are approached literally, African behavior makes no sense. Why set out portions of food for people who are not there? Because we are making a statement about the necessity and value of their spiritual presence, a statement which can be made materially because of the relationship between spirit and matter. Why should a carver make a sacrifice to the spirit of a tree from which he cuts? Because he is part of a culture which perceives the interrelationship and interdependence of all beings within the universe. If we take or destroy, we must give or rebuild; for there is one spiritual unity which joins us all, and, if we do not ritualize this truth, we will end by destroying ourselves.

The African universe has great depth and many dimensions. Its order is sacred. The parts within it relate in such a way that each is a reflection of the whole. In my being, as a person, I am a reflection of the universal order. That sacred order is constantly being communicated to us, through natural phenomena, through life, through experiences, through nature and natural events. A tree can therefore be understood as an expression of the sacred, a storm as a communication from the divine. The presence of a river or a mountain can bring the divine closer to us. They are ideal locations for ritual (prayer), since in their proximity we are able to transcend to sacred time and space.[6] African symbolism seeks to get at the essence of things; we are not satisfied with superficialities. The symbolic mode makes it possible for us to perceive the material manifestation of spirit. The symbolic nature of the African world view allows us to apprehend, through metaphor, the ambiguities and richness, even paradox, of phenomenal existence. The logic of rationalism does not do that. Through symbolism the universe can be approached in all its richness and potentiality. Imagine what it is reduced to by those who perceive only on a literal and material level.

The African-American, in his or her being, represents the embodiment of the confrontation of two divergent world views: a spiritual ethos inheriting a sacred, cosmic world view forced to adjust to a materialistic society in inhuman circumstance. What happens when the spiritual ethos of peoples of African origin is entrapped and exploited by an oppressive, materialistic society whose culture seeks to dominate them? Do they lose their integrity? Does their ethos and world view become distorted so that they are no longer recognizable as Africans? Do they indeed become Europeans? Or is it possible that a legacy of powerful metaphysical conceptions gives them the ability to revitalize themselves in spite of great suffering and imminent devastation? Is it possible that their souls are continually replenished by *ntu*—the universal life force?

MAAFA: THE HOLOCAUST (DEHUMANIZING CIRCUMSTANCE, HUMAN RESPONSE)

Maafa signifies, "Disaster, or great misfortune," in Kiswahili. The trade in African lives and the enslavement of African beings by Eu-

ropeans constituted the most thoroughly destructive act ever to be per-
petrated by one group of people upon another. That is so because of a
combination of factors which created a unique historical circumstance.
To begin with, within the setting of our enslavement, the ideology of
white supremacy was systematically reinforced by a set of interlocking
mechanisms and patterns which functioned to deny the validity of an
African humanity. This system of African oppression and denial was
buttressed by a materialistic, aggressive world view, and an increasingly
intense technically ordered society which sought to make Africans simple machines in the service of Europeans. European ideology dictated
that Europeans create inferior objects so that their self-concepts could
function positively within the context of their value system. Functioning
positively meant relating as superiors to inferior beings. If they could
not make themselves feel superior they were nothing, defeated in terms
of their own ethos and world view in which pleasure was derived only
from power and control. The shock of slavery was traumatic. The culture
from which we had been taken was humanly oriented, organized on the
basis of the recognition of the human need for love, warmth, and
interrelationship. Even the large state-organized societies were fundamentally kin-based in terms of the daily lives of most of the people.

The system and circumstance of slavery in New Europe sought to
destroy African values, African self-images and self-concepts. The African universe was disrupted. It became dysfunctional as the sense of
order that it offered dissolved. For the overwhelming majority of those
brought to North America and their direct descendants, the benefits of
African culture were stripped away—not one by one—but brutally, in
one sudden and total act. Family, language, kinship patterns, food,
dress, and formalized religion were gone. What replaced them was the
order of slavery. The object of the new order was to demonstrate the
African lack of values. It turned our humanity into weakness. To be
European was to have value, to be African was to be without personal
worth. And instead of the security of a kin-based society which imparted
emotional strength and positive self-images to its members, the slave
order created and depended on a constant state of terror. As long as
you denied your Africanness, your humanness, and pretended that you
did not mind watching others suffer around you, you were relatively
safe. Fear was the great immobilizer.

For the African, slavery meant chaos. The evil order of white supremacy and black exploitation was chaos to the African sensibility.

The imposed order of the whip, the subtle dehumanization of paternalism implied chaos and death to the African spirit. Herein lies the miracle of black existence in New Europe. Out of nothingness we built a world. In an environment which denied black being, we insisted on being.[7] Oppressed by dehumanizing circumstance we still found something in which to recognize enough of ourselves to revitalize our souls—to create new selves. From the very first we gave expression to the divine in us for it was our humanity. It was out of this expression of divinity that a reformulated, African-derived cultural expression was to emerge, a cultural expression peculiar to the North American circumstance, of necessity influenced by Europe, influenced by the harshness and paternalism of the slave condition, influenced even by the denigration of the African heritage. The expressions which emerged were our language, our music, our dance, our thought patterns, our laughter, our walk, our spirituality. These were the vehicles through which the African ethos expressed itself in America.

They took the material aspects of our culture and prohibited the continuance of our traditions. They took our drums—unconsciously understanding their meaning? Put in terms of the African world view, they attempted to isolate us, to cut us off from our source of spirit. For the African, this set of circumstances was disastrous. For us spiritual isolation implied permanent death. Our very existence was in jeopardy. To survive as Africans, to survive spiritually, we had to create meaning. We had to re-create order in the midst of chaos. According to the European world view, to be African was to be nothing. We were forced therefore to create something different, some form, within a modality compatible with the African world view through which we could make contact with the source. We needed to be energized. What an impossible task—to make sense of senselessness, yet that is what African value demanded. That is what Stanley Elkins and others do not understand. The trauma of slavery stripped us, but not of everything. It was the fact of being stripped which forced us to rely so heavily on a world view, that aspect of culture which creates order.[8] That world view, in turn, forced us to make just enough sense of the insanity of slavery, to create just enough of a belief-system to enable us to reestablish on foreign ground that driving energy for a continued vital existence which is the birthright of all descendants of Africa.

Faced with the realities of slave existence, we had to find ways of expressing, energizing and revitalizing the spiritual being we had salvaged from the wreckage of the holocaust—the effects of which were to last for more than 400 years. For unless this spirit was expressed, it could not be renewed. And if it were not renewed, the circle would not be complete and it would die. Out of the chaos and trauma of slavery, the spirit of Africa was reborn in the form of the African-American ethos.

The ultimate expression of the African world view is the phenomenon of ritual. Only through ritual can death be understood as rebirth. It is through ritual that new life was given to the African spirit. We performed and experienced ritual drama in North America. The modality of spontaneous ritual drama was foreign to the Euro-American ethos and therefore could not have come from that source. We performed the "ring shout" in the "hush harbors," the "night sings," and the "prayer meetin's."[9] Away from white surveillance, when we could, we would come together. We would gather slowly, a few at a time, at night—a special time for us. Night was special not only because the day's work was over, but also because night is when spiritual energies and powers are most potent. We gathered and enjoyed the warmth of our commonness, of our togetherness. We would form a circle, each touching those next to us so as to physically express our spiritual closeness. We "testified," speaking on the day's or the week's experience. We shared the pain of those experiences and received from the group affirmations of our existence as suffering beings. As we "laid down our burdens" we became lighter. As we testified and listened to others testify, we began to understand ourselves as communal beings, no longer the kind of person that the slave system tried to make of us.[10] Through our participation in these rituals, we became one. We became again, a community.

We also created vehicles for expressing the spirit and gaining strength which could help us during the day, in the midst of toil under the eyes of the masters and overseers. The African metaphysic does not distinguish sharply between sacred and mundane experience. As we worked in the fields when the sun was at its hottest and our backs hurt the most, when we felt the least like human beings, someone would break into a song. The song would catch on until it moved throughout the field, and its beauty would touch our spirits and say to us, "You can create and feel this beauty. You must be human. You have meaning."

Those very first songs in the fields were "fields-hollers," work songs, "sorrow songs," spirituals and blues all at the same time. To express beauty in the midst of ugliness is not to make a statement that exploitation, human misery, or slavery is beautiful. In the profanity of slave existence, the African ethos discovered its own sacred being through the vehicles of song and ritual, music and dance. Suffering became an opportunity to express spirit, and through its expression its existence was reaffirmed. African-Americans spiritualized the material world the Europeans had built. Our singing didn't say that our suffering was beautiful. It said that our condition was real, and in feeling its reality we felt our souls. (A totally different emphasis from Descartes' "I think therefore I am.") That is what it means to be a spiritual people. And that's why the spirituals, and the blues which would follow, are part of a continuum. As James Cone says, they are not contradictory. They are complementary. We needed both to express the whole truth.[11] Our rituals, our songs, our music and dance, became vehicles through which to contact the divine, media through which we reached the spiritual source and so received sustenance and energy from the knowledge of our specialness.

Ritual drama in African society is a multidimensional mechanism of cultural expression. It can be understood on metaphysical, religious, communal, and psychological levels simultaneously. Ritual drama involves the repetition of a sacred act performed in a prescribed manner. It is religiously understood, therefore, as an imitation of divine beings or of our revered ancestors. Events are placed within the context of a harmonious order and so are sacralized. We understand them better because they are placed within a familiar mode. That is the function of religion. Metaphysically, the sacred repetition of ritual implies extraordinary ontological definitions. Ritual during slavery brought the spirits and our ancestors to us. In spirit possession we became the spirits.

African ritual drama is used to make transitions smooth, so that they will not disrupt the continuity of personal and communal life. In slavery we used ritual to avoid permanent trauma and to make the transition from Africa to America. Cyclical, sacred time is achieved through ritual and we used it as a mechanism for renewal, replenishment, redefinition and rebirth. African ritual is a statement of continuity, unity, and community. When the life of the group is threatened, ritual is used to psychologically and emotionally strengthen its members by creating a sense of order which will better enable them to deal with their problems in a constructive way. Ritual drama kept us sane and gave us the courage to live. Ritual functions positively to deal with the anxieties, apprehensions, and ambivalencies which are endemic to human experience and to place them in proper perspective. It is cathartic, and catharsis is necessary for renewal. It is this philosophically profound, multidimensional cultural mechanism which we as Africans used in New Europe so that our spiritual being might periodically gain new life. African-American Ritual drama, so essential to the black ethos, accounts for the enduring strength and vitality of Africa in North America.

The "hush harbors" of the African slaves were the forerunners of the black church service, the penultimate expression of formalized African-American ritual drama. What are the spiritual, philosophico-religious, and communal dynamics and effects of that service to which black culture owes so much? Black church ritual takes place in sacred space, therefore, special things happen. The self can be transformed. We come prepared to be "uplifted," and to become a part of a sacred community..."one more time". We enter with a sense of expectation—ready and anxious to participate. The congregation gathers: the deacons, the choir, and the musicians are present. The preacher is among them. There is little if any separation between these groups, for just as with the hush harbors, the words exchanged in greetings have already begun to redefine us as one communal body.

The music starts and it begins to take us up and out of our powerless selves. It relaxes us and soothes us—like a healing balm, it starts to make us feel good all over. We sing, and the sound that our voices make together stirs us. It sounds good. We wait for the preacher to begin. He is a "performer" of sorts, but his job is to transform us into an actively participating group. In African-American ritual drama, there is no passive audience, calling the spirits correctly implies total involvement. For the ritual to be successful, the preacher must move us to the point that we come outside of our ordinary selves. We must leave ourselves in order to give of ourselves fully. He begins. He speaks, but it is not so much the meaning of the words which is important; it is their sounds which make the magic. He punctuates them, putting them together in musical phrases which have tonal variation. The phrases rise and fall. He pauses, he hesitates, he whispers, he moans and grunts. He repeats, and he listens for our response. We have begun to participate, because his words have touched something in us and so we say "Amen" ... and then we say it again. And throughout the variation of his many words, phrases, sounds, the preacher repeats particular ones at certain intervals. We punctuate his performance with our "Amens"

of approval. And while his head starts to jerk and his feet leave the
floor, our bodies are swaying. He is helping us and we him, in an
intimate reciprocal relationship.

We are helping each other to find the rhythm. Rhythm conducts us
to the point of spiritual being and eternality. Barrett says that it is the
"essence of the Universe," the fluid which connects all being.[12] It is
that which presents the universe as cosmos. Rhythm is *ntu*, the universal
life force. To be touched by it, to find it, is to be energized.

The preacher becomes a poet, like a musician, he leads us to the
rhythm, but he cannot find it without us. He develops his theme and
uses his voice and his body in such a way that we build slowly from
the less to the more intense. He cannot move too fast lest he leave us
behind. We have to find it together. But he can tell by our sounds of
approval that we understand, that we are with him and he must move
one. So we move together, feeling our closeness more and more in-
tensely, allowing the rhythm to take us as we move faster and faster,
higher and higher . . . until we burst out of our corporeal beings. Until
we experience spiritual ecstasy. Until. . . . What do we say? Until we
"get the spirit." That is the African-American way of saying that "the
gods have come." The height of religious expression, the most profound
metaphysical statement, for a person of African descent is that eternal
moment of joy in which we feel ourselves to be the receptacle of spiritual
being. "Filled with the holy ghost." Church people have given an
African interpretation to this European terminology. It describes the
phenomenon of spirit possession and is the objective of all African
ritual.

The preacher will make some "speak in tongues," others do a special
dance, and the fortunate ones will demonstrate the physical manifestation of spirit within them by characteristic behavior and movements
of their bodies. They will become testaments to the presence and closeness of the spirits. But something will have happened to all of us who
are present, as well. For there is no closer bond that a group of black
people can feel than that which comes from the experience of feeling
and expressing our deepest emotions together. The group becomes a
sacred community once again, and so its members gain strength from
communal experience. The ritual becomes an affirmation of their communal identity and so a reservoir of psychic, even political strength.
Paul Carter Harrison understands.

The mode was beginning to reveal itself now that everyone was part of its creation. Possessed, the audience had moved outside of its conscious relationship with self ... and spurred by ancestral spirits, became urgently united around the ecstatic definition of a singular image: the power of blackness.[13]

The spirits have come among us, have renewed us, and have been strengthened by our praises.

Personally, these experiences provide us with occasions to express deep-felt emotions. We are a spiritual/emotional people. The expression of that spirit and those emotions is a necessity of existence. African ritual drama, wherever it is found, is an affirmation of humanness. Human emotion is not embarrassing for us. We are not ashamed to be "moved." Through the ritual of the black church we experience rebirth—psychic, emotional communal, and spiritual renewal. Periodic rebirth is eternal life. Through our rituals, beginning with the "hush harbors," we African-Americans achieved the impossible. We defeated the death of oppression. We survived as spiritual beings and as *Africans*. Ritual drama is for us, above all, an affirmation of life!

"This little light of mine, I'm gonna let it shine...." But what about those of us who have long since left the church, those of us for whom Christian terminology and conceptualization have no meaning? Are we African-Americans without Ritual drama, and so without African spirituality? The answer, of course, is an emphatic "no." Black life abounds with rituals through which we renew ourselves for struggle, rituals through which we redefine ourselves as African by giving collective expression to the African ethos.

In the 1960s civil rights movement when we joined hands in a circle and sang our songs together, physically powerless in confrontation with a powerful and violent enemy, we were performing ritual. We found in each other the spiritual strength to neutralize an otherwise immobilizing fear. The demonstrations themselves were rituals. Through participation we experienced a transcendence beyond the humiliating reality of black life in the hard-core South.

Malcolm was a preacher. He was a teacher and an artist as well. The sight of him, the sound of his voice, his presence inspired many black rituals. The tradition and style of the black Baptist minister spilled over into other arenas of the black experience. Nowhere was this genius better exemplified than in Martin Luther King, Jr. It manifests itself in the ability to touch the African-American ethos: to move our spirits! To raise us to heights and to put us in touch with the essence of our being.

Our funerals have traditionally been rituals, not in any ordinary sense, but in the sense of African-American ritual drama. The group is called together from wherever its various members have migrated. The ritual is performed according to prescribed regulations, one enactment following another, until the family is transformed once more into a sacred community bound by a common experience, then cleansed, energized, and raised briefly to spiritual heights through their ability to experience and express the suffering within. The family renews its kinship ties, and the deceased is aided in his or her transition to another phase of existence. Crisis is understood communally. The order is restored. Things are put right. "We sent him off well."

We have always come together for ceremony and celebration on the many occasions which are special to us. The times when we want to say, "We are family!" Carleton Molette says of African-American ritual drama:

One of the purposes is to celebrate the affirmation of a sense of community, a feeling of togetherness. . . based upon the assumption that *we who are gathered here to participate in this event are and being together.*[14]

We have always "partied," and sometimes those parties have been successful rituals. A ritual is a happening, an event.[15] It is a moment of eternity in which the right set of circumstances combines to create that special experience. It can occur anywhere (providing the right beings are present and the time is right), but more easily in some settings than others. A class can become a ritual experience.

But we have not always been watchful. We have often displaced our sacred ritual dramas with distorted counterfeits in which the renewal of energy becomes dissipation of productive energy and transcendence becomes escape. The present disco form, for instance, crowds our consciousness. This form waivers precariously between health and sickness, depending on its context and frequency. Ritual drama was meant to punctuate existence, not to become our total existence.

In his brilliant work *The Drama of Nommo*, Paul Carter Harrison argues for the use of the mode of ritual drama by black playwrights in rejection of the approach of Western theatre, which is designed to please a non-African aesthetic, a non-African ethos. Essentially, he says, if you want to reach a black audience, learn from the pros. Use the modality of African ritual drama as the black church has done so successfully.[16] Harrison uses the terms which Janheinz Jahn has taken from Alexis Kagame's profound analysis of African philosophical conceptions. *Muntu* (human-beingness), *kintu* (thing), *hantu* (time and place), *kuntu* (modality)—these terms categorize all being; cosmically joined through participation in *ntu*, the universal life force which imparts being and reality to them. Ritual drama is the *kuntu* through which African *muntu*ness is best expressed and given life. *Nommo*, the world, represents the activating principle which Muntu uses intelligently to set forces in motion. The ability of being to affect—strengthen or weaken—another, is referred to as the *magara* principle.[17] Kagame has made it possible for us to express African conceptions in African terms. We must follow this example.

We have said that the *kuntu* (modality) of ritual drama allows for the ultimate expression of the African-American ethos. The potential of the ritual experience can be either manipulated and wasted in a political vacuum, or it can be ingeniously focused as an organizing and liberating force. In any case, it is through ritual drama that African-American spirituality has perpetuated itself.

KUCHEZA NGOMA: COMMUNING, SHOUTING AND FEELING THE RHYTHM

Kucheza ngoma, to dance to the drum (Kiswahili) means communing, shouting, and feeling the rhythm. Outside of the church, our most effective rituals occur during musical performances. Music is the most powerful catalyst of African-American spiritual expression. The reason involves a very deep and critical discussion.

"Black people have natural rhythm." "They love to dance." "All Black people can sing." These were the remarks which caused us pain in the 1940s and 1950s as we faced the white world individually, trying so hard to be "accepted." We did not want to hear anything which set us apart, which distinguished us from the dominant culture. We did not understand, then, that it is precisely our uniqueness, the very special character of our ethos, which is our strength. There is much truth hidden in these statements, although, like all generalizations with pejorative intent, they obscure meaningful reality. Neither we, nor the whites who voiced them, understood their deep and even philosophical significance.

Rhythm, dance, and song are quintessential aspects of the cosmic African universe. Through them we participate in that universe. And it is that participation which continued in the diaspora and which belied the fact of assimilation. Participation, on the level of soul or the essence of being, implies relationship to a spiritualized African universe, and not confinement within a materialized European one.

The concept "soul" is essential for any understanding of the phenomenon of African-American music as well as for the black response to Euro-American domination. Via commercialism in Western society, ideas become reduced to mere words and words easily lose their meanings through profane use and overuse of the media. Capitalists have taken the idea of "soul"—a sacred concept in the African-American world view and made it banal. "Soul" is the poetic expression which in one word encapsulates the complexity and depth of the African-American ethos. For Leonard Barrett, "soul signifies the moral and emotional fiber of the Black man." The potency of this quality makes it a "force" which, he says, demonstrates "strength, power, intense effort and will to live":

Soul-force is that power of the Black man which turns sorrow into joy, crying into laughter, defeat into victory. It is patience while suffering, determination while frustrated and hope while in despair. It derives its impetus from the ancestral heritage of Africa, its refinement from the bondage of slavery, and its continuing vitality from the conflict of the present.[18]

"Soul-force" is the basic ingredient of black survival.

On a philosophical level, "soul" indicates a conception of human nature in opposition to that generated by the Western world view. This conception is at the bedrock of African-American musical response. The rationalistic epistemology of the Western metaphysic necessitates a particular view of the essential nature of man. The essence of man's being becomes "thought" in isolation from other functions, sensations, and responses.[19]

As Western society, through the centuries, became more and more rationalized and rationalistic, its theorists valued the mode of objectification more and more. This value spilled over into the culture as a whole. Emotional response, identification, and involvement became of less and less value, until these tendencies generated by a scientific world-view, affected peoples' abilities to feel and to express feelings. It is precisely that quality of human response to which the concept "soul" refers. Moreover, it is that ability of the human being to feel, which is, in terms of the African world view, essentially human. But that ability is not set in contradistinction to thought; rather the two—thought and feeling—are understood to be inextricable and to be necessary for an accurate perception of reality. African epistemology and its attendant view of the essence of man brings us closer to a phenomenological approach to learning. It thereby defies the doctrinaire and ideological rationalism of the West. As Molette puts it:

The Afro-American aesthetic does not operate on the characteristically moti-vated, resulting in elevated behavior, or emotionally motivated, resulting in base behavior. The Afro-American aesthetic places a very high value upon emotionally motivated behavior; or another term that might be used to describe it. . . would be spiritually motivated behavior.[20]

Ethically and politically, the Platonic view of man further exacerbates these tendencies toward the dehumanization of man through a basic distrust of human nature. This view holds that most people if uncon-trolled will do evil, and that it is only through control by the more rational individual that justice can be obtained.[21] According to Plato, this same controlling mechanism is to operate within the human being, where baser emotions are to be controlled by reason. At a later period European society projected the concept onto the stage of intercultural relations, raising it to an ideological level. The more rational cultures, the civilized, were to control the less rational cultures. The Christian view of man is thus influenced. It tells us that human beings are basically and initially sinful and that their salvation comes only through the denial of their true and natural selves.

Soul is the essence of man in the African view. It is that aspect of him which expresses his union with the universal order and through it with all being (*okra, se, emi, chi*).[22] Therefore, to touch our soul is to touch us most deeply. What is it that joy and suffering have in common? They are both felt deeply. As James Cone says:

Black Music is unity music. It unites the joy and the sorrow, the love and the hate, the hope and the despair of black people; and it moves the people toward the direction of total liberation. It shapes and defines black being and creates cultural structures for black expression. Black music is unifying because it confronts the individual with the truth of black existence and affirms that black being is possible only in a communal context.[23]

Few have understood what music is to us. Remember that in African religion we gain our strength from communication with the spirits and from being touched by them. Remember also, that, ontologically, we gain meaning, force, and being through relationship with the universal life force, by feeling ourselves to be a part of the whole. Our music manifests that relationship, as it puts us in tune with the universe. It explains to us the mysterious workings of the universe and ourselves as cosmic beings. Our music calls the spirits. They force us to play it. It in turn forces them to show themselves, to come, to be close to us, to touch us and teach us. As in ritual, in music the human and the divine meet. When this happens we are energized and strengthened. We sing while we work. We hum while we cook. We listen to Aretha when we are down. Is it any wonder, then, that most of our music finds its roots in the church? In our sacred music joy and suffering merge. When we see beauty in the world, we sing. When we want to express how much faith we have in spirit, we sing. When the world is ugly and life is hard, we sing. Suffering did not give birth to the blues. Black suffering gave birth to the blues, just as black suffering and black hope gave birth to the spirituals. As Africans we say everything in music. As Africans, we use music as a vehicle for history, love, work, sadness, joy, celebration, philosophy, belief, and ritual. We use music as a primary means of communication. In Harrison's words:

Black music speaks to black people in concrete terms even when spoken language fails to communicate; it connotes, where words may not be able to, the emotional matrix of black experience, its elaborate negotiation of human relations and ambivalences, as well as its memory traces of race identity.[24]

For us, dance is inseparable from music. A.M. Opoku, the Ghanaian dance historian says, "it is life expressed in dramatic terms."[25] And as Barrett points out, for Africans in the diaspora dance as a form of nonverbal communication was crucial for two reasons: Along with music, it is the only language in which we could converse, and music and dance were the only media capable of expressing African metaphysical conceptions, too complex for verbal symbols.[26] In African ritual the ancestors join us through dance. Metaphysically, then, we transcend time. In Barrett's words, we "become immortal." Through dance we experience reality as immediate to us; that is, we are identified with the universe. Again, being one with reality means that we are not removed from it, as is the goal of Western objectification. In this relationship of identity we have reached our goal, metaphysically, religiously, emotionally, intellectually, phenomenologically.

DENIALS OF AFRICAN-AMERICAN HUMANISM

Traditionally, African culture is an extremely well-ordered construct, since it is informed by a world view characterized by the themes of unity and harmony, of wholeness and equilibrium. The health of the society within that context depends on the maintenance of a balance between complementary forces. When that balance is upset, for whatever reason, the order is threatened and otherwise neutral forces can become dangerous to the community. Witchcraft, for instance, becomes most powerful and therefore destructive at critical junctures, when the life of the group is undergoing crisis. The society, at these times, is in disequilibrium. It is the role of the priest to help to restore harmony. Rituals are also powerful in this role, as they function to restore order when chaos threatens.

This characteristic of African society makes it especially vulnerable to any change which is imposed unnaturally or from without. When the mechanisms within it are not capable of absorbing these influences into harmonious change and natural growth, the environment becomes altered. The more radical the alteration the more distorted become traditional aspects of the society as its members attempt to adjust. The intrusion of the European in Africa altered the mode within which Africans had to exist. Colonial domination distorted traditional forms. Former mechanisms for the maintenance of health no longer worked, sometimes even themselves becoming unhealthy or oppressive. The wisdom of the elders became oppression of the young. Witchcraft became predominant and more powerful, causing people to be obsessed with fear of it. The strength of and love for tradition led to destructive rivalry between language groups...and we could go on. The mode—the context—was itself inhuman; how was a humanistic world view to equip us to cope? The motherland is now more than ever tortured by the effects of the violence caused by European cultural and economic domination.

African-Americans have also suffered affronts to their African sensibilities.[27] Our very spirituality all too often surfaces as an inability to deal within the context of Western oppression, within an exploitative, materialistic, and materialized world. Too often deep spirituality implies an overabundance of faith in people and institutions who do not deserve it. Sometimes our true natures become twisted and contorted in our efforts to minimize the effects of exploitation and oppression. We have even repudiated the very values by which our forebears survived. Harrison talks about "the hustler mode." The work of the hustler, like the sorcerer in traditional society, is "erosive to the stability of the society." He operates according to an individualistic rather than a communalistic ethic.[28] The pusher of narcotics is a blasphemy, adapting so well to the world of black exploitation that he hates his people and, consequently, himself. He is an African who kills children, who, every day, works to diminish the life force of an entire community. He contradicts his own being. The junkie is the victim who victimizes himself. He robs himself of energy. He loses his *muntu*ness. His soul becomes a grotesque image of the African spirit. In turning on himself, he turns on those closest to him. He robs his mother, who ironically is the only person who still recognizes him as human. He then robs other black mothers and turns this aberration into a way of life.

Unfortunately, there are all kinds of "pushers," "junkies," and "hustlers" in black life, just as there are more subtle forms of "dope" and "prostitution." Our communities have become only "neighborhoods." The value images are gone. The teachers are gone. The counterbalancing forces are ineffective. There are no "elders," no priests, and so our children are suffering. They become enraged through disappointment at finding that what they have come from the spirit world to possess no longer exists. They turn on their parents, who have already abandoned them, and then they turn on themselves. Children of "hustlers" become "hustlers," and we are locked into despair.

We live in the chaos of North America, and so we lack the discipline inherent in traditional Africa. Yet, we have not become thoroughly European. Even in our dehumanization, our ethos is African. *We are a spiritual people, living in a profane society.* The question is, which is more powerful, the mode or our spirituality? Western academia teaches our young scholars that African philosophical conceptions are nonsense.

At the same time, Western rationalism denies the cosmic nature of our souls. Western religion has strong rationalistic tendencies, and within it African religion is reduced to "animism." We are bombarded at every turn by psychological assaults on our African selves. There is only one solution and that is to change the mode. It is the essential nature of Western-European society which threatens our existence—not just its mechanism, not only its exploitative nature, nor its white racism alone. As it is, sacred dance becomes disco, divine music becomes a fifteen-pound radio slung over a shoulder, and power of *nommo* is dissipated by jack-leg preachers. The entire mode must be changed. We must create an environment within which our Africanness can be healthy and productive.

TUMALIZE DUARA: THREE HUNDRED AND SIXTY DEGREES

African culture is amazingly resilient. In spite of the most culturally destructive forces in history, it has not disappeared. African-American humanism is derived from the humanistic nature of the African world view, and grows out of the African conception of the human being. It is an attitude toward life which stresses the importance of spiritual/ emotional experience. Man's ability to have power over and to exploit others is not paramount. Rather, human interrelationship and interdependency are recognized as primary needs and part of what validates human experience. African-American humanism values the survival of the group as actualized through the birth of its new members and the rebirth of its antecedents.

African humanism rejects the concept of "art for art's sake" and replaces it with "art for life's sake." African-American humanism expresses itself as a concept of the universe in which spiritual realities can be perceived and as a belief in spiritual forces which interrelate all beings and affect us in our daily lives.

Some will say that the ideas expressed herein constitute a mythology, but then we must understand the political function of myth. A myth is not a "lie"; rather it is the highest statement of truth. It is a truth which mobilizes and unifies, a truth which states the ideals of a people. All ideologies are founded on myth; all social analysis becomes the mythology of some culture.

The African-American experience must be used to turn spirituality into a political strength rather than the political deficit it has been historically. Our spirituality must be anchored to sharp political analysis and critical thought. In this way we can achieve the balance necessary for rediscovering ourselves as African people. In Kiswahili, *tumalize duara* (let us complete the circle).

NOTES

1. Gregory Bateson develops the idea of "ethos as an anthropological concept" in the context of his discussion in *Naven* (Stanford, Calif.: Stanford University Press, 1958), pp. 27–88.

2. For explanations of this concept among the Dogon and Fon peoples, see Marcel Griaule and Germaine Dieterlen, "The Dogon," and P. Mercier, "The Fon of Dahomey," in *African Worlds*, ed. Darryl Forde (London: Oxford University Press, 1954), pp. 33–47, 106–29.

3. Leonard Barrett, "Soul-Force: African Heritage," in *Afro-American Religion* (New York: Anchor, 1974).

4. John Mbiti, *African Religions and Philosophies* (New York: Anchor, 1970), p. 127.

5. See Stanley Diamond, *In Search of the Primitive* (New Brunswick, N.J.: Transaction Books, 1974), p. 198.

6. Alexis Kagame, *Philosophie Bantu-Rwandaise de l'être* (New York: Johnson Reprint, 1966); Janheinz Jahn, *Muntu* (New York: Grove Press, 1961), p. 101. Also see Mircea Eliade, *The Sacred and the Profane* (New York: Harcourt, Brace and World, 1959), pp. 116–18 especially.

7. Contrary to Eugene Genovese's contradictory and confusing argument in which he says that "Southern paternalism necessarily recognized the slaves' humanity," part of the problem here is Genovese's use of empty rhetorical abstractions; see Eugene Genovese, *Roll, Jordan, Roll* (New York: Vintage Books, 1976), pp. 3–7. Contrast this with Malcolm's comments on the "Message to the Grassroots" record album (James Cone, *The Spirituals and the Blues* [New York: Seabury Press, 1972]).

8. Barrett, "Soul-Force," p. 60.

9. George Rawick, *From Sundown to Sun Up* (Westport, Conn.: Greenwood Press, 1972), p. 33.

10. Barrett, "Soul-Force" p. 155.

11. Cone, *The Spirituals*, p. 11.

12. Barrett, "Soul-Force," p. 83.

13. Paul Carter Harrison, *The Drama of Nommo* (New York: Grove Press, 1972).

14. Carleton Molette, "Afro-American Ritual Drama," *Black World* (September 1973), p. 9.

15. Paul Carter Harrison, *Kuntu Drama* (New York: Grove Press, 1974), p. 7.

16. Harrison, *The Drama of Nommo*, pp. 5–17.

17. Janheinz Jahn, *Muntu* (New York: Grove Press, 1967), chapter 4.

18. Barrett, "Soul-Force," pp. 1–2.

19. Eric Havelock, *A Preface to Plato* (New York: Grossett and Dunlap, 1967).

20. Molette, "Afro-American Ritual, Drama," p. 9.

21. "Human nature will be always drawing him into avarice and selfishness, avoiding pain and pursuing pleasure without any reason, and will bring these to the front, obscuring the juster and the better; and so working darkness in his soul will at last fill with evils both him and the whole city" (Plato, *Laws* Bk. 50: 875C). This tendency is also found in Paul's doctrine (Christian) in which there is a radical opposition between the flesh and the spirit, always implying that man is not in harmony with himself.

22. These are Twi, Fon, Yoruba, and Ibo terms respectively for the part of the person directly from the creator and is symbolized as the vital breath of life.

23. Cone, *The Spirituals*, p. 5; Cone's analysis of the spirituals and the blues and their relationship is creative: see Chapter 6 especially.

24. Harrison, *The Drama of Nommo*, p. 62.

25. Barrett, "Soul-Force," p. 73.

26. Barrett's discussion of this point amounts to revelation. It is the most profound statement I have ever encountered in the literature mode of the very deep significance of music, dance and rhythm for the African ethos; see pp. 82–83.

27. Harrison's discussion of the change from the traditional mode to an alien and oppressive mode, and the effect of that change on our behavior is very perceptive. See Harrison, *The Drama of Nommo*, pp. 20–25.

28. Ibid.

14

THE AFRICAN ESSENCE IN AFRICAN-AMERICAN LANGUAGE

MOLEFI KETE ASANTE

The almost total absence of visible African artifacts in Afro-American culture has led to a general belief that nothing of Africa survived the tyranny of American slavery.[1] Prohibited by "Christian" slave owners, following their individual consciences, from participating in traditional ceremonies and rituals, the African in the United States for the most part did not develop complete formal African art forms. In fact, the African "artists" functions were nearly meaningless in such an alien context. While the visible artifacts of religious sculpture gradually disappeared, the linguistic and communicative artifacts were embellished and sustained the African's creativity when more conspicuous elements of African cultures would have produced immediate and violent repression. This chapter outlines the complex verbal behaviors which constitute continuity and a relationship between West African languages and African-American English.

Despite the preponderance of pidgin and later creole among early Africans in America, little investigation into the structure, history, context, or possible relationships with West African languages was ever undertaken. Considered as "corruptions" of English or as the "babblings of children," the language used by the Afro-American was dismissed as unworthy of investigation. Furthermore, the persistent and prevailing idea among early American scholars as well as laymen argued that Africans had no culture. Such a view served as a successful impediment to a discussion of relationships between Afro-American and African languages.

Writers such as Melville Herskovits and Janheinz Jahn have been vigorously attacked, not so much for their method as for the inferences to be drawn from their methods. On the basis of field research in African cultures, diasporan and continental, they challenged many interpretations about the African connection. In effect, along with W.E. B. Du Bois, Alain Locke, and Carter Woodson before them, they provided novel interpretations of old materials.

A considerable intellectual meanness had to be combatted by the initial cadre of communicationists examining the continuity of black language behavior from Africa to America. The racist assumption that black pidgin reflected an innate inability of Africans to learn English was current at one time.[2] In fact, as Herskovits points out, the linguists who studied pidgin often had no knowledge of African languages and therefore could not make informed interpretations. Lorenzo Turner augments this position by exposing the inaccuracies within the work of linguists quick to give assurance that there are no African survivals among Black Americans. In the work of Mervyn Alleyne and the sociolinguists we have begun to get a clearer picture of the African contribution to English.[3] Alleyne particularly has demonstrated linguistic continuity in the West Indies.

In 1922, Ambros Gonzales, like many white American linguists, misunderstood the Gullah language and arrived at the wrong conclusion. He cites a list of words that were purported to be of African origin. Most of the words identified by Gonzales are either English words misspelled or African words interpreted as English words that blacks could not pronounce. Gonzales was thoroughly confused about what he was studying, as Turner points out:

Many other words in Gonzales' glossary which, because of his lack of acquaintance with the vocabulary of certain African languages, he interprets as English, are in reality African words. Among other Gullah words which he or other American writers have interpreted as English, but which are African, are the Mende *suwangc*, *to be proud* (explained by Gonzales as a corruption of the English swagger); the Wolof *lir*, *small* (taken by Gonzales to be an abbreviated form of the English *little*, in spite of the fact that the Gullah also uses *little* when he wishes to); the Wolof *benj*, *tooth* (explained by the Americans as a corruption of bone); the Twi *fa*, *to take* (explained by Americans as a corruption of the English *for*).[4]

The point made by Turner is that white American linguists refused to consider the possibility that blacks used African words in their vocabularies. In fact, the evidence demonstrates that whites unfamiliar with either African languages or Gullah made expansive generalizations which tended to support their preconceived notions about black speech habits. Writing in the *American Mercury* in 1924, George Krapp said "It is reasonably safe to say that not a single detail of Negro pronunciation or Negro syntax can be proved to have other than English origins."[5] Other writers who voiced nearly the same judgment regarding the presence or absence of African survivals in black American speech supported the notion of an absolute break with African culture.[6] It was inconceivable to them that either phonological, morphological, or semantic interference could have existed where Africans retained their language behavior in confrontation with English.

These writers represented the prevailing American notions about race, cultural retention, and African intelligence. And while Herskovits and others were gallant in demonstrating the presence of Africanisms in black America, they frequently concentrated on artifacts which proved insufficient to carry the burden of cultural continuity. Despite claims that Herskovits' work had a negative effect on the discussion of culture because he exaggerated differences between blacks and nonblacks, his primary thesis was essentially sound.[7] It was, of course, an unpopular position because several writers, including the sociologist E. Franklin Frazier, were captivated with the idea of more or less nondistinction between cultures and races. The emphasis was upon making blacks Anglo-Saxons, as Frazier's student, Nathan Hare, eventually put it. But blacks were culturally different, and, whether one argues that this difference resulted from African retention and syncretism of other cultures, the point is unchanged. In fact what should have occurred, but did not, was the systematic and empirical testing of culture-related data to explicate Afro-American language behavior.

That something of the African backgrounds of Black Americans survived in their speech is not difficult to argue despite the intense efforts to prove that blacks were incapable of cultural retention because of slavery. However, no displaced people ever completely loses the forms of their previous culture. That is, the specific artifacts may differ from those used at a prior time, but the essential elements giving rise to those artifacts are often retained and produce substantive forms in the new context. Thus I contend that Black Americans retained basic components of the African linguistic experience rather than specific artifacts. It follows, therefore, that to seek the distinctive retention of African words in Black American speech as Turner, Herskovits, and Romeo Garrett have attempted to do in the past, is to search amiss. What they have sought to do would make interesting, provocative, and valuable additions to our knowledge, but it is not convincing from the standpoint of cultural survivals. It is cast in too narrow a mold, and often depends upon the continuity of specific words from several ethnic regions of Africa. Although African lexical items can be found in limited supply among African Americans, they do not make the argument for a more general retention of African linguistic behavior among most Black Americans. Earlier writers seemed to have preferred to make African lexical discoveries in African-American language; they are, after all, easily identifiable phenomena. What my research suggests is that combinations of classes of sounds, units of meaning, and syntax behaviors are to be considered as survivals rather than a concentration on any single one of these factors or simple lexical characteristics.

But the relationship between African languages and African-American speech behavior can be more clearly ascertained on a primary level in the "communication style" of the person. While this is a difficult concept to define, it means simply the verbal and nonverbal behavior patterns that distinguish one person from another. In fact, whole groups may be distinguished in such a manner. On a secondary level, there are observable relationships in the substantive social fabric of language behavior, i.e., proverbs, riddles, dozens, and call and response. The combination of the communicative styles and "folkloric modalities" constitute an approach to the sense of a language. It is in this sense that language in Afro-America is uniquely more African than European, other factors aside. This is not a rejection of linguistic structure, inasmuch as I hope to demonstrate that certain structural matters underscore my basic thesis.

Recent linguistic studies have defined a language variously referred to as Black English, African-American English, and more appropriately as Ebonics, which consists of systematic rules different from English as it is popularly learned and spoken. The cohesive grammar of Ebonics has features shared with popular English, and with other dialects of English. However, the most significant fact is that it has some features which are found only among Ebonics speakers. At least one researcher believes, "Systematic differences in Black English [sic] which occur

only within that language system, may be the result of interaction between coastal West African languages of the Niger-Congo language
family and the dialects of English encountered by black people when
they first arrived in America.''[8] In such cases, however, it is highly
unlikely that no individuation of those unique systematic differences
appeared in other dialects of English. The interaction of African languages with English dialects has not been shown to be significant in
the singularity of certain grammatical rules present in Ebonics. A more
plausible answer is that Ebonics contains structural remnants of certain
African languages, although the vocabulary is overwhelmingly English.

If we accept the creolization theory that Ebonics developed as a result
of language interference, isolation factors, and nonpopular linguistic
models, then it is possible to trace the language from pidgin to the full
coming to be of another language. According to the creolization theory,
a pidgin language has two characteristics: (1) its grammatical system
is sharply reduced, and (2) it is not the native language system of those
who speak it. On the other hand, when pidgin becomes the native
language of those who use it, it becomes a creole language.[9]

Thus the language spoken by Africans in the New World was greatly
influenced by the phonological and syntactic structures of their first
languages. Whatever semblance of English they learned had the un-
mistakable imprint of African languages, much like the English spoken
by average French people would be rendered in many instances in terms
of French phonology and syntax. These Africans were, for the most
part, not linguists learning languages but lay persons acquiring an instrument for their survival. And the limited English vocabulary and few
sentences needed for the task of staying alive were extremely usable
and useful in dealing with whites. But the mastery of English morphology and syntax lay in the future. Pidginization as a first step toward
creolization occurs throughout the African's history in America. Morphological, phonological, and grammatical principles underlying popular English have constantly played havoc with the African past. The
diagram below illustrates the process of structural retention in Black
American speech behavior.

Inasmuch as African-Americans are descendants of a great many
different ethnic and linguistic groups, if we are to talk about communication styles, constructions, or pre-verbal forms, it is necessary to
identify as precisely as possible the area where most African-American
ancestors originated. Slave trade records provide us with information

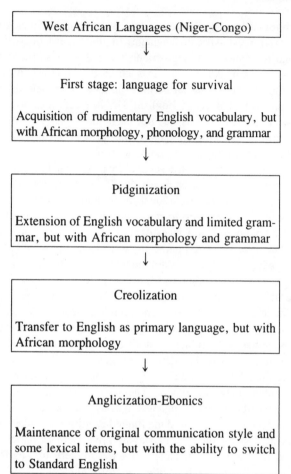

West African Languages (Niger-Congo)

↓

First stage: language for survival

Acquisition of rudimentary English vocabulary, but with African morphology, phonology, and grammar

↓

Pidginization

Extension of English vocabulary and limited grammar, but with African morphology and grammar

↓

Creolization

Transfer to English as primary language, but with African morphology

↓

Anglicization-Ebonics

Maintenance of original communication style and some lexical items, but with the ability to switch to Standard English

regarding areas from which slaves were taken. The Atlantic slave trade was permitted for nearly two hundred years in the United States. Every state was affected at some point, although the majority of Africans landed in the Southern States.[10]

The languages spoken by most of the African linguistic groups are considered to be in the Niger-Congo family. Several similarities between these languages and Ebonics are so clearly observable as to deserve immediate mention. The verb systems of Efik and Ewe differentiate between a habitual aspect and an aspect of completion. Thus it is possible in Efik to express an action which occurs habitually in the present, past, or future with time determined by context rather than by vocal inflection. Ebonics also uses aspect rather than tense in some verbal constructions. Perhaps Richard Long's preliminary analysis of the *Uncle Remus* Dialect best demonstrates work done in recent years on the relationship between Ebonics and African languages. He provides us with the following comparative paradigm between the Niger-Congo verb system and Ebonics.[11]

Niger-Congo Verb Tenses	English Translation
Present	he go
Near past	he gone
Remote past	he been gone
Future	he going to go
Aspect of progress	he going
Aspect of completion	he done gone
Past aspect of repetition	he been going

While Long gives us an interesting point for departure, he does not draw too clearly any definite relationship between the two languages; furthermore, the future tense-aspect of his construct translated as "he going to go" is probably incorrect. Whether this expression appears because of Joel Chandler Harris' recording of it in *Uncle Remus* or because of Long's wish to hear it so, it is questionable as the sole expression in Ebonics for the future. A more common phrase is "he gon go" to indicate future. Based upon the use of this expression in the author's own family in South Georgia, I conclude that it is likely that in other Gullah or Ogeechee regions the same is true.

A more useful investigation has been made by William A. Stewart who observed the lack of verbal inflection in Ebonics to show the difference between simple present and past.[12] Thus "I see it" in Ebonics may mean "I see it" or "I saw it", depending upon the speaker's context. One cannot surmise from this that a difference between the categories is nonexistent because the present and past negatives demonstrate the presence of both grammatical categories. For example:

Present	Past
I see it	I see it (I saw it)
I don't see it	I ain't see it

Brewer says, "Twi, Igbo, Ewe, Efik—all Niger-Congo languages
—Jamaican Creole, and Gullah all exhibit a similar lack of inflection
to show time. Present, past, and sometimes future time are indicated
by context rather than by verbal inflection."[13]

Gullah (Ogeechee)	I de go	I go, I went
Jamaican Creole	Yesterday me buy salt fish	
Ewe	Mayl	I go (no particular time)
Igbo	Àdâ bù abo	Ada is (was) carrying a basket
Twi	əFa	He takes (present, past, all times)

Furthermore, the Ebonics verb system has four perfectives whereas
English has only two.[14] While the present and past are similar in the
two grammars, Ebonics also has a completive perfect and a remote time
perfect.

Completive (near Past)	I done walked
Remote time	I been walked

Dwyer and Smith describe West African pidgin English in a way that
makes an interesting comparison to the Ebonics perfectives.[15] The essential point to be made is that two aspect markers occur before the
verb: *de*-continuing or habitual action and *don*-completed action; the
word *bin* is used as a past tense marker. It is not just West African
pidgin English which possesses the habitual and continuative aspect.
One sees similar elements in Efik and Ewe verbal construction. Thus
in Efik any verbal construction can have a habitual counterpart. In Ewe
na is suffixed to the verb: *nayine*, "I generally go."

Clearly morphological and grammatical connections are demonstrated
between Ebonics and West African languages. However, the primary
argument of this chapter is that it is in speech communication style
generally, even as Anglicization occurs, that the Afro-American retains
his essential Africanness. Precise discovery of lexical items is not necessary to argue continuity. Jack Berry states, "Almost every one of the
languages spoken South of the Sahara is tonal, using pitch distinctions
to differentiate words in much the same way European languages use

stress.''[16] That Afro-American language behavior is characterized by a significant control over vocal inflection and modulation is fairly well established.[17] The Black American means something precise by his pitch, e.g., in the pitch of words such as "Jesus," "Man," "Say," etc. Vocal color plays a vital role for the black public speaker, particularly the preacher, who uses various intonations and inflections to modify or amplify specific ideas, concepts, or emotions. Harmonizing is a principal function of black speech behavior, and every attempt is made to reach internal harmony, the blending of sounds and ideas, for effectiveness. Thus the audience frequently responds with interjections, "Amen," "Speak," "Pray on," and "Tell the truth." This is similar to the Igbo, "He speaks" or "Let him speak," "Speak on" or "he has spoken." There is a certain noticeable communicative style which is transmitted in the tone, rhythm, or pitch of voice in these cases. In fact, the so-called black voice can be recognized by other Ebonics speakers by pitch and tone. Thus, the more prevalent African rhythm, tone, and pitch are in the vocalization, the more distinctly African is the voice. One is tempted here to suggest that whites in some southern United States communities, having learned the peculiar intonations and sounds of their African nurses, speak with African tone and pitch. On the other hand, some blacks speak with an almost precise European intonation pattern with no trace of African vocal color. This behavior indicates that language interference has affected the speech of blacks and whites alike in the United States. One cannot be sure even how long the communicative styles of African will remain. The time may come when we will only be able to observe rare instances of the pitch, rhythm, and tone of Africa. In a real sense, the linguists' early ecstasy over African lexical retentions, e.g., "ok.," "okra," "go-go," etc., was the beginning of a general merging of African lexical items into the general American vocabulary.

It is now necessary to expand upon the role of syntactical features of Ebonics as indicators of a linguistic relationship with African languages. Such an expansion will explicate certain communicative processes which cannot be explained by retention of lexical items alone. It is for this reason that greater insight may be gained by a detailed treatment of two types of syntactical phenomena: (1) serial verb construction and (2) the usage of tense and aspect. Serial verb-like constructions appear in Ebonics quite frequently. In some West African languages several verbs are used to express actions that require only one verb in English. John Bendor-Samuel describes the Gur branch of Niger-Congo:

Strings of short clauses characterize Gur syntax. Long clauses with a large number of nominal phrases are very unusual. Frequently complex clauses are broken down into a sequence of two or more clauses. Indirect objects, benefactives and instrumental phrases are avoided. Thus Vagala uses a two verb sequence in a construction such as *u é ù té ǹ* literally 'he did it gave me' for 'he did it for me,' and Basari similarly has *ù ná kí tu m* literally 'he did connective gave me.'[18]

This type of serialization appears in many West African languages. Ayo Bamgbose says serial verbs refer to the combination of verbs found in many West African languages where all the verbs share a common subject in the surface structure.[19] For example, he cites:

Twi:
> *òdè sìká nó màà mè*
> He take money gave me
> "He gave me money"

Vagala:
> *ù kpa kíyzèé mòng ówl*
> He took knife cut meat
> "He cut the meat with a knife"

Yoruba: *ó mú iwé wá*
> He took book come
> "He brought a book"

The fact that serialization exists in West African languages has been clearly established, but it is also necessary to indicate that there are surface variations in the structure of serialization across languages. The description of Ewe is one example:

A peculiarity of Ewe is that we often find a row of verbs one after the other. The chief features of this are that all the verbs stand next to each other without being connected, that all have the same tense or mood, and that in the event of their having a common subject and object, these stand with the first, the others remaining bare: should a conjunction stand between two verbs, the subject and object must be repeated.[20]

Furthermore, Bendor-Samuel also makes generalizations about serialization in the Gur branch of Niger-Congo:

In most languages this serial construction has certain clear markers and though there are many differences from language to language usually the following characteristics are marked:

1. The series shares a single common object which occurs before the first verb in the series and is not repeated within the series.
2. There are no conjunctions between the verbs.
3. Nominal phrases functioning as object may occur after any verb in the series when the object changes, though it is not usual to find more than two such phrases. When the object of two or more verbs is the same it is never repeated and usually occurs after the first verb.
4. Adverbial phrases may occur after a verb but only one phrase (nominal or adverbial) usually occurs between verbs in a series.
5. There are severe restrictions on the forms of the verbs in the series. Categories like future, negative, imperative etc. are only marked once for the whole series and in some instances are never found in such a series at all.

Some languages have conjunctions occurring with the series. Dagbani has two conjunctions which occur with such a series, *ka* and *n*. In Dagaari there are two such conjunctions which occur quite frequently. Bemoba has one conjunction that occasionally occurs. In Vagala two conjunctions may occur. Sisala has one conjunction which frequently occurs, and in Konkomba similarly there is one frequently occurring conjunction.[21]

Thus it is apparent that serial verb constructions vary considerably in surface structure but are characterized by the general principal that several verb phrases appear in a single surface structure prediction.

Westermann agrees that semantics is a common principle of serial verb usage.

In English these consecutive verbs are partly rendered by composite sentences. But very often several Ewe verbs may be expressed by a single verb in English.

The explanation of this is that the Ewe people describe every detail of an action or happening from beginning to end, and every detail has to be expressed by a special verb: they dissect every happening and present it in its several parts, whereas in English we seize on the leading event and express it by a verb, while subordinate events are either not considered or rendered by means of a preposition, adverb, conjunction, or a prefix of the verb.[22]

The semantic relationship between the verbs within a given construction is particularly important. It is apparent from the examples cited above that two verbs are utilized to convey what would normally be expressed by a single verb in English. This is the dissecting quality of African linguistic expression. The West African speakers analyze events by considering their component parts.

The same tendency toward analyzing actions by considering their component parts can be seen in Ebonics. Some sentences of Ebonics speakers utilize several verbs, while standard English has available for use a single verb to express the complete action. For example: *I took consideration* and *j'ined* de lawd. This expression can be paraphrased as *I accepted religion*, or *I became a Christian*.[23]

The most noticeable difference between this sentence and its English equivalent is that in the English version the fact that the person pondered the issue or thought about joining the church or accepting religion is not evident in the surface structure of the sentence, but by virtue of his having accepted, which is, by definition, "to receive with consent something given or offered," the person must have had to think about it, and decide whether or not to accept or reject this particular faith. In English, it is the main verb which is usually focused upon, and this is usually the verb which surfaces; therefore, on the surface of the English translation of the above sentence we get the verb *accept*.[24] On the other hand, the Ebonics speaker, tending to surface a larger number of verbs to express the same action, surfaces the verb participle *took consideration*, for the act of having thought about or pondered, and *joined*, for the actual step taken in accepting that faith. The Ebonics speaker here seems to want to express each event, as does his counterpart in many West African languages. We see a similar phenomenon in: (command) "Turn loose and drap down from dar," or English, "Come down from there." It is interesting that the Ebonics speaker, when commanding that someone should come down from out of the tree, finds it necessary to tell the person to first turn the tree branch loose and then drop down from it. Again, note the tendency to segment the action, and more importantly the fact that this segmentation appears on the surface, in the form of two verbs. Alternatively, for the English speaker, it is sufficient to focus on the main action, that of falling or dropping from the tree. Another example from the film made for the federal project is: "I *hear tell* you went home." [English: "I hear that you went home."]

Again, the Ebonics speaker is found describing every action and each event is expressed by a single verb. In this sentence the speaker states that he has been hearing a certain thing, but also states on the surface that *someone is telling* that which is heard. This serial verb construction is a clear example of the serial verb principle for several reasons. The verbs stand adjacent to each other without being connected. Furthermore, only one of the verbs can be inflected for tense, whereas if they were simply two sentences, one embedded into the other, both could be inflected for tense. This also holds for many serial verbs in African languages. Additional variations may yield:

I *heard tell* you went home.
I *will hear tell*, if you do that.

On the other hand, inflection of the second verb will yield ungrammatical sentences like:

I *hear told* you went home.
I *heard told* you went home.

If this sentence were said to be simply, as a result of an embedding transformation on the component sentences, *I hear it* and *Someone tells/ says*, producing *I hear that someone tells other people* (as also there would have to be a rule deleting the complementizer *that*), then sentences like the following could be generated where either or both verbs can be inflected for tense:

I *hear tell* that you went home.
I *hear* it, (somebody) *told* that you went home.
I *heard* it *told* that you went home.

A similar analysis can be made for the sentence: "I *made do* with what I had," ("I used what I had.") where only the first verb can be inflected for tense, but never the second. Another example of this would be the sentence: "*Go* home *go see* about those children." ("Go home and attend to those children.") This sentence is interesting in another respect as well. That is, it is used with or without the first *go*. Upon hearing a sentence of this type, one would automatically assume that *go* is an imperative, indicating that the person being given the command should move in a certain direction away from the speaker, while *see about* means to attend to. But here, *go*, expressing a command to move away from the speaker, is used in the same sentence with *go see*, showing that some type of serial relationship holds between *go* and *see* in this prediction. We cannot claim that it is simply the imperative *go* and the imperative *see*, because *go* exists as a command in initial position in this sentence, alone. Sentences presented below tend to have a serial-like construction and may be evidence of the same function semantically as the serial verb constructions of many West African languages.

He *picked up* and *went* to town. (He went to town.)
I'll *take* a switch and *beat* you good. (I'll beat you with a switch.)

Clearly, it is a tendency for African-American speakers, like some West African speakers, to describe every detail of an action by using a special verb.

The tense and aspect quality in African-American English has been cited by several writers. Lorenzo Turner notes that the Ogeechee or Gullah speakers, much like speakers of many West African languages, attach little significance to the actual time when an event takes place, on the contrary, the manner of the action is stressed. Turner offers examples of West African languages which follow this pattern:

In the Ewe language, for example, the verb is unchangeable. Tense and mood forms are made by a combination of several verbs or of verbs and nouns, and it is difficult to distinguish between tense and mood. One verb form, designated by many grammarians as the Aorist, does not indicate any particular time but can represent the present, past or even future, according to the context.

In Mandika the actual time when an action takes place is of less importance than the nature of the action as regards the completeness or incompleteness. Accordingly, there are three aspects of the verb: the first represents an action without reference to its completeness or incompleteness; the second describes an action which is being continued; and the third describes one which has been completed.[25]

It has been found that there is no distinction between past and present indefinite forms of the verb among Yoruba speakers. Where it is necessary to make a distinction between past and present, the African uses an adverbial of time. For example, *Ó kéré* may be translated as "It is small" or "It was small," depending on context. If we add the adverbial *telèfi* ("previously"), it would have to be translated "It was small." This form conveys the meaning of completed action. It holds also in

Yoruba that the *n* formative, which marks the verb for progressive or iterative action, can be either present or past time, depending upon the time referred to in context.

Thus, tense and aspect are not linked in many West African languages. In some cases, the syntactical systems are such that they focus on aspect. As in Hausa, aspect is marked by grammatical formatives while tense is marked by either context or adverbials of time. Therefore, aspect can be used without reference to tense in many languages.

Slave narratives from Alabama reveal numerous constructions in which tense is superseded by aspect. Certainly there exist mechanisms in Ebonics whereby aspect may be expressed without tense. For example, "He *clumb* de tree to shake de simmons down whilst I *be pickin* em up." In this sentence the speaker, having made reference to tense in the initial clause, doesn't repeat his tense marker on the verb phrase of the second clause. Nevertheless, the speaker has not neglected to indicate the manner of the action of the verb phrase in the second clause. If we consider the English form of the above sentence: "He *climbed* the tree to shake the persimmons down, while I was *picking* them up," we find that the tense formative is redundant in the second clause.

The following sentences employing *done* indicate the extent African-American English uses the preverbal particle: "All my chilluns *done*" indicates the extent Ebonics uses the preverbal particle:

All my chilluns *done* died or wandered away.
'Fore I knowed it I *done* fell slap to sleep.
Hell *done* broke loose in Gawgy.
He couldn't tell us much about what *done* happen.
When ole marsa come back he *done* got his arm shot off, but he lef befo' dem overseers go, ca'se dey *done* whupped dat ole 'oman what come wid us to deaf.
Mr. Lincoln *done* said we was free.

Labov in writing about similar constructions says that the meaning is clearly "already" and therefore *done* becomes a perfective particle. Labov states also that *done* is used in certain sentences, with a meaning of intensification, as in the sentence following: "After I don won all that money. 'Cause I'll be done put—stuck so many holes in him he'll wish he wouldna' said it."[26] While there may exist cases where the perfective meaning is obscured, in most cases the preverbal particle *done* is an aspect marker in African American English, marking the verb for completed action, without reference to time.

Contrary to Labov's claim that *have* and *done* are interchangeable in their roles as perfective particles, most African-American English speakers make a semantic distinction between these two perfectives. *Done* appears to carry a consistent meaning of completion.

The following sentences taken from Charlie Smith by Sukari Salone show the preverbal form marking of *done*.[27]

I eat anything that's *done*.
Is the food *done*?
It's béen *done*. (It's been completed a long time ago.)
(´) = stress
I *been done* went.

In these instances *done* clearly means completed action, and trying to replace it with an alternative perfective would yield ungrammatical sentences, thus revealing the difference in status between the forms using *done* and those using *have*. For example:

It's been *have*.
I *been have* went.

There are two forms of the word *been* in Ebonics: (1) without stress, used simply as a past perfect as in "He been married," connoting that he has been married but is no longer so, and (2) with added stress as in "He béen married," connoting that he married a long time ago, and is still married. The following sentences from Ebonics demonstrate the use of *been:*

My ole man *been* dead goin' on twenty years.
Ca'se I *been* belongin' to de church for fifty-five years.
Just left up to dem, I'd 'ave *been* dead.
All my chilluns *done* died or wandered away an' my old man *been* dead goin' on twenty years.
My pappy's name, I don't know ca'se he *done* been sole to somewhares else when I was too little to recollect.
But effen he *had a been* caught. . . .

Replacing *done* by *have* and *had* in the fourth and fifth sentences respectively yield different semantic interpretations.

It appears that *done* is itself a verbal aspect of completed action, without reference to time, as opposed to the perfective (have/had/has) which is marked for time. Salone properly reasons, that this has been overlooked in other studies dealing with Ebonics because "something is lost in the translation," so to speak. To translate an Ebonics sentence using *done* into other dialects of English, one would of necessity use a perfective form, thereby also marking the form for tense. For example, the sentence "I done ate" in Ebonics means literally, "I completed the action of eating," where the preverbal *done* specifies nothing in reference to time. This form *done* can as well exist with the perfective form which is marked for time.

I *would have done* ate.
I *had done* ate.
I *will be done* ate.

In translating the *done* sentence into standard English, one would use the perfective, as in "I have eaten," which does carry information about completed action, but also carries information about the relationship of the action in time. And, in doing this the speaker of standard English assumes that the Ebonics speaker is also implying a specification for time, which according to the evidence is incorrect.

Finally, the African-American speakers tend to use a continuation form without reference to time, especially after the time has been made reference to in a previous clause of the sentence, as in the examples which follow:

He *clumb* de tree to shake de simmons down whilst I *be pickin* em up.
I *seed* sompin a-comin' down de road 'bout dat high, 'bout size a . . hit *keep acomin* an' *keep agitten* bigger an' bigger an' closer an' closer.

Contrasting the standard English equivalents, we find additional tense markers.

He *climbed* the tree to shake the persimmons down, while I *was picking* them up.
I *saw* something coming down the road about that high, about the size of a . . .
it *kept coming* and *kept getting* bigger and bigger and closer and closer.

As can be seen, while the standard English speaker must inflect all verbs for tense, the Ebonics speaker does not feel the need to be redundant in expressing tense, but he nevertheless is redundant in expressing the manner or aspect of the action, even to the extent of utilizing frequently an archaic English form, *a plus gerund* (probably on plus gerund) from which implies an interactive meaning.

This chapter began with an admission that the followers of Turner, Herskovits and Garrett were too narrow in their perspectives to adequately substantiate the continuity of Africanisms in African American English. However, I have argued that the communication styles of African-American speakers constitute the real continuity with the African sense. The linguistic factors analyzed in detail in this chapter are supportive of the basic proposition. African American speakers have maintained this fundamental sense of culture despite the imposition of European cultural values and styles. Retention of lexical items constitute one part of continuity, but the major burden of African American English has been carried by communicative processes, i.e., African American manner of expression, supported in the main by serialization and the unique use of tense and aspect. Neither of these phenomena has any analogue in the English language and therefore provides further proof that Ebonics derived in large part from the genius of West African languages.

NOTES

1. The work of Professor Robert Thompson has demonstrated the survival of West African carving and sculpturing techniques. Particularly manifest in the coastal regions of Georgia and South Carolina, West African wood sculpture techniques are generally considered to be among the major artifacts retained by Afro-Americans. Thompson, an historian of Afro-American art at Yale University, has indicated a strong belief in artistic retention. For a similar view see Judith Chase, *Afro-American Arts and Crafts* (New York: Van Nostrand, 1971). In addition, Karimu Asante's work on the survival of movement, as in dance, further demonstrates continuity.

2. Melville Herskovits, *The Myth of the Negro Past* (Boston: Beacon, 1969), p. 276.

3. See Mervyn Alleyne, "The Linguistic Continuity of Africa in the Caribbean," in *Topics in Afro-American Studies*, ed. Henry J. Richards (Buffalo, N.Y.: Black Academy Press, 1971), pp. 119-34. Alleyne argues that if African elements appear in African American speech it is inescapable that they belong

to the African base. He isolates four broad communicative channels operating
in African American speech development:

Africans ──────────────▶ Africans ──────────────▶ Europeans

Africans ──────────▶ Africans   Mulattoes ──────────▶ Europeans

Field Slaves ──────────▶ Artisans ──────────▶ Domestics ──────────▶ Europeans

Rural ──────────▶ Urban Proletariat ──────────▶ Middle Class ──────────▶ (White)

4. Lorenzo Turner, "West African Survivals in the Vocabulary of Gullah,"
presented before the *Modern Language Association*, New York (December,
1938).

5. George Krapp, "The English of the Negro." *The American Mercury*,
vol. 2 (1924), p. 190.

6. See, for example, H. L. Mencken, *The American Language* (New York,
1936), pp. 112, 523; Reed Smith, "Gullah," *Bulletin of the University of South
Carolina*, no. 190 (1926), pp. 22–23; Guy Johnson, *Black Yeomanry, Folk
Culture on St. Helena Island, South Carolina* (Chapel Hill: University of North
Carolina Press, 1930), pp. 49–51.

7. See Norman Whitten and John Szwed, *Afro-American Anthropology*
(New York: Free Press, 1970), p. 29.

8. Jeutonne Brewer, "Possible Relationships between African Languages
and Black English Dialect," a paper presented before the Speech Communication Association, New Orleans, December 29, 1970. It has been generally
recognized by communicationists and linguists that the problem of grammatical
interference is highly controversial and complex. Uriel Weinreich, *Languages
in Contact* (Paris: Mouton, 1970), attempted to resolve some of the issues.
However, Weinreich's work is an exploration of language contact phenomena
between chiefly European languages rather than an outline of possible linguistic
symbiosis between Africans and European languages.

9. Robert Hall, *Pidgin and Creole Languages* (Ithaca, N.Y.: Cornell Uni-
versity Press, 1966), p. xii. See also Ian Hancock, "West African and the
Atlantic Creoles," in *The English Language in West Africa*, ed. John Spencer
(London: Longmans), pp., 113–22.

10. Herskovits, *The Myth of the Negro Past*, p. 47. Philip Curtin, *African
Slave Trade: A Census* (Madison: University of Wisconsin Press, 1969), is
perhaps the most reliable work on the number of slaves brought to America.
Prior to Curtin, estimates had ranged from 50 million to 10 million. Curtin's

view is that about 9.5 million slaves arrived in the New World. The mortality rate for captives would mean nearly 50 million people were affected.

11. Richard A Long, *The Uncle Remus Dialect: A Preliminary Linguistic View* (Washington, D.C.: Center for Applied Linguistics, 1969), p. 6.

12. William A. Stewart, "Urban Negro Speech: Sociolinguistic Factors Affecting English Teaching," *Florida FL Reporters*, vol. 7 (Spring 1969), p. 50.

13. Brewer, "Possible Relationships between African Languages and Black English Dialect."

14. Ralph Fasold and Walt Wolfram, "Some Linguistic Features of Negro Dialect," in *Teaching Standard English in the Inner City* (Washington, D.C., Center for Applied Linguistics, 1970), pp. 61–62.

15. David Dwyer and David Smith, *An Introduction to West African Pidgin English* (Lansing, Mich., n.d.), p. 132.

16. Jack Berry, "Language Systems and Literature," in *The African Experience* edited by John Paden and Edward Joja (Evanston, Ill.: 1970), p. 87.

17. For a discussion of the generative uses of vocal inflection, see Arthur L. Smith, "Socio-Historical Perspectives in Black Oratory," *Quarterly Journal of Speech* (October, 1970), pp. 264–69.

18. John T. Bendor-Samuel, "Niger Congo, Gur," in *Current Trends in Linguistics*, vol. 7 (The Hague: Mouton, 1969).

19. Ayo Bamgbose, "On Serial Verbs and Verbal Status," paper read at the Tenth West African Language Congress, Ibadan, 1970.

20. Dietrich Westermann and M. A. Bryan, *The Languages of West Africa* (London: Oxford University Press, 1952).

21. Bendor-Samuel, "Niger Congo, Gur," p. 17.

22. Westermann and Bryan, *The Languages of West Africa*, p.

23. The examples used in this section are taken from *The Federal Writer's Project, Slave Narratives: Alabama*, Film E 79, Reel 1, Berkeley: University of California Research Library, 1965.

24. Sukari Salone, "The Case for an African Influence in African American English," paper read at Linguistics Seminar, UCLA, 1972, p. 6.

25. Lorenzo Turner, *Africanisms in the Gullah Dialect* (Chicago: University of Chicago Press, 1949),

26. William Labov, *A Study of the Non-Standard English of Negro and Puerto Rican Speakers in New York City* (New York: Columbia University Press, 1968).

27. Salone, "The Case for an African Influence," p. 15. I am indebted to Salone for her interviews of Charlie Smith in 1972. Mr. Smith died in 1974 at over 130 years of age. The accent mark over *béen* indicates stress.

15

THE RHYTHMS OF UNITY: A BIBLIOGRAPHIC ESSAY IN AFRICAN CULTURE

MOLEFI KETE ASANTE AND KARIAMU WELSH ASANTE

Numerous intellectuals have seen the necessity of explaining the relationship of African cultural data to that of other regions of the world. Furthermore, there has been an abiding curiosity about individual African societies so much so that more than half of the anthropological and cultural studies done outside of North America have been done in Africa. In coping with the enormous corpus of this work, we have divided this chapter into two principal parts: philosophical writings on culture and political writings on culture. Our division is necessarily rough and subjective since much of the work done on African culture crosses both divisions. We have not attempted to discuss every single field study ever written but to examine the major arguments contained in some key volumes.

Philosophical Writings on Culture

These are works that explain the unity of African thought or show the common philosophical approaches employed by people of African descent. Among the comprehensive attempts to introduce readers to the main philosophical contours of African thought, E.A. Ruch and K.C. Anyanwu, *African Philosophy*, is the best example. Although the introductory essay in the volume asks, is there an African philosophy? the authors spend considerable time examining European philosophy and discoursing in general on myth and rationality. Consequently, it is only at page seventy-six that we are confronted with an answer to the question. Anyanwu writes with deftness in this essay that "the knowledge of the African cultural reality is but 'enlightened rationalism' of knowledge emancipated from the African cultural world."

In contrast to *African Philosophy* is John Mbiti's *African Religions and Philosophy*. Mbiti's aim is to demonstrate how African religions and philosophy are derived from traditional folkways. However, because he is educated as a Christian, the religion of his formal education intrudes into his discussion of African religions and philosophy. Nevertheless, Mbiti's book served to spark a lively debate around the question of the African worldview. As Dona Richards has contended he failed to understand completely the worldview of Africa or Africans and consequently his definitions of reality are often based on European conceptions. Mbiti seems a prisoner of an opposing ontology to most African thinking. He follows some of the early formulations of Western anthropologists when he contends that the African has no conception of the "abstract future." The ideology of progress, so European in its tone, captures Mbiti's mind and he no longer understands "rebirth" or the "ancestors," calling the ancestors at one point the "living dead." Dorthy Pennington, of course, sees value in some of Mbiti's clearer perceptions.

Janheinz Jahn's *Muntu: The New African Culture* begins with the idea that all African culture is one. Using the concepts of African language and culture, he examines *nommo*, the generative quality of the word as the source of much that is considered African. The oral tradition finds its roots in the concept of *nommo*. Nothing exists in African culture apart from the spoken word, according to Jahn. His is an enlightened view of the relationship of Africa to the spoken word. Thus, Muntu takes us from the African continent to the Caribbean and the United States to put us in touch with the culture in the diaspora.

Perhaps Cheikh Anta Diop's *The African Origin of Civilization* is the scholarly masterpiece that started researchers looking deeply into the African past. There has been research in earnest on Africa since the fifteenth century, but prior to Diop few, if any, African writers seemed interested in the issue of African origins of civilization. Diop's arguments rest on the works of historians of antiquity and his own linguistic and anthropological findings. Of course, there is little doubt in the mind of Diop that ancient Egypt, Axum, Meroe, and Nubia were African kingdoms which gave civilization to the world. As a philosophical undertaking, *The African Origin of Civilization* represents the first major breakaway from the traditional European and Eurocentric conceptions of Africa. Now the radar studies of the Sahara made in 1981 by the space shuttle Columbia reveal the remains of ancient African civilizations in southwestern Egypt and northwestern Sudan more than 40,000 years old. On November 13, 1983, the *New York Times* reported corn grinding tools buried under the sands. This seems to prove much of Diop's theory.

Following Diop, writers such as Theophile Obenga, the Congolese scholar, have investigated the cultural foundations of African life. Obenga's *L'Afrique dans l'antiquité* demonstrates the extensive contributions Africans made to the ancient world. But Obenga is not alone in following the lead of Diop in this direction, other francophone Africans have taken up a similar position. Sissoko's *Les Noirs et la culture* is another example of this line in the philosophy of culture. J.J. Maquet gives us a European view in *Africanity: The Cultural Unity of Africa*. Maquet's work is in a vein similar to Jahn's; both were European scholars seeking to express African unity. Maquet takes that baton and carries it to the inner sanctum of "Africanity" in order to distinguish an African essence. According to Maquet, Africanity is the fundamental element in Africa's cultural unity and it appears in all art forms as well as the thought patterns of Africa.

Africa's Gift to Humanity is one of J.A. Rogers' masterpieces on the contributions of people of African descent to world history. Prior to Rogers, several historians had attempted to assess the "gift" of Africa to the world. Leo Frobenius' *L'Histoire de la civilisation africaine* is an intellectual triumph in the history of African culture from one point of view. Frobenius' work has been little appreciated or used in the United States by all but the experts in African history. Leo Hansberry, John Henrik Clarke and John Jackson have gone a long way toward examining Frobenius' ideas in the light of more recent research. What is lacking in Frobenius is made up in the works of Diop, Obenga, and Ki-Zerbo. Where Frobenius was careful, Delafosse was reckless, and in *Les Civilisations nègres-africaines*, the author misses the connection between African regions. There truly is no Africa north and south of the Sahara; the Sahara is Africa, and people live in the oases of the Sahara.

M. Fortes and E.E. Evans-Pritchard edited a volume called *African*

Political Systems published in 1940. Their aim was to discuss the traditional political institutions of several African nations. Since only Liberia and Ethiopia were independent countries in Africa at that time, the writers concentrated mostly on the indigenous systems of British colonies. Fortes later worked with G. Dieterlen to write *African Systems of Thought*, published in 1965. Fortes and Dieterlen's work deepened the intellectual consideration of African philosophy. Fortes and Dieterlen provide ample evidence of African philosophical systems. Although this work is marred by its occasional Eurocentric lapses, it is a significant document.

P. Tempels' *La Philosophie bantoue* and Marcel Griaule's *Dieu d'eau*, translated in English as *Conversations with Ogotommeli*, are standards in the chronicling of traditional philosophies by Europeans. Griaule's thirty days and thirty nights with Ogotommeli reveal the complexity of the Dogon culture which Griaule observed and recorded. In both of these books the underlying structure of African thought emerges and the reader can see the unity of the cultural systems. Consequently, it is no longer possible for writers to say that Africans are essentially without complex cultural systems. Just as historians have had to reinterpret their views of African history after numerous archaelogical finds, the anthropologists are forced to reconsider some of their earlier false beliefs. It is no longer fashionable to speak of the Zulu or Asante people as "warlike" because they defended themselves in the face of British invasions, particularly when they were confronted by some of the most "warlike" people the earth had seen. In a similar vein, since Tempels and Griaule recorded the philosophical traditions of select African cultures it has become impossible to speak of Africa as having no philosophy. Beyond their records, however, are the numerous articles that have been written on different aspects of African philosophy.

Several writers have expressed Pan-African views in their writings, that is, their political views have become a part of their intellectual enterprise. Theophile Obenga has written in *Pour une nouvelle histoire* that the human race began in Africa. He surveys the evidence on the history of the human race, citing scores of dates and numerous scholars from Africa, Europe, and America to make his case for a new history. Mbonu Ojike's *My Africa* is descriptive and personal, but its political content emerges in its insistence upon the cultural uniqueness of the continent. Similarly, the major philosophical and cultural work of Leopold Sedar Senghor is also a political statement. Senghor's *Negritude et humanisme* is the most comprehensive work on negritude. In this book he outlines what he sees as the fundamental difference between Europe and African cultures, demonstrating how Africa relies on passions, feelings, and emotion, and Europe relies on reason. Senghor does not engage in extremes, only in tendencies, and although he has been mis-used to suggest a sharp dichotomy between reason and emotion, he never intended that misunderstanding. J.A. Sofola's little known but powerful *The African Culture and the African Personality* devoted considerable space to the discussion of traditional values. As a sociologist with a keen insight into cultural manifestations of values, having always been interested in how Africans maintained sanity in the face of European assault, Sofola writes sympathetically about how African personality differs from the European. If one could criticize this pioneering work in English it would be by saying that Sofola occasionally seems to be "proving" the existence of the African personality which, according to the position we have taken, needs no defense.

Le Monde africain noir by J. Ki-Zerbo is a useful account of the history and civilizations of Africa. Ki-Zerbo astutely weaves the fabric of the ancient African civilizations showing the unity of the African past. His work demonstrates the same unswerving commitment to the restitution of African history as that of Obenga and Diop. Diop's *Cultural Unity of Black America* is a profound examination of the cultural constituents which make it possible for Africa to achieve political unity. Preeminently preoccupied with the ineffectual uses of power among African nations, Diop proposes regional and Pan-African approaches to the question of weakness. Since Africa possesses an enormous amount of the world's natural and physical wealth and since there exist so many similarities between peoples, Diop can see no reason why Africa should not have a single government.

The Destruction of Black Civilization by Chancellor Williams has commanded unique attention among African scholars. Williams' contention is that the civilizations of Africa were systematically pillaged by both Arabs and Europeans. He holds that only the unification of African ideology can re-create the nobility that once characterized the people who built the great kingdoms of Egypt, Nubia, Meroe, Axum, Cush, Ghana, Monomatapa, Mali, and Songhai.

Political Writings on Culture

The books we have identified under this heading are those that seek an active orientation to cultural issues. They are not devoid of philo-

sophical examinations but rather they suggest measures for reconstructing and re-energizing African cultural unity. Cheikh Anta Diop also
stands at the beginning of this tradition, as well, inasmuch as he is the
single most influential voice in the new historiography. John Henrik
Clarke's *Marcus Garvey and the Vision of Africa* is an Afrocentric
analysis of the political philosophy of the greatest mass leader in the
history of African Americans. Clarke, an eminent historian, applies the
insights of recent and past history to his interpretation of Garvey. From
this position he is able to suggest universal African grounds of Garvey's
philosophy.

Afrocentricity: The Theory of Social Change by Molefi Kete Asante
is an ideological statement of the unity of African culture and the need
for new consciousness. *Afrocentricity* contends that there are two types
of consciousness, a consciousness of oppression and a consciousness
of victory to create liberating motifs and messages which occupies the
major portion of this work. Asante examines previous attempts to unify
Africans in America and concludes that consciousness must precede
unity.

A number of works by South African writers has appeared dealing
with the issue of their blackness in a white society. Among the volumes
in this vein are Credo Mutwa's *My People*, N. C. Manganyi's *Being-
Black-in-the-World* and Jordan Ngubane's *Ushaba: The Hurtle to Blood
River*. Mutwa also wrote *Africa is My Witness*. While these writers are
essentially concerned with the condition of the African in South Africa,
they nevertheless provide valuable critiques of how African culture in
their society connects to that of other Africans. These works are similar
in character to the numerous books which explore individual cultures,
e.g., N.A. Fadipe, *The Sociology of the Yoruba*, and Wande Abimbola,
The Ifa Divination Poetry.

The African-American scholar Maulana Karenga has published an
Introduction to Black Studies, a first-rate survey of the major principles
which support the cultural unity of Africa. Karenga's is an insightful
examination of history, culture, mythology, and creativity. In one sense,
it is to African-American culture what Adesanya's work is to Yoruba
culture and yet both works suggest the universality and cultural similarities of African people.

In a similar stream are the numerous works of Abdias do Nascimento,
the father of African Brazilian historiography. Nascimento's *Mixture
or Massacre: The Genocide of a Race* and his brillant *Sitiado em Lagos*

are devoted to connecting the African in Brazil to the continent. He delves into the myth of Brazilian race relations in *Racial Democracy in Brazil* to show that the aim of the government in Brazil has always been to de-Africanize blacks and to make them "lighter" through miscegenation. Nascimento expertly explores the rhetoric of Brazilian authorities who insist that blacks can change their status by becoming more white. Never are whites counseled to become "more black" in order to be accepted. Nascimento is a Pan-Africanist who asserts the African character of the Brazilian nation. In doing this he has reached across the Atlantic for links between the Yoruba in Salvador and the Yoruba in Ife.

Kwame Nkrumah wrote extensively on the politics of African states, searching always for the unifying principles in African thought. In *Consciencism* Nkrumah states a political philosophy for Africa. It is his view that African philosophy contains a moral-political substance that makes the unity of African thought and action concrete. Harmony with society, nature, and one's fellows is the principal aim of African philosophy. In prosecuting his view, Nkrumah demonstrates the three main influences upon the modern African conscience: African, Euro-Christian, and Arabo-Islamic. He characterizes traditional African society as egalitarian and on the basis of this argument, he contends that any African philosophy must be based on authentic roots. Socialism is the most valid expression of the African political conscience, according to Nkrumah. Thus his is a political action handbook which explores the relationship of society to philosophy and vice versa.

Julius Nyerere's *Ujamaa: African Socialism* sets out the condition for African socialism. He explores in depth the divergence of African socialism from European socialism, demonstrating the originality of the African theory and method. Nyerere's political ideology becomes the ground for his nationalism. In effect, the father of African socialism remains a schoolteacher as he provides a platform for achieving *ujamaa*. The didacticism of *African Socialism* exists because it is meant to be a very practical volume.

Kenneth Kaunda's *Humanism in Zambia and a Guide to Its Implementation*, published in 1968, was a crystallization of his ideas regarding the authentic soul of Africa. Much of Kaunda's ideology is deeply based in Christian theology, nevertheless, he sees the implementation of African humanism, not to be confused with European humanism as the best road to African advancement.

The richly diverse literature on Africa will only continue to grow. There are now more African scholars than ever before writing on the subject of cultural unity. The legacy of Diop on the continent and Clarke in the diaspora will be maintained and strengthened by young Afro-centric scholars now appearing in the pages of *Journal of Black Studies*, *Western Journal of Black Studies*, *Présence Africaine* and other journals dedicated to the rhythms of African unity. In the unity of African thought one finds one more example of the harmonizing of the world's cultures, for ultimately earthlings share the uniqueness of this planet.

REFERENCES

Abimbola, Wande. *Ifa Divination Poetry*. New York: NOK, 1977.

Asante, Molefi Kete. *Afrocentricity: The Theory of Social Change*. Buffalo, N.Y.: Amulefi, 1980.

Clarke, John Henrik. *Marcus Garvey and the Vision of Africa*. New York: Random House, 1974.

Delafosse, M. *Les Civilisations nègres-africaines*. Paris: Stock, 1925.

Dieterlen, G. *African Systems of Thought*. London: Oxford University Press, 1965.

Diop, Cheikh Anta. *The African Origin of Civilization*. Westport, Conn.: Lawrence Hill, 1974.

————. *Cultural Unity of Black Africa*. Chicago: Third World Press, 1978.

Fadipe, N. *The Sociology of the Yoruba*. Ibadan, Nigeria: University of Ibadan Press, 1970.

Fortes, M., and E. E. Evans-Pritchard, *African Political Systems*. New York: Oxford University Press, 1970.

Frobenius, Leo. *L'Histoire de la civilisation africaine*. Trans. H. Back and D. Ermont. Paris: Gallimard, 1936.

Griaule, Marcel. *Dieu d'eau [Conversations with Ogotommeli]*. London: Oxford University Press, 1975.

Jahn, Janheinz. *Muntu: The New African Culture*. New York: Grove, 1961.

Karenga, Maulana. *Introduction to Black Studies*. Inglewood, Calif.: Kawaida, 1982.

Kaunda, Kenneth. *Humanism in Zambia and a Guide to Its Implementation*. New York: Harper and Row, 1968.

Ki-Zerbo, J., *Le monde africain noir*. Paris: Présence Africaine, 1963.

Manganyi, N.C. *Being-Black-in-the-World*. Johannesburg: Ravan, 1973.

Maquet, J.J. *Africanity: The Cultural Unity of Africa*. New York: Oxford University Press, 1972.

Mbiti, John. *African Religions and Philosophy*. New York: Doubleday, 1970.

Mutwa, Credo, *My People*. London: Kahn & Averill, 1966.

Nascimento, Abdias do. *Mixture or Massacre: The Genocide of a Race*. Buffalo, N.Y.: Afrodiaspora, 1979.

———. *Racial Democracy in Brazil*. Ibadan: Sketch Publishing, 1977.

———. *Sitiado em Lagos*. Rio de Janeiro: Editoria Nova Fronteira, 1981.

Ngubane, Jordan. *Ushaba: The Hurtle to Blood River*. Washington, D.C.: Three Continents, 1979.

Nkrumah, Kwame. *Consciencism: Philosophy and Ideology for Decolonization and Development with Particular Reference*. London: Nelson, 1964.

Nyerere, Julius K. *Ujamaa: The Basis of African Socialism*. Dar es Salaam: Tanganyika Standard, 1962.

Obenga, Theophile. *L'Afrique dans l'antiquité*. Paris: Présence Africaine, 1973.

———. *Pour une nouvelle histoire*. Paris: Présence Africaine, 1980.

Ojike, Mbonu. *My Africa*. London: Blandford, 1955.

Rogers, J.A. *Africa's Gift to Humanity*. New York: H. M. Rogers, 1961.

Ruch, E. A., and K. C. Anyanwu. *African Philosophy*. Rome: Catholic Book Agency, 1981.

Senghor, L. *Negritude et humanisme*. Paris: Présence Africaine, 1956.

Sofola, J. A. *The African Culture and the African Personality*. Ibadan: African Resources Publishing Co., 1973.

Tempels, P. *La Philosophie bantoue*. Paris: Présence Africaine, 1961.

Williams, Chancellor. *The Destruction of Black Civilization*. Chicago: Third World Press, 1974.

ABOUT THE CONTRIBUTORS

KARIAMU WELSH ASANTE is founder and director of the Center for Positive Thought, the School of Movement, and co-founder of the Museum of African and African American Art and Antiquities in Buffalo, New York. She was the founder and first artistic director of National Dance Company of Zimbabwe during her tenure as a Fulbright Professor, 1981–82. She has written numerous scholarly articles and is a Ph.D. student at New York University. A well-known choreographer, she has choreographed for Kariamu and Company and other professional dance companies. She is lecturer in Afro-American dance at Temple University.

MOLEFI KETE ASANTE is Chair and Professor of African and African American Studies, Temple University, Philadelphia. He is the author or editor of twenty-two books, including *Afrocentricity: The Theory of Social Change* and *Contemporary Black Thought*. Dr. Asante holds editorial positions with eight journals and is the editor of the *Journal of Black Studies*.

SAMUEL OSEI BOADU is Assistant Professor, Texas Southern University. He has contributed scholarly articles to journals of communications and language in America and Africa. Dr. Boadu's current research interests include mass media effects on African societies, the structure of media content, and emphatic responses to cultural messages. He is Associate Editor of the *Journal of Language and Communication Arts*, and visiting professor at Texas Southern.

FELIX BOATENG is Director of Black Studies at Eastern Washington University. Dr. Boateng's interests include educational policies in African countries, methods of disseminating traditional educational approaches, and similarities of cultural methods among African peoples. His scholarship has appeared in the *Western Journal of Black Studies* and the *Journal of Black Studies*. Dr. Boateng was one of the founding editors of *Western Journal of Black Studies*.

JOHN HENRIK CLARKE is Professor, Department of Black and Puerto Rican Studies, Hunter College of the City University of New York. He is the author or editor of more than a hundred books and articles on the African world. Considered by some to be the dean of Afro-American History, Dr. Clarke is one of the leading intellectuals in the African community of scholars. He served as an Associate Editor of *Freedomways* and serves on numerous boards and international commissions.

MAULANA KARENGA is Director, Institute of Pan African Studies in Los Angeles. He has taught at several major universities and has lectured at nearly two hundred colleges and universities in America, Africa, and Asia. He is the author of sixteen books and numerous articles on African culture and politics. His latest work is the popular *Introduction to Black Studies*, a fundamental text at many universities. The creator of Kwanzaa, the holiday, Dr. Karenga writes extensively on cultural reconstruction.

ABDIAS DO NASCIMENTO is a federal deputy of the National Congress of Brazil, a former professor of Afro-Latin Culture at the State University of New York at Buffalo; and the Director of the Institute of Afro-Brazilian Studies and Research, Pontifical Catholic University of São Paulo, Brazil. A leading African-American intellectual, Nascimento founded the Black Theatre Movement of Rio de Janeiro in the 1940s and is an artist, musician, poet, historian, and playwright.

EGHOSA OSAGIE is Professor and Head, Department of Economics, University of Jos, Nigeria. Dr. Osagie has contributed many articles to scholarly journals in Africa and North America. He has been an advisor to the ECOWAS community of West African government, the Nigerian government, and the Nigerian school system. His economic texts are used in the grade levels of the Nigerian school system. As a principal economist in Africa, Dr. Osagie has conceptualized practical and theoretical models.

DORTHY PENNINGTON is Associate Professor, Department of Speech and Human Relations, University of Kansas, and Associate Director, Institute of African Studies. She has published extensively in the area of intercultural communication and interracial relations. Her work appears in both communications and African studies journals. Among her publications is *Intercultural Communication*, a textbook widely used in the United States. Dr. Pennington's work on the African and Afro-American concept of time has been cited by numerous authors.

DONA RICHARDS is Associate Professor, Department of Black and Puerto Rican Studies, Hunter College, City University of New York. Dr. Richards has published in *Journal of Black Studies*, *Présence Africaine*, *Western Journal of Black Studies* and numerous other journals of the African world. Her research appears in monographs and chapters in various books including *Contemporary Black Thought*. Examining the dominant themes of European culture as they relate to the African world, Dr. Richards is a tafik in Afrocentric analysis.

WOLE SOYINKA is Professor of Drama at the University of Ife, Nigeria. Perhaps the premier playwright of the African world, Soyinka commands great international respect for his poetry and prose as well. His breadth of vision has been eulogized by many critics. Dr. Soyinka has published numerous books, plays, and novels, all examining human emotion. A past president of the African Writers Association, Professor Soyinka has greatly influenced the thinking of contemporary writers.

MWIZENGE TEMBO is on leave from the Institute of African Studies at the University of Zambia, Lusaka. He is at present completing his doctoral studies at Michigan State University. Tembo's interests are in African personality theory, Afrocentricity, and Africanity. He has explored the full range of these theories in several publications.

INDEX

270 INDEX

① Immediacy of unmediated
experience — the lived
moment — unlike

② Past — egwugwu — ancestors
are part of the timelessness
of the past — connections.

③ Unitied spiritual
Totality ┬ ancestral spirits
├ ogbanje — child
├ Ani —
└ ~~anin~~ chi —